A Garden of Bristlecones

D0732669

Environmental Arts and Humanities Series

A Garden of Bristlecones

Tales of Change in the Great Basin

MICHAEL P. COHEN

University of Nevada Press: Reno, Las Vegas

Environmental Arts and Humanities Series Editor: Scott Slovic

This book has been funded, in part, by a grant from the Nevada Arts Council, a state agency.

University of Nevada Press, Reno, Nevada 89557 USA
Copyright © 1998 by University of Nevada Press
Watercolors, title page, and chapter opener line art © 1998 by Valerie P. Cohen
All rights reserved
Manufactured in the United States of America
Design: Carrie Nelson House
Library of Congress Cataloging-in-Publication Data
Cohen, Michael P., 1944–
    A garden of bristlecones : tales of change in the Great Basin /
Michael P. Cohen.
        p. cm. — (Environmental arts and humanities series)
    Includes bibliographical references (p.   ) and index.
    ISBN 0-87417-296-9 (pbk. : alk. paper)
        1. Great Basin bristlecone pine. 2. Great Basin bristlecone pine—History.
3. Forest ecology—Great Basin. 4. Natural history—Great Basin. I. Title.
II. Series
QK494.5.P66C64   1998   97-23933
585'.2—dc21   CIP

The paper used in this book meets the requirements of American
National Standard for Information Sciences—Permanence of Paper
for Printed Library Materials, ANSI Z39.48-1984. Binding
materials were selected for strength and durability.

07   06   05   04   03   02   01   00   99   5   4   3   2

♻ Text of this book printed on recycled paper
60% total recovered fiber   10% postconsumer fiber

This book is dedicated to Sam Allen (1928–1997)

Long ago I began asking myself "What would Sam, my editor, think?" every time I wrote. He understood exactly what I was trying to express, knew where I had stumbled, and knew how to make the writing ring true. Our relationship went far beyond the professional. Sam has been like a father and co-author to me, and now he is a part of my own mind.

bark smells like pineapple: Jeffries
cones prick your hand: Ponderosa

nobody knows what they are, saying
"needles three to a bunch."

turpentine tin can hangers
high lead riggers

"the true fir cone stands straight,
the doug fir cone hangs down."

—wild pigs eat acorns in those hills
cascara cutters
tanbark oak bark gatherers
myrtlewood burl bowl-makers
little cedar dolls,
        baby girl born from the split crotch
              of a plum
           daughter of the moon—

foxtail pine with a
clipped curve-back cluster of tight
      five-needle bunches
  the rough red bark scale
and jigsaw pieces sloughed off
        scattered on the ground.
—what am I doing saying "foxtail pine"?

these conifers whose home was ice
age tundra, taiga, they of the
      naked sperm
do whitebark pine and white pine seem the same?

    a sort of tree
    its leaves are needles
    like a fox's brush
(I call him fox because he looks that way)
    and call this other thing, a
      foxtail pine.
                —Gary Snyder, *The Back Country*

". . . of all problems, none disquieted him more, and none concerned him more than the profound one of time. Now then, this is
the *only* problem that does not figure in the pages of *The Garden.*
He does not even use the word which means *time.* How can these
voluntary omissions be explained?"

I proposed various solutions, all of them inadequate. We discussed them. Finally Stephen Albert said, "In a guessing game to
which the answer is chess, which word is the only one prohibited?"
I thought for a moment and then replied:

"The word is *chess.*"

"Precisely," said Albert. "*The Garden of Forking Paths* is an enormous guessing game, or parable, in which the subject is time. The
rules of the game forbid the use of the word itself. To eliminate a
word completely, to refer to it by means of inept phrases and obvious paraphrases, is perhaps the best way of drawing attention to it."

—Jorge Luis Borges, "The Garden of Forking Paths," *Ficciones*

CONTENTS

Watercolors by Valerie P. Cohen, following page 218
Bristlecone and Sky
Red Daybreak
Mother Courage
Desert Range
In the Wild Animal Park
Bristlecone with Curly Root
Two Thousand Years Later
Bristlecone on the Edge

Maps

Valerie wanted to spend a few more days drawing old trees in the White Mountains of California and I went along. It was August but felt like spring, and so I took a walk in the woods. One of my friends reminds me that I once advised against the use of field guides. Without a guide, this time I went astray from the straight road and found myself at a loss. I had no idea where I was. Midway in life's journey, alone in an arduous wilderness, faced with a question, "How shall I say what wood that was?" I wanted to know what others had learned about the trees around me and their strange world near timberline. One thing led to another. A few months later I visited the Laboratory of Tree-Ring Research in Tucson, Arizona.

I would not have been wondering about bristlecone pines if people like Valerie had not done so before. I have been a scientist, and almost everything I know about these trees comes from technical literature that also reminds me of this past in my life. My present experience with these woods constitutes a kind of spiritual fact-checking. Some of the results of Valerie's experience and my own are in this book.

This book is about human encounters with one species, the Great Basin bristlecone pine (*Pinus longaeva* D. K. Bailey). People have come to the Great Basin from many regions, and their stories dramatize many changes in people and in trees. "Nobody knows what they are. . . ." I have always admired the subtle humor of Gary Snyder's "Foxtail Pine," a poem more relevant to the subject than a casual reading may make it appear. Never mind that he calls his tree a foxtail pine: it could be a bristlecone pine.

The Great Basin bristlecone pine embodies an arid environment. Some individual trees, living under highly austere conditions, approach 5,000 years of age. They usually grow near or with limber pines, the two species creating a modern subalpine forest, which has a complex and interesting history. Americans have not noticed these trees or the forest in which they live until very recently. During most of the human encounter with the Great Basin, bristlecone pines have been far above purview. Now that the belated study of these trees has become part of a re-evaluation of American history, these trees have called out unique modes of inspection, and not just from scientists.

The story of human knowledge is short when compared to the history of these long-lived trees. Nevertheless this book is rooted in modes of human knowledge. Early in the 1950s, a small group of men uncovered the longevity and sensitivity of specific trees and quantified the relations of old trees with their environment. These men, predominantly from the University of Arizona, called themselves dendrochronologists, and, as the name suggests, they were interested in measuring "tree time," but they were always interested in a great deal more. When these scientists began to read and record the changes they found embodied in the growth rings of the trees, over a period of two decades they made the bristlecone the most intensely studied of conifers.

So this book is rooted in a set of stories of modern people in search of a readable past, and though the trees may embody some of that past, the way they have been read and their record rewritten constitutes my focus. Reading and writing are always double. What people learn from studying the trees intersects or crosses the way people use trees to express themselves. This is an Emersonian issue. Emerson believed in a "radical correspondence between visible things and human thoughts," between natural and spiritual facts. His belief is the taproot for traditions of American nature writing.

I believe that human language creates meaning. That is the subject of the introduction to this book. To say that human methods of inquiry "created" the bristlecone pine is more than a slight simplification, but it has a kernel of truth. That kernel is my theme: the book in your hand elaborates the figures from that theme. From my perspective, the insistent attempts to read history out of these trees constitute a shared project of creative reading, and sometimes the methods of reading are obscured by the figures of speech used by the very authors who have read so carefully and well.

Dendrochronologists sought records of change. They hoped to read the trees, to find out a great deal about the conditions under which bristlecone pines grew, and to construct a narrative of change stretching over many millennia. It was not simply the trees' longevity but their apparent sensitivity to change that made them the target of so many detailed investigations that were self-consciously and rigorously engaged in abstracting a record from trees, and finding meaning in it. These matters are introduced in chapters 1 and 2.

Now, nearly forty years after Edmund Schulman discovered that the bristlecone was the "world's oldest living thing," images of bristlecones and their tree-rings are published pervasively, sometimes as decorative figures, and sometimes to represent ideas of eternity and change. They have been associated with Great Basin natural history, as images of "first nature," unchanged by humans and worthy of human respect. Chapter 3 illustrates a case in point.

As figures, the old trees fall into two groups. To speak in linguistic terms, a bristlecone can be conceived as a "metonymy" of the Great Basin. Metonymy, a figure of speech, entails the substitution of the name of an object closely associated with a word for the word itself, and involves continuous association from whole to part. Through processes of language, bristlecone pines have been embodied in words with accumulated symbolic associations. Broadly speaking, the bristlecone has come to be used as a metonymy indicating or embodying ideas of the perseverance and memory of the natural world of the Great Basin. Chapter 4 shows how scientists have confronted what they conceived as a continuous organic relationship between the tree and its environment.

Because the past is not simply a chronology but an idea, bristlecones have also served as metaphors for the past. Constructing a metaphor is a different procedure from making a metonymy. Metaphor is a form of analogy between discontinuous entities, ascribing to the first object one or more qualities of the second. People sometime ascribe analogous qualities to trees and humans, qualities relating to ideas of time and change. Metaphor shapes trees and humans by mirroring them. We often speak of the tenor and vehicle of a metaphor. The bristlecone has become a vehicle which holds a flow of human meanings attached to it, by analogy. For instance, I teach at a university whose insignia includes an image of the bristlecone pine, under which appears the motto "Learning Lives Forever." To speak in a more narrow scientific sense, the climatic record of the bristlecone pine has been correlated to records read from other sources, sometimes as a set of global continuities, and more recently as a set of discontinuities. Chapter 5 introduces the problem of discontinuity in natural history, as read from bristlecone tree-rings.

Chapters 6 and seven attempt to integrate the work of a variety of disciplines, to tell some of the histories of the bristlecone. These "natural histories" are figurative, in the sense that the bristlecone becomes the hero or main character in the narratives.

It would be convenient if there were sharp distinctions between continuous and discontinuous histories of this tree, or relations between ideas of this tree. But close analysis of these figures of the bristlecone reveals what would otherwise be hidden in stories about knowledge. When constructed as a set of metonymies, the trees may embody natural history, and as metaphoric images, may seem to offer themselves as vehicles for human thought. People create figures of speech, tell stories, and abstract the histories of these trees. People ask certain kinds of questions, and answer them in certain ways. Figures of speech and figures of thought may be more or less rigorous; when analyzed as human constructs, they reveal the people who make them. The cultural role of the bristlecone is the subject of chapters 8 and 9.

I began by wondering about trees, but soon wondered about figures the bristlecone made in modern human thought, as a set of images of the past, and the implications of these figures. The distinctly modern human history of bristlecones, as they have been used to embody natural history in human terms, led to a consideration of the way people have decided to act toward these trees, and use them. Chapters 10 and 11 deal with the relationship between towns and parks and the history of bristlecone reserves. Chapter 12 constitutes a meditation informed by the histories of the bristlecone. It resides on the edge between public knowledge and private responses.

This is a book about "nature writing," an ambiguous expression suggesting two possibilities: that "nature" writes its own history, and that humans can read and rewrite or transcribe that writing. Recent years have seen well-written and -documented depictions of the natural history of the Great Basin for the lay reader. Stephen Trimble's *The Sagebrush Ocean: A Natural History of the Great Basin,* Donald K. Grayson's *The Desert's Past: A Natural Prehistory of the Great Basin,* and Ronald M. Lanner's *The Piñon Pine: A Natural and Cultural History* are scrupulous narratives. There is a wealth of more technical literature about bristlecone pines and the Great Basin, much of it published very recently. Some titles seem, on first glance, very unlikely. *Packrat Middens: The Last 40,000 Years of Biotic Change,* edited by J. L. Betancourt, T. R. Van Devender, and P. S. Martin, reveals the fascinating processes by which the Great Basin is coming to be known and the implications of this recent knowledge.

I have tried to be scrupulous in focusing upon these sites of human knowledge and on the modes and methods by which their information is constructed, especially by language. This has called for a certain skepticism, mistrust, or suspicion of the language used by authors I admire. It is a language I sometimes use myself. I read in Trimble's book that bristlecone pines are "witnesses to the entire span of the 'modern' biological world of the Great Basin." But I know that trees do not literally bear witness. With Grayson, I might say "Plant and animal communities appear stable and real to us only because we do not live long enough to observe differently. Bristlecone pines, which do live long enough, know better." I share these sentences, but the last one makes no literal sense. More properly, reading the bristlecone pine record is a human activity that may disabuse "us" of false appearances which come from the human lack of longevity. Neither is it true, strictly speaking, that the wood rat "is today helping scientists decipher the past," thanks to "its penchant for museum keeping," as Ronald Lanner wrote in *The Piñon Pine*. It would be nice if the bristlecone bore witness, or knew better, or the wood rat helped scientists and kept museums. But nature likes to hide.

I pick these figures of speech from the works of writers who are admirable and well-known scholars of Great Basin prehistory. What human modes of inquiry are hidden behind those figures? To focus on modern ideas, I write in a modernist mode, which calls for scrutinizing closely such figurative language and the kinds of crises it creates.

What dendrochronology calls "principal investigators" I will call readers and writers. Dendrochronologists, paleoecologists, paleobotanists, and others have plotted the histories of the trees, have written and have rewritten the histories of human interaction with these trees. Later writers have used these methods of reading and writing to decipher other histories. Narratives use each other, and later ones have often absorbed the language, structure, and premises of earlier stories to refigure Great Basin natural history.

The histories scientists have read out of bristlecones have, in turn and often unexpectedly, come into conflict with stories humans have told about their own past and present. Histories read out of the trees and of the trees have altered conceptions of human cultural identity. In our age, archaeologists have discovered a human history more diverse and less linear than previously imagined. Biogeographers have come to see that our biological environment is more recently created and less stable than they used to think. Paleoclimatologists have realized that the conditions under which we live are not typical even of the recent past. These disruptions of a simple continuity between the present and the past illustrate a complex and sometimes disturbing dialectic between social and natural history, best expressed as a set of crises of human consciousness and more common than is supposed among those who try to reconcile human and natural history through close study.

It is that process of study, and the kind of crisis it creates, which shapes the structure of this book. The bristlecone, as I describe its history, is a crisis tree. It has yielded a set of stories revealing changes, stories that sometimes seem to repeat themselves but are slightly different and are a form of incremental repetition, perhaps like the patterns of tree-rings. These stories are interesting, but they do more than entertain. They are stories for people who like to know where their ideas come from. Not the tree itself but the idea of the tree constitutes the subject for this book. The tree, however, is real and not ephemeral.

A Book of Changes

Do whitebark pine and white pine seem the same?

The Bristlecone Pine as a Text

What makes these trees, residents of the timberline all across the high ranges of the Great Basin, worthy objects of human attention? That they are widespread? That there were once more of them? That they are long lived? Age, in itself, is not a criterion for value or wonder. For instance, creosote bushes in the Mojave Desert create large circular clones over many thousands of years, and some may be nearly 12,000 years old. The original stems, however, are no longer present, and the rings of vegetation, called circular clones, are empty inside. Frank Vasek determined the age of these by extrapolating present rates of growth back into their absent past. Creosote rings are old, but their history cannot be read.

On the other hand, the tree-rings of bristlecone pines constitute a possibly coherent text. The age of old bristlecone pines can be measured precisely by the numbers of their annual growth rings, as if the trees create their own rule: the rings themselves are not regular like the markings on a ruler and seem to reveal more than age. But what? To ask "what?" makes them seem impressive. Dendrochronologists ask what history these trees embody in their wood, living and dead, available like texts for scientific study. Because the trees are treated as texts, my own inquiry focuses on those who are impressed—the history of human use and inquiry, human knowl-

Population I

Population I

Population II

Population III

Population IV

KILOMETERS

2000 and 3000 Meter Contours Shown
Latter bounds High Country shown in Black

Base map details with permission of the
American Geographical Society

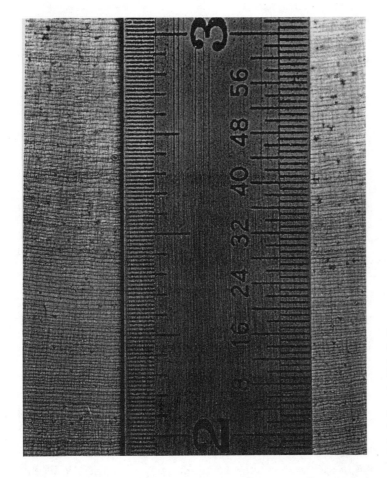

Cross section of bristle-cone pine (*Pinus long-aeva*) from 10,500 feet in the White Mountains of California. It took 140 years to gain a one-inch increase of the radius. Dark dots are resin canals. (U.S. Forest Service)

edge, and human conceptions of change. The questions people have learned to ask of these trees have been framed in the latter half of the twentieth century and make the history of this inquiry about the old organism modern.

Humans perceive these trees as ambiguous signs, inhabited by signs. When I speak of a sign, I am using, albeit somewhat loosely, a concept developed by modern linguistics. The compound and complex sign "Great Basin bristlecone pine" is made up of two elements in relationship: (1) the words of the name are *signifiers* attached to (2) the mental concept or idea people have of this tree and its place—what is *signified*. The signifier and signified are only meaningful through their relationship. They have no meaning apart from each other. This relationship between signifier and signified has changed and is historically unstable. People have used other names for the same tree and have changed their ideas about the tree since the early 1950s, when Donald Culross Peattie imag-

(opposite) Geographical distribution of *Pinus* subsection *balfourianae*. (D. K. Bailey, "Phytogeography," *Annals of the Missouri Botanical Garden*, 1970)

ined that old specimens lived nearly a thousand years, and a U.S. Forest Service publication declared them useless. People still disagree about the bristlecone pine's salient features, though they count the same tree-rings, inspect the same needles, and measure the size of congruent cones.

In this relationship between *signifier* and *signified,* there is a gap between the two elements, a difference. The tree knows nothing of this gap. A tree exists and is real. Though it has no natural name, and no person possesses a complete and adequate idea of its total essence, it does have a natural existence. Problems of identity, name, and the meaning of its existence are entirely in the realm of human signification.

At any given time and place in the history of this human inquiry, it should be possible to discern a triangular play among the three elements: an actual kind of tree, a signifying name, and a set of human ideas of the tree. The second and third elements change historically, and their relationship to each other changes, as I have said. Given sufficient time—which is quite beyond human experience—the tree changes too. As people signify with names and ideas, they reveal and hide aspects of the dynamic tree itself, but they are always engaged in the activities of reading and writing, decoding and encoding.

The way this tree is inhabited by human thought is dramatized by two methods used to study it. One inspects the tree from the outside, looks at salient external features as they relate to its environment, and one attempts to perceive the tree from the inside, dissecting the internal tree, its patterns of tree-rings, chemistry, and genetic structure. The methods of internal study, practiced by a set of scientific communities, have generated highly specialized languages but must eventually refer themselves to the external tree. For example, dendrochronologists attempt to link the tree-rings to climatic events shaping the life of the tree. They use these signs to read out a portion of the history of the earth embodied by the tree.

Signs have a life of their own. Meaning radiates, like waves from a stone dropped in a pool. The Great Basin bristlecone pine has acquired a broad cultural meaning, in whose life revelation and concealment play against each other. The way the tree's life has been read with rigor by scientists is interesting, but the life of received ideas about this tree is impressive too, and the figures of this tree in human society are fascinating. The Great Basin bristlecone pine, itself the central figure of this book, is an elaborate and dynamic figure indeed. It enters many stories and sometimes dominates them. Often the resolution of these stories, as in any good tale, is deferred.

There can be no fixed, essential meaning or final authority in the knowledge of trees. The possibility of promised meaning and the impossibility of keeping the promise are at war. But take people to the bristlecone groves and they want to choose a tree. Asking which is the "real bristlecone" leads to an unending series of answers about the meaning of a tree, none entirely satisfying, and all creating new questions. In this sense, the Great Basin bristlecone pine is like a really good book, a classic to be re-read periodically throughout life, offering an unending dialogue between the reader and the text.

Common Names

The Great Basin bristlecone pine has gone by many aliases. Since the late nineteenth century, when the tree acquired its first modern names, these have been divided into common names written in English and scientific names written in Latin. The history of these names constitutes one set of forking paths. At other times, people spoke of these trees in ways which are incompletely known. People have visited bristlecone forests for nearly as long as people have inhabited the Great Basin, which is estimated presently at greater than eleven thousand years. No doubt people who burned bristlecone wood thousands of years ago, in hunting camps high in the White Mountains of California, had a name for this tree and stories about it.

Over a longer view, covering at least forty million years, the bristlecone has been a different tree at different times. During these millions of years of tenure in the Great Basin, its outer appearance altered in subtle ways and its inner structure was transmuted too, as it evolved in a world which changed. These shifts in identity create difficulty for those who seek to name it. Like many western species— like life itself—the bristlecone pine has an inside and an outside. Through its history it has been a shape shifter and polynomial.

To begin with names. The Great Basin bristlecone has gone, for most of its modern human history, by the scientific name *Pinus aristata* Engelmann. The common name, bristlecone, comes from *aristata,* the species' original scientific name—still used for its close relation in the Colorado Rockies—and means "bristle" pine, refer-

Pine cones. Above, left to right, Sierra foxtail, Great Basin bristlecone, Rocky Mountain bristlecone. Below, cone variation in foxtail pines. (D. K. Bailey photo)

ring to the delicate prickle at the end of each scale of the cone. It has been called foxtail pine because its foliage is like that of its neighbor to the west, and called hickory pine, primarily by people in Colorado, because its wood is so dense. Its first scientific name came from trees collected in the Rockies, and because of the method of collection, the Great Basin bristlecone was not distinguished from its relative to the east until nearly a century later.

The bristlecone pine has always been caught between scientific and common modes of perception. In 1970, about a decade after scientists began to investigate it rigorously, the species in the Great Basin was renamed *Pinus longaeva* D. K. Bailey, because it was not the same as its relatives to the west and east. *Longaeva,* because it had already been identified as the oldest living tree on earth.

People commonly speak of "ancient bristlecones," conflating individual trees with the species. But not every bristlecone is ancient. People speak of the species as if it were the oldest living organism, or thing. They speak of old, elder, or ancient bristlecones in the same redundant way people sometimes say "Ancient Anasazi." People hardly know what to say.

The problems of naming suggest the following desire: if only one could be careful enough with language, one could give the tree a dense and compact name, so appropriate that shape and sense connect inextricably, identifying the tree itself in unambiguous

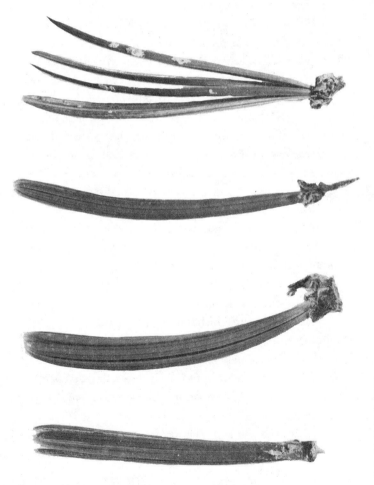

Pine needles. Top to bottom, Rocky Mountain bristlecone, Great Basin bristlecone (Utah), Great Basin bristlecone (White Mountains, California), foxtail (Sierra Nevada). (D. K. Bailey photo)

terms. But this is not possible, because a question of identity engages the individual tree (who), its characteristics or features (what), its habits (how), its region (where), a history in which it figures (when), and its meaning (why). The question of identity includes an ever-widening set of issues with the tree at the center.

Distinguishing Features

People are taught by guidebooks and by folklore to recognize the Great Basin bristlecone pine by its five needles per fascicle, bound or bundled tightly together, needles an inch to an inch and a half long, stiff, radiating around the ends of branches in dark clusters, producing a characteristic dense appearance. The needles are leaves, and as the term *fascicle* indicates, they are bound together at their junction like the leaves of a book and grow in signatures of needles, five to a bunch. Each signature marks a new portion of the tree's story.

The shape of the clusters of needles is sometimes likened to the bristles on a bottle brush, or the hair on a fox's tail. The tail of the fox is thick-haired and bushy. It is prized by humans for its stylishness and its reddish brown and yellow color. But to speak of a fox is to speak also of its behavior, wily, sly, crafty, and perhaps deceitful. If the Great Basin bristlecone pine were named for its foliage, it would be called—and has been called—the Great Basin foxtail pine, a name which indicates its kinship to the foxtail pine of California (*Pinus balfouriana* Greville and Balfour).

The bristlecone pine acquired its first name, however, as a result of its cones. Male catkins grow about 0.4 inches long, red-purple: a catkin, named for its resemblance to a cat's tail, is an inflorescence. Female cones are dark purple when new—though some begin a yellow-green—and fade to brown when ripe. They are ovoid rather than conical, about three inches long. They perch on the ends of branches, dripping with pitch, and open after two years, revealing, open or closed, the long delicate incurved prickles for which the pines are commonly named. It is, for instance, easy to distinguish these from the cones of neighboring limber pines (*Pinus flexilus*) by this one feature.

The seeds are small and compressed (0.3 in.) with a terminal wing, light brown and translucent, frequently mottled, broadest at the middle, about twice the seed length.

This way of speaking focuses attention by selecting distinguishing details. Students may use a "key" to delineate kinds of pine trees primarily by the character of needles, their number and anatomy. Then students consider the shape of cones, seeds, and the anatomy of the xylem, the supporting and water-conducting tissue of vascular plants. This orderly method of description, though dense in concrete observation, selects and reduces the detail of the tree. The purpose of this method is double, to sharpen distinctions, and to reduce clutter in the subjective mind making them.

People use the venerable system of botanists, assuming that certain details call for intense scrutiny and create essential distinctions. These details create a structure of thought; they lead to subjects of inquiry and sets of questions. The seeming permanence of the system of botanical classification suggests that these subjects and questions will remain fixed. But naming and classification are always contested, and the present systems are landmarks of earlier contests. People always notice one thing or another. All methods of observation select detail and for that reason can be considered somewhat arbitrary.

Does a tree's foliage look like a bottle brush, or like a fox's tail? People use language; scientists try to use it with precision, poets to use it with elegance; historians ask how the language came to be and what its changes reveal about its speakers.

The trees are also seemingly bristly in another sense: they seem all elbows, and perhaps uncommunicative. A typical tree grows fifteen to fifty feet tall, its form described this way in Clarence Hall's *Natural History of the White-Inyo Range*: "Trunk commonly thick and contorted or split, but straight when young; very stressed trees may have large spreading crowns almost shrubby in appearance; old trees commonly spike-topped, with strip bark growth." Bristlecone bark is light to reddish brown.

This kind of description shows how some people seek the tree's identity by looking at its larger configuration or pattern instead of focusing on small details. Its stark and striking appearance constitutes a gestalt which may have a basis in the origin of the tree's vegetative organs—bluntly put, the way limbs grow and the way their growth is influenced by their environment. Writers repeatedly use the adjective "irregular" for the bristlecone. Even young trees are rarely symmetrical. Bristlecones present a shaggy appearance, their foliage unevenly distributed around the trunk.

People see them as persons, noticing that the way their limbs grow—beginning in elbows and ending sometimes in sky-reaching, pointed, naked arms—gives a characteristic appearance to certain older trees. They are not crooked so much as they are bowed or bent, seeming to submit or yield to the environment, but resisting it too. The death of limbs and signs of the loss of limbs, so evident in older trees in exposed sites, suggest that these trees, as bodies, have complex articulations with their environments.

Distribution in the Present

Where they are is, from another perspective, what they are. Bristlecone pines are now distributed across the subalpine regions of the Great Basin, from California into the Colorado Plateau of Utah, at elevations of about 9,500 feet to 11,650 feet above sea level, their range occasionally extending down to 8,500 feet and lower in special circumstances. Because they are often found growing alongside the limber pine (*Pinus flexilus*), Ronald Lanner, an expert on the region's ecology, has characterized the quintessential Great Basin forest as the Limber Pine–Bristlecone Pine Zone, noting that the limber pine grows dominant in the north and the bristlecone pine in the south. Bristlecone forests are best developed and dominant on certain soils, on dolomite or limestone, especially along the southern half of the White Mountain summit surface. The bristlecone forest thrives in a world unambiguously wild, in "first nature," its way of life influenced as little as it is possible for humans to imagine.

Great Basin bristlecone pines are, in the most radical sense, strangers because of the way they live and where they live. People do not grow up in environments surrounded by these trees, but come to them casually or deliberately as visitors. What makes them interesting, in part, is their *not* being easily accessible, lovable, or "human." They are like ice, or wind, and an observer may remember even in the hour of death that first incursion of the tree upon consciousness. That incursion or inroad of the bristlecone on consciousness leads backward. In the human history of these trees, observers keep going back to them, hoping to ask the right questions and finally understand something about change and longevity.

These trees live way up high in the sky, but they are also at the bottom of environmental history, which, as Donald Worster writes, interrogates "the role and place of nature in human life." They are at the bottom of environmental history because historians must have some ideas about nature itself, as it functioned in past times.

The Region

This book focuses on ideas generated from the study of bristlecone pines growing in the Great Basin, a region named in 1844 by John Charles Frémont (1813–1890) because it seemed unnatural. He was thinking of the region as a hydrographic unit. Everything, he thought, flows in, dries up, disappears, or dies. This apt if grim hydrological distinction crosses the human history of the region, as a paradox. As Donald Grayson and Stephen Trimble point out, there are other ways to name or describe the natural Great Basin. Most of these superimpose another aspect of geography upon the hydrographic unit. As a physiographic region, it is defined by its topography, marked by the Sierra Nevada on the west, the Columbia Plateau on the north, the Colorado Plateau on the east, and more arbitrarily by the Mojave Desert of southern California and southern Nevada. The floristic Great Basin is defined by a complex assemblage of plants, upon which some biologists superimpose the vertebrates.

Because they focus on the bristlecone pine, the stories in this book are drawn primarily from the Great Basin of modern human history. These stories neglect the rich and complex ancient human history and modern ethnography of the region. Because they are focused on the uses people have made of the natural history of the region, these stories cannot avoid the extent to which the modern Great Basin contains a great deal more than natural history.

The Region and the West

The modern human history of the region begins with extraction. People have been taking materials and abstractions out of the Great Basin for more than a century. In the mid-nineteenth century, the region became a source of wealth, of currency, itself material and abstract. Silver and gold were made to flow out of the region. In the late twentieth century, as the region has become a source of knowledge, this process of abstraction has been no more a natural phenomenon than the abstraction of currency.

At present, the Great Basin of the bristlecone pine is predominantly federal land, and certain areas are increasingly managed from a perspective which makes these lands a repository, an archive where records are kept or the land retains values lost elsewhere. Such decisions are belated with regard to human and natural his-

tory yet reflect one part of the process of regionalization of the
western United States.

But between the islands of mountains people have also been
putting things into the Great Basin: cities, railroads, highways in
the nineteenth century; something more disturbing in the twentieth century. A map of the current region reveals substantial sectors
devoted to modern military activities. Hill Air Force Range, Wendover Range, Dugway Proving Grounds, and the Deseret Test Center are marked "no public access" on the official Utah highway map.
In Nevada, large military installations include Fallon Naval Air
Station and its associated bombing ranges, Nellis Air Force Bombing and Gunnery Range, the land around the Hawthorne Army
Ammunition Plant, and the Nevada Test Site. These military reserves have become repositories of the weapons of modern warfare.
It is generally but not entirely true that the military has appropriated the basins of the Great Basin but found no use for the high
mountains.

The Great Basin, as repository of natural or unnatural knowledge, might contain a parable of what Ann Ronald, in the book
Earthtones, calls America's "regrettable assessment of what is valuable and what is not." For her the natural beauty contrasts to a
human horror of military reserves, and the region wears a paradoxical aspect of Hyde and Jekyll. Just as there are many versions of the
Great Basin, there are many versions of the West, and they are not
congruent. But what West does the bristlecone pine inhabit?

One West, created in 1892 by Frederick Jackson Turner (1861–
1932), is a set of the human histories of European immigrants. His
regional histories of the West demonstrate parallelism in cultural
development, where a frontier repeats itself, which may suggest
cycle, or recycle. Some newer western historians, neo-Turnerites like
William Cronon, George Miles, and Jay Gitlin in *Under an Open
Sky: Rethinking America's Western Past,* focus on the transitions from
frontier to region, continuing to think of the West as a process. They
find *connectedness,* not isolation: frontier areas are both *connected*
and *remote.* These historians sometimes compare the processes of
human history to a biological process called species shifting, the
movement and exchanges of organisms. In recent human terms,
they think, the processes defining the West include market making, land taking, boundary setting, state forming, self-shaping—
processes which result in both homogenization and separation of
human groups. The human history of the region in which the

bristlecone pine is embedded includes these processes, which may seem at first glance like a laundry list applicable to all histories, and perhaps even natural history.

Recent human impacts on the region have been dramatic. Much of the biota of the Great Basin has undergone catastrophic change at the hand of modern humans. During the "Exploitation Pageant," the era of 1860–1890, the piñon-juniper forests were stripped in ever-widening circumference around mining towns, the radius of desolation revealing the extent of the mineral boom.

During the same era, range cattle literally consumed the sagebrush grasslands, "one of the last great vegetation resources to be suddenly, radically, and irrevocably changed by the introduction of domestic livestock," writes James A. Young in *Cattle in the Cold Desert*. In this late nineteenth-century pastoral experiment, the grasslands were tested by a system of ranching which put as many cattle on the range as possible, until losses of livestock became too great to bear. Miners and cattlemen showed little concern for a "vanished primeval flora." As Young has written, "the plant communities did not bend or adapt; they shattered." The bristlecone pine remained above most of this activity, virtually untouched.

More recently, and more pervasively, widespread and disastrous atomic testing has created less visible and less easily measurable but more devastating effects. These disturbances to the life of the region are coupled with the toxicity of so-called conventional weapons. Certain modern techniques of mining call for unearthing large tracts of landscape and have also created problems for life in the Great Basin. These problems are not visible *in* the bristlecone forests, where little human disturbance is evident, but *from* the forests, high in the mountains of the Great Basin, the results of human acts spread out below, like a map of disturbances.

Temporary Isolation

The Great Basin has been altered in major ways, and that process, which includes especially land taking, boundary setting, and market making by military and corporate entities, continues. What these entities have recently ignored has acquired value because it has been left alone. Mostly, people were and are afraid of this cold desert, especially its mountains. They shifted into it with discomfort primarily because they have also been acquisitive and aggressive. In the nineteenth and twentieth centuries the Great Basin has seen boom and bust with a vengeance, the booms larger and the busts coming quicker than anywhere else on the continent, and yet the cycle has been remarkably discontinuous, too, and can hardly be called a cycle at all. For the Great Basin is also the natural home of the ghost town, of the machine—as Patricia Limerick has written—abandoned in the desert. There are ranching ghost towns, mining ghost towns, and military ghost towns. And each of these experiments in Great Basin culture has left both visible and invisible changes to the region.

The future may present a pattern both different from and the same as the past. Recreation is coming even to the Great Basin—strange as that may seem—because people are coming, and the nature of that recreation has to do with the nature of the modern world. In 1994 the president of Walt Disney Company was killed in a helicopter crash while skiing in the Ruby Mountains. As it happened, a friend of mine died with him. Helicopter skiing is at the same time ephemeral and industrial, calling for no resorts. Its technology, evolved from the elaborate and expensive machinery of twentieth-century war, suggests that recreation in the Great Basin, now consisting of a few brief raids on the country, will settle here someday.

The phenomenon of helicopter skiing compares and contrasts with the solid and yet virtual reality of the theme park hotels of Las Vegas, which are designed to keep people inside and alter the human senses of time and space. But that is another story.

Despite these major disturbances of life in the Great Basin, it appears that few people have settled the interior of the region or changed it much in the last century. The sparseness of population and austerity of the land create a complex of perceptions. I have lived for some decades on both the eastern and western edges of this world, and have been afraid of solitude and time that seem to emanate from the natural history of the region. In the Great Basin of the mind one meets Chronos, who eats his children. The Great Basin's natural history is filled with things not like us, things which seem out of the past, as frightening as eternity, suggesting time out of mind. Because I came to this region after the bomb was brought here, the things that humans have done to the region also play a role in my complex response to the landscape. The landscape is saturated with human acts which seem terrible, and not like us. Even the people I meet often seem damaged, fragile, or strange, and I worry about them. I notice the sores on the hands of a waitress in Caliente, or the strange stoop of a man walking through a hotel lobby in Tonopah. The Great Basin continues to tug at my imagination.

Much of the recent history of the region has occurred in the mountains. Shift perspective and you observe not a Great Basin but a region of mountains where time and light are exposed, as minerals, water, timber. In the great American desert of the Great Basin, travelers climbed up dry streambeds, higher than they wished, and, if lucky, found their watery sources. Some climbed into the mountains looking for exposed ledges of silver chloride, until they could see out to a few of the hundreds of other hazy ranges whose fuzzy edges suggested endless time and space. I have spent more time in the mountains of the region than in the valleys. Perhaps this has been a way to hide from modern realities too frightening to confront on a daily basis, but it has also exposed me to another reality. The mountains of the Great Basin contain the bristlecone pines, and the people who study these trees begin their thinking about natural history in the mountains.

Longevity, Use, and Wonder

For those who study it, nothing has come to embody a great abundance of austere time and space more completely than the Great Basin bristlecone pine, the world's oldest growing tree, which has flourished above disturbing human activities. Young trees of a thousand years of age are not particularly remarkable. But the old ones: if you saw them, you would not call them flourishing, exactly. Like much of the life in the Great Basin, they look to be barely surviving: they look to be survivors from some past era, or explorers of the limits of life. They are both, and extravagant too.

Because of their age, they do not belong to California, Nevada, Utah, or any modern political entity, but are, like the Great Basin, a place between worlds. These trees inhabit a region not comfortable for human beings, a region of time out of mind. There were aboriginal people who hunted high in the mountains, people of unknown origin and fate, but probably none dwelled there earlier or as long as some living trees or groves. Even Paiutes are relatively late comers to the region of the bristlecone.

In my lifetime, people have continued to adjust their attitudes toward these trees. Before people knew how old the bristlecones were, the species seemed worthless. I offer the following description from "How to Know the Trees of the Intermountain Region," a publication by the U.S. Forest Service, printed in 1940.

Bristlecone Pine

(Pinus aristata)

This species of pine is rare in the Intermountain Region, being found chiefly on sterile or poor soils.

It is found in a few places in southern Utah and Nevada on rocky slopes at high elevations. This tree is also known as foxtail or cattail pine as the needles stay on the twigs for many years making long tail-like branches.

Although sometimes cut for firewood, this tree has no commercial value. This tree can be observed in its native state at Cedar Breaks (southern Utah) where it grows along the edges of the cliffs.

The questions people ask, you might say, determine the answers they get. These trees, by their knotty and twisted appearance and reality, now evoke questions of time, space, and change, but they have not always done so. Because they elicit and tangle central modern concerns of humankind, the stories of humans who have sought to know them make impossible any quick and efficient untying of scientific and mythic, mathematical and aesthetic, historical and folkloric strands. As Emerson once said of the Sequoia, another species of old tree, "The wonder is that we can look at these trees and not wonder more." Humans have wondered more.

CHAPTER 1

Somewhere Between Colorado and California

The Death of Frederick Creuzefeldt

In late August of 1853, near Cochetopa Pass in southern Colorado, a German botanist named Frederick Creuzefeldt cut two branches from a pine with which he was not familiar. The tree grew in a scanty forest of a kind that would be called *krummholz* in the early twentieth century, named for the crooked, elfin character of the stunted trees that grew under harsh conditions, high in cold mountains. The branches he collected bore no cones. Collecting this sample was not an important event in Creuzefeldt's life, and he probably did not reflect upon it. He would be dead a month or so later.

Consequently, the record of the encounter of a European immigrant and bristlecone pine in the new world is clouded. A map depicting the places where other men and similar trees met marks sporadic events in diverse places, sowed across the Rockies, Colorado Plateau, Great Basin, and mountains of California, and across the years in no regular pattern.

According to Donald Culross Peattie's *A Natural History of Western Trees,* Creuzefeldt, who discovered the bristlecone, came from St. Louis with a professional and scientific Pacific Railroad Survey led by Captain John W. Gunnison. The crux for the survey was Cochetopa Pass (10,032 feet in elevation), because Gunnison was

Rocky Mountain bristlecone. (D. K. Bailey photo)

directed to find a southern route for a railroad crossing the Continental Divide. Virtually all western surveys of this era included a botanist who would collect specimens and send them for identification to eastern centers of learning.

Frederick Creuzefeldt was a tough fellow, and this was not his first journey to the Rockies. He had been one of the strongest members of the party John C. Frémont recruited for a disastrous survey of the 38th parallel in 1848. Creuzefeldt's story is normally taken as a footnote to the pertinent histories of Frémont's and Gunnison's explorations, of exploration serving empire and science serving exploration.

Because Frémont had made himself newsworthy, his story is more completely and heroically told by historians. By 1848, when he was sent west by his father-in-law, Senator Thomas Hart Benton, he was past his glory days as a self-styled "Pathfinder" and publicizer for westward expansion. Five years after he "discovered" the Great Basin in 1843, he seemed to feel that blazing a trail over the Rockies for the iron horse would make him a hero once again. He was funded by St. Louis businessmen who wanted a southern railroad to San Francisco.

Frémont chose to surmount the southern Rockies in 1848, but his ignorance of the geography and his choice of an unfortunate season for mountain travel doomed his party. The party's scout, Old Bill Williams, has been blamed for leading Frémont's thirty-three men into heavy snow and bitter cold; by December, somewhere near the headwaters of the Rio Grande, the men were no longer seeking Cochetopa Pass or glory, but trying only to survive. They began to freeze to death.

The day after Christmas 1848, Frémont dispatched Williams and his three healthiest men to acquire supplies in Taos, return, and rescue the expedition. When one member of the rescue team expired, so the story goes, he may have been eaten by Frederick Creuzefeldt and his fellow rescuers. Eleven men perished from exposure to the elements.

Five years later, Gunnison approached the southern Rockies. He chose a better season for mountain travel and crossed the high pass safely. But a month later, while camping on the banks of the Sevier River in western Utah, Gunnison's party wandered into a war between Mormons and Indians. Members of the Pahvant group attacked the survey early one morning while the cook was preparing the breakfast fire. He was the first to die.

This happened on October 2, 1853, near Fillmore, Utah, though some historians place the event incorrectly in space and time. Confusion is understandable because at the edge of the Great Basin, the Sevier River runs north up one mountain valley past Manti, and then reverses itself near Fillmore, finally disappearing into a dry lake.

Gunnison died riddled with Paiute arrows, and Frederick Creuzefeldt pitched forward beside the fire next to his leader, one of the eight victims of the so-called Gunnison Massacre. The bodies were mutilated by coyotes and other animals before they were recovered twelve days later. Gunnison could be identified by his iron-grey hair, and his body was removed. Creuzefeldt was not identified and was buried anonymously with his fellows on this spot, memori-

Foxtail pine, Paul Land-acre relief print. (from Peattie, *A Natural History of Western Trees*, 1953)

alized by a monument thirty miles west of Fillmore, well into the Great Basin. Gunnison is memorialized in Utah and Colorado by towns, a river crossing, a reservoir, a butte, a county, a national forest, and two valleys. Nothing is named for Creuzefeldt.

The Disappearance of John Jeffrey

John Jeffrey (1826–1853), a solitary Scottish botanist, formerly gardener at the Royal Botanical Garden in Edinburgh, was sent to North America in 1851 on a collecting expedition. In 1852 he plucked

Bristlecone pine, Paul Landacre relief print. (from Peattie, *A Natural History of Western Trees*, 1953)

a limb containing cones from a tree inhabiting the Klamath Mountains of northern California. This was the Colorado bristlecone's western relative, the foxtail pine, which is more prolific in the southern Sierra Nevada. Jeffrey's sample can be found in the herbarium at the garden. Jeffrey himself, as Peattie describes him, "was always a lonely man, collecting far out ahead of civilization, claiming few friends." He vanished without a trace the next year while walking east from San Diego across what is sometimes called the Colorado Desert at the southeastern corner of California. He may have crossed the Colorado and died in New Mexico.

The foxtail pine (*Pinus balfouriana* Greville and Balfour) acquired its name from John Hutton Balfour (1808–1884), curator of the Royal Botanical Garden, one of the men who described Jeffrey's limb. Because Jeffrey collected a branch containing many fascicles of four needles, and these were used for the description and illustration of the foxtail pine, it was not until 1880 that anyone noted the similarity of Jeffrey's and Creuzefeldt's samples.

The Foxtail–Bristlecone Pine Complex

Brigham Young had shipped the murdered Creuzefeldt's branches east, where they were preserved in herbaria by the Princeton botanist John Torrey (1797–1873) and his protégé at Harvard, Asa Gray (1810–1888). To identify a tree, however, botanists require needles and cones and to know the original location for the samples. Otherwise, the provenance of the tree cannot be verified by later investigators.

Three coneless branches of the Colorado bristlecone seem also to have been collected on Frémont's second expedition to California in 1843–44. The precise source of these samples is unknown as well, but they were probably collected near South Park, Colorado. They are preserved in the U.S. National Herbarium and the Gray Herbarium at Harvard University.

It is poetic to imagine that the bristlecone was collected on the same expedition that led to Frémont's discovery of the Great Basin. However, the specimens of 1843 and of 1848 are insufficient for complete identification of a species. George Engelmann (1809–1884) of St. Louis wrote the first complete published description of the Colorado bristlecone pine (*Pinus aristata* Engelmann) in 1863, using samples collected by C. C. Parry in 1861. The specimen Engelmann used, and named *aristata* for its bristled cone, is now in the collection at the Missouri Botanical Garden in St. Louis.

The story of the bristlecone begins in difficulty because it marches forward in a halting manner. Fragments of this tree found in places largely conceived as obstacles to transcontinental travel passed or were bypassed from hand to hand and from the dead to the living. Because of this very peculiar, almost ritualistic chain of evidence, the bristlecone pine was first identified and named in an arboretum east of the Mississippi from samples stored in an herbarium by Engelmann, who probably never saw a tree of the species. Those who confronted the tree sometimes died. Creuzefeldt passed

Hydrographic Great Basin. (Map by Deborah Reade from Trimble, *Sagebrush Ocean*, 1989)

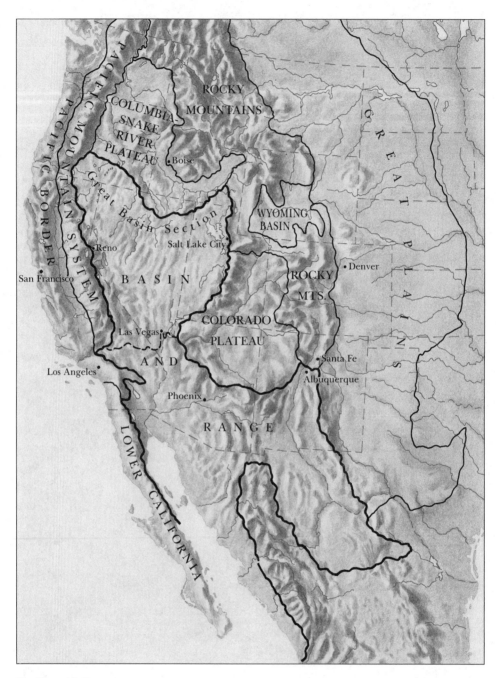

**Physiographic Great
Basin. (Map by
Deborah Reade from
Trimble, *Sagebrush
Ocean*, 1989)**

out of history—or into it, perhaps—as a collector, and Engelmann, who named the tree by virtue of his skill in the science of systematic classification, passed into the history of bristlecone taxonomy by appending his name to the name of the tree.

In 1880 Engelmann created an orderly system by which pines might be categorized, published as *Revision of the Genus Pinus*. He stressed characteristics of appearance, sometimes corresponding to the age of a tree, including bark, colors of woods, positions of stomata, and differences in needles. He focused particularly on the differences of structure to be found in the needles—"of the greatest importance for the classification of pines"—and the position of resin ducts within them. He also focused on the shape of cones and forms of the cone-scales.

As part of his system, Engelmann placed the foxtail-bristlecone pine complex within a single species named, on the basis of priority, *Pinus balfouriana*. "*Pinus balfouriana,* Jeffrey, and *Pinus aristata,* Engelmann, of the Colorado Rocky Mountains, are identical in leaf structure and in flowers and must be united," he wrote, "though the cone of the former is elongated, often even cylindrical . . . while the other has an oval cone with thinner scales and awnlike prickles." (The awn is the delicate prickle that terminates the grain sheath of barley, oats, and some grasses.) "In Utah and Nevada," he noted, "a form occurs with cones like the latter, but with short, stout, re-curved prickles."

Between the samples from Colorado and the samples from California there was a gap which represents on a map the unexplored Great Basin. Because Engelmann's samples were incomplete, he had no way of seeing what that gap might hide, and a paucity of samples did not allow him to apply his own salient criteria for identification. The needles of the western species glisten and those of the eastern species are dusty looking. The differences in appearance reflect deeper underlying structural differences in the populations of trees from which the samples come and outline the edges of a gap in human knowledge which remained open for nearly a century because it did not seem very important.

A Theory of Discovery

Who discovered what and how? In stories of collectors, preservers, describers, publishers, classifiers, and systematizers, the individuals seem in retrospect less important than the process in which they participated, a process behind the scenes, so to speak, while the "winning of the West" took center stage. The foxtail-bristlecone pine complex was discovered by no one man, but was uncovered as a by-product of that American procedure called exploration, driven by the imperialism of men like Thomas Hart Benton, the ambition of those like John C. Frémont, the nationalism of Scottish botanists, the curiosity of Germans, and whatever solitary force drove John Jeffrey.

Why did empire builders patronize botanists? There were, of course, utilitarian reasons. Exploration was also driven by the idea of preserving the wild species that would disappear before progress. In herbaria, archives of western flora in eastern and European academic centers, men like Asa Gray and George Engelmann desired to theorize systems of classification and meet the challenges European and especially Darwin's science offered to their understanding of the new world.

For some time, American historians have followed William Goetzmann, who conceived of exploration as an activity with a "mission, not as a sequence of discoveries." Exploration is "programmed," he wrote in *Exploration and Empire*. The "purposes, goals, and evaluations of new data are to a great extent set by previous experiences, the values, the kinds and categories of existing knowledge, and the current objectives of the civilized centers from which the explorer sets out on his quest." It is no accident that Jeffrey and Creuzefeldt were Europeans, or that the latter was engaged by Benton's railroad survey. European scientific culture discovered the bristlecone pine in the service of American imperialism. Which is how Creuzefeldt, a German botanist, happened to be killed on the bank of the Sevier River by Indians native to the Great Basin.

Scientists did not serve only pure knowledge, especially in the West. The interests of developers, especially of the railroads, selected and determined the importance of problems worthy of attention. Yet there is no railroad over Cochetopa Pass. Peattie linked the character of people and trees. He thought of the foxtail pine as being solitary like its discoverer, but was imagining the foxtail as it grows in the Sierra, not where Jeffrey collected it, in the Klamath Range. Jeffrey was remembered by his employers for a very different pine named after him (*Pinus jeffreyi* Greville and Balfour). Creuzefeldt has been forgotten. Memory is selective and can give its own shape to the past. But exploration can also alter or decenter the very powerful culture from which it proceeds. Trees can disrupt theories of history too.

Identification suggests knowledge of something, for itself and of itself, yet this is almost never true because identification always implies a history of discovery and a relationship between observer and observed. The tree in this book has gone by many different names, and its literature, scientific and popular, refers to it by some no longer in use. Bristlecone, foxtail, hickory pine. *Pinus longaeva,* the name given in 1970 as a result of extensive research in the field and in herbaria by Dana K. Bailey, is perhaps its final and lasting name, but probably not.

Alvin Noren and the Uses of Bristlecone Forests

If, on the other hand, knowledge comes not from exploration, discovery, or naming but from long use, and is established in situ, the trees of the foxtail-bristlecone pine complex, of the family *balfouriana,* have supplied humans in their desires for fuel, power, decoration, and containers, have served to provide shade, perhaps control erosion, conserve water, and produce free oxygen.

To detail some local uses in the Great Basin: young, long (ca. 40 feet) logs can be found as the walls of nineteenth-century cabins. Bristlecone beams can be found shoring up mines, and they made durable power poles at the turn of the century for the Aqueduct, Tonopah, and Goldfield power lines. Light but resinous, the wood is soft but tough and resistant to the elements. Forest rangers used bristlecone wood for signposts. The close-grained wood was utilized in a unique way by the Russian immigrant and scholar of conifers Nicholas T. Mirov (1893–1980), because he was also an artist. He cut and incised bristlecone blocks, suggesting a great deal about knowledge when he printed images of bristlecones with bristlecone blocks.

As for power of a more tangible sort: more than one author notes that the downed scraps of long-dead bristlecones make excellent fire. It would not be unreasonable to imagine a shepherd or cowhand working the high slopes of the White Mountains burning seven-thousand-year-old fragments of history to warm his feet. There were, according to the U.S. Forest Service, plenty of shepherds in the White Mountains of California at the turn of the century, their fires smoking up the high slopes of the mountains and visible from the Owens Valley. Ten-thousand-year-old pieces of bristlecone wood have been retrieved in the White Mountains from campfires made by people thousands of years ago.

By accident, I once cut up a downed bristlecone for firewood on a white rocky ridge of the Markagunt Plateau, and since then I have noticed a number of authors confessing to having done the same. I had a permit from the Forest Service, but it was—I find this strange to write—for Jeffrey pine. My ignorance or carelessness was published by the seven hundred or so rings that marked the ends of the rounds I loaded in my truck. So pitchy and dense, they made the best kindling I ever split. And the fragrance! It filled my house. No doubt these uses or abuses of old wood are instructive. The real discovery of the bristlecone occurred perhaps when humans were locating a hierarchy of uses for this limited resource; then they began a negotiation of their relation to this tree.

According to the lore of the bristlecone, in the late 1940s Alvin E. Noren (1892–1974?), Inyo District ranger in the White Mountains, harvested a load of bristlecone wood. He had planned to mill the wood in Bishop for kitchen paneling and cabinets he was building for his home in Big Pine. Late at night, by the light of his kerosene lantern, he inspected the cut ends of his logs and realized the harvest of years he had loaded into his truck. Noren paneled his home with bristlecone wood and crafted particularly fine cabinets. After counting the rings, however, he had other thoughts and began the process by which the first bristlecone reserve was instituted at the western edge of the Great Basin, in the White Mountains of California.

Noren was a native Californian of Swedish ancestry. He was fifty-five years old when he measured the largest bristlecone and named it The Patriarch. He was tall, slim, erect, with glasses astride a long nose. His blue eyes had a look of far distances. His white curly hair was closely cropped, his chin firm, ears pointed, and lips thin. He was curious about those trees, and in 1947 sent The Patriarch's dimensions to Nick Mirov at the University of California at Berkeley. Mirov came to the White Mountains, where he confirmed Noren's measurements, collected bristlecone seeds for the Forest Service's research station in Placerville, and also painted oil landscapes of the Sierra.

Before Noren retired in 1954, he was able to institute a small reserve around the Patriarch Tree and see the tree he measured added to the American Forestry Association's list of big trees.

An Accounting of Trees

A very specialized use has evolved from looking closely at the rings of trees. Under the magnified gaze of dendrochronology, the bristle-cone pine, discovered almost accidentally in the course of human history, has become a guide for reading this history. Counting tree-rings—an ancient and venerable practice—has been credited to Leonardo da Vinci, who conceived in around 1500 A.D. the project of determining "the nature of past seasons" from tree-rings. But there are even earlier references to this practice. Dendrochronology as a precise science became a distinctively American exercise early in the twentieth century, when Andrew Ellicott Douglass (1867–1962), a young astronomer at the University of Arizona, began to compare variations in annual precipitation to the thicknesses of annual tree-rings.

Douglass's story has been told primarily by his students, many of whom became eminent scientists, and one of whom became president of the University of California. All stress Douglass's versatility and speak of him as a visionary, a man of telescopes and microscopes, with cosmic and microscopic interests. As an astronomer, he was primarily interested in establishing a regular and cyclic relation between climatic and sunspot phenomena, as recorded by the sequences of narrow and wide rings in climate-sensitive trees. His secondary interest—really a means to his vision—was to establish a master sequence of tree-rings by matching the overlapping tree-ring patterns of dead and live trees in the Southwest.

Douglass started with cross sections and radial sections of trees. Later, about 1920, he began to use a Swedish increment borer to withdraw cores and count the tree rings of live Douglas fir and ponderosa pine. The Swedish increment borer is an elegant tool that allows humans to see into trees without cutting them down, by removing a pencil-thin section. Although the hole remains visible, the tree's sap plugs it almost immediately, and the hole seems to do no harm to the tree's health. Devised by economic foresters to measure the growth of plantation trees, it has become the principal tool of dendrochronology.

One bores by twisting a sharpened tube which screws its way into the heartwood of the tree. The bore is the hole left, the core is what the borer seeks. It is hard work, a laborious two-handed job, done by feel, calling for delicacy as well as power. In the early days, the borers were about fifteen inches long, but for very large trees the foresters in Sweden designed meter-long tools which could remove cores of up to forty inches. The idea is to penetrate the wood perpendicular to the growth of the tree. Often, and especially with old trees, the difficult question is where to bore, and how many times, in order to get a set of cores with a continuous sequence of rings from the origin of the tree's growth to its most recent ring. This is an exercise in intuitive solid geometry.

A romantic fascination with the interior of trees is suggested by the penultimate paragraph of *Walden*: "a strong and beautiful bug . . . came out of the dry leaf of an old table of apple-tree wood, which had stood in a farmer's kitchen for sixty years . . . from an egg deposited in the living tree many years earlier still, as appeared by counting the annual layers beyond it." Using a widely known folktale, Thoreau evokes some promise of a lost past that might re-emerge in the present and makes the point explicit when he asks, "Who does not feel his faith in a resurrection and immortality strengthened by hearing of this?" But this is to beg his own question.

Late in life, Thoreau practiced a disciplined sort of amateur dendrochronology, counting the tree-rings of stumps—many of which he sawed himself—to detect an order of events, and "unroll the rotten papyrus on which the history of the Concord forest is written." He also wrote in his journal that it was "easier to recover the history of the trees . . . than to recover the history of men who walked beneath them." He was deeply—and as it turned out fatally—engaged in tree-ring study in the late fall of 1860. According to his biographer, Walter Harding, he spent the afternoon of December 3, 1860, on his knees, counting rings on stumps of trees. "It was a bitterly cold day," writes Harding, "and before it was over he had contracted a severe cold—the beginning, as it turned out, of his final illness."

Like Thoreau, when a modern dendrochronologist burrows into a tree he turns the story of the bug inside out. Like Thoreau, he wishes to do more than count rings. Many well-known American conservationists have read tree-rings. Thoreau, John Muir, and Aldo Leopold especially. All three found that the exercise engaged a crossing of human and natural history. In the "Good Oak" section of *A Sand County Almanac,* Leopold imagines that he plunges into and re-emerges from past human history as he cuts through his log, where he finds an "allegory for historians in the diverse functions of saw, wedge, and axe." The saw works across the years, the wedge radially, and the axe on a diagonal, each offering the historian a different perspective.

The modern, scientific method of reading tree-rings developed by Douglass seems deceptively simple because it is essentially literary. For the dendro-reader the rings constitute a text, something that has meaning and structure and can be decoded. The tree encodes and records, the scientist decodes and discloses. As with any text, there can be certain gaps or inconsistencies: a scrupulous reader must create a master plot from many trees by comparison and inference.

Dendrochronology is based on the uniformitarian principle espoused by James Hutton in 1785—"the present is the key to the past." Though uniformitarian principles are not entirely historical, because they cannot allow that the past is different from and strange to the present, Edmund Schulman (1908–1958), a prominent student of Douglass's at the University of Arizona, spoke of the quest for "an absolute time-scale for a particular region," by "the construction of a master tree-ring chronology anchored in the present." Standing at the origin of his inquiry, but at the latest chapter of the tree's story, the scientist reads backward, toward the beginning; at the end of his inquiry he reaches the origin of the tree's story, and perhaps of his own.

Beginning early in the century, Douglass engaged in reading what he called the "records of the trees," which he imagined they had jotted down like memoranda "at the close of each fading year." He waxed poetic about these records as "a magic key to mysterious books." In the Southwest, the central mystery was a chronicle of precipitation. Douglass's single purpose, unwavering throughout his long career, was to predict future precipitation on the basis of the past.

Trees, Cities, and History

It was almost by accident that Dr. Clark Wissler of the American Museum of Natural History heard Douglass speak on dendrochronology in 1914. People use trees to build cities, Wissler realized, and dendrochronology might offer a solution to a "perplexing archaeological problem, the dates of occupation for the great abandoned urban centers of the prehistoric Southwest." He sent seven large sections of roof beams from northern New Mexico to Douglass in 1916. The beams were primarily ponderosa with an occasional

Douglas fir. In 1919, Earl Morris sent six beam samples from Aztec, New Mexico.

The dating of ancient cities was a diversion for Douglass and went slowly. He began to study wood from Pueblo Bonito of Chaco Canyon in the early 1920s. In 1922, the National Geographic Society contributed $7,500 to fund a "beam expedition." For the Society, research played a subsidiary role to a marketing plan and an article for the magazine with black and white photos, some hand-tinted. Because the subject of the article was keyed to the discovery of Pueblo Bonito's date of origin, more money followed, which was enticing to Douglass, a dendrochronologist without a laboratory.

Douglass sought cycle and prediction, yet the way archaeology swayed him from his principal aim was in retrospect no swerve at all. The pertinent contemporary questions for archaeology in the Southwest were multifaceted. (1) How old were the ancient cities? (2) Why were they abandoned? (3) Where did the people go? The second and third questions would lead back to precipitation. The real message or mystery Douglass wanted to unlock related the history of humans in the arid environment of the Southwest to the future of humans who wanted to make homes there.

After decades of counting backward, Douglass had, by sampling many ponderosa trees with overlapping chronologies, established the procedure of *cross-dating*, of matching distinctive synchronous patterns of rings in separate living and dead trees of a single species found in a specific region. In 1929, at a site near Show Low, Arizona, Douglass achieved a sufficiently continuous tree-ring chronology to put a precise date on the construction of not just Pueblo Bonito, but more than forty ancient cities. Using a complete series of rings from ponderosa pine spanning nearly a thousand years, he revealed not only the ages, but also established a record that could reveal climatic fluctuations of an era covering the so-called Anasazi cultures. The final event is widely known and celebrated as "Bridging the Gap," or the "Crossing of the Gap." When Douglass matched the pattern of tree rings in a "master chronology," he linked the prehistory and modern history of the Southwest. Native American history became part of a continuity with European American history.

A single sequence constructed from many cores—single because it applies to only one geographical region, the Southwest—allowed the beginning of both dendrochronology and dendroclimatology. The chronology seemed firm: the climatological cycles Douglass hoped to read were unambiguous. Yet like most readers, Douglass desired not just a chronicle but a plot. He believed in but could never describe his compelling pattern of climate, and questions of cyclicity continue to be debated.

Nevertheless, for some environmental determinists his dendrochronology could become dendrohistory when certain patterns in tree-rings correlated with well-known historical anomalies. For instance, the narrow tree-rings found for the latter half of the thirteenth century, presumably caused by drought or cold weather, might be used to explain why the great cliff dwellings of the Southwest were abandoned. Still, cultural anthropologists and archaeologists have hesitated; it is a tenuous inference, reading the tree record with such determinism back into a record of human responses to environmental change.

So, by the late 1930s dendrochronology was affixed—albeit ambiguously—to human history. On the Colorado Plateau, this history could extend to the pre-Columbian era, a period sufficient to date such archaeological sites as Mesa Verde. Such a chronology was insufficient for human history in a broader worldwide context, because it was too short and too local.

Climate and Tree-Rings

Douglass worked primarily with ponderosa pine in Arizona and New Mexico, but trees which grew much older than ponderosas enticed him. The monumental sequoia (*Sequoiadendron gigantea*) of the western Sierra Nevada seemed to grow past its third millennium. It was one of Douglass's favorite candidates for study in the late teens and early 1920s. Because old sequoias appear so sturdy and monumental, they seem a symbol of a certain theory of natural history in themselves. Sequoias allowed Douglass to develop further his technique of cross-dating and extend the ponderosa chronology several thousand years. He had established a thousand-year pre-Christian sequoia chronology by 1920. But the sequoia, growing on the west slope of the Sierra, is well watered and consequently insufficiently sensitive to changes of climate. Dead sequoia wood lasts about a millennium before decaying. Other pines and some firs are more readable for records of climate change, but do not live long or last long after they die.

Douglass got funding for dendrochronology from John C. Merriam of the Carnegie Institution. In the 1930s, people all over the world were fascinated by his absolute chronology. Douglass became briefly renowned, and the results for the University of Arizona were impressive too. He established the Laboratory of Tree-Ring Research in Tucson in 1937 and enlisted students in his discipline. He had already enlisted Edmund Schulman, in 1932, and Waldo S. Glock, in 1935. In 1939 the lab and office found a home under the football stadium. There, until 1960 when he was ninety-two, Douglass pursued climate in tree-rings, never wavering from his fervent desire to establish a method for long-range weather prediction predicated on data correlated with sunspot cycles.

Edmund Schulman was Douglass's best hope to carry on the work of climate and tree-rings, seeking the elusive cycle of astroclimatology. He was in many ways modern where Douglass had been Victorian, quantitative where Douglass had been intuitive. Douglass spoke of "scientific instincts" and "literary instincts." Schulman assembled and sorted data. He was not interested in archaeology, but in climate and tree-rings. He picked up many of the pieces of this problem and brought a new rigor to their analysis. Because he was interested in reconstructing climates of the past, Schulman began to see how tree-ring data were subject to successive improvement, or re-reading.

It became clear to him that to contain a great deal of history, the wood of a tree must be old enough to reveal a great many years and the tree's growth sensitive enough to create patterns. That is all, but it is a great deal, simple and complex. Framing a set of questions, Schulman began to investigate what he termed "overage conifers" in the western United States. His survey was by no means random, since he, unlike Douglass, was conversant with modern biological and ecological thought.

Schulman wanted a pure science but took his funding where he could get it. In 1941, for instance, early in World War II, the Los Angeles Bureau of Power and Light, which managed Boulder (Hoover) Dam, asked the Scripps Institute of Oceanography to study flows of the Colorado River, hoping to step up power production at the dam. Scripps asked Schulman to predict, on the basis of one year's study of dendrochronology of the Colorado River Basin, what the flow would be. He made remarkably specific estimates of the frequency of drought, but cautioned that these kinds of studies led to predictions that would never be more than statistical probabilities.

After the war, especially with the establishment of the National Science Foundation (NSF) by Congress in 1950, there was serious funding for tree-ring studies. By the late 1950s, the International Geophysical Year of 1957–58, inspired in part by a prediction of a big year for sunspots, and punctuated by the first man-made satellites, opened up even more money. In 1956 Schulman was among the first researchers at the University of Arizona to receive an NSF grant. He knew where he would focus his studies and how dendrochronology could be used in what were coming to be called the geophysical sciences.

From 1939 on, he had spent every summer in the field. Right through the war years he conducted his search, narrowing his field to include the "special characteristics of the oldest individual trees." He also discovered that high-altitude species lived longest and began to establish his concept of "longevity under adversity." Certain high-altitude trees tended to be short of stature yet wide of diameter; they appeared gnarled or spiraled, sparsely foliaged, and their bark shrank—the cambium-edges retreating laterally to a narrow strip. These trees were likely to be found on thin or patchy soils, particularly on limestone, and only at certain parts of the species' range.

Recognizing in 1954 that "trees of great longevity . . . found recently are all from environments strongly limited with respect to moisture or temperature or both," and certain that pine trees may exceed two thousand years of age, he wanted to know "to what may we ascribe the great longevity."

Sequoias, precisely because they seemed not to exhibit longevity under adversity but longevity under optimum growing conditions, continued to fascinate him as they had Douglass. As Schulman wrote in 1954, "some believe [sequoias] may enjoy perpetual life in the absence of gross destruction." John Muir had reported counting 4,000 rings on a sequoia stump. Modern scientists can neither affirm nor deny this number and have found no sequoias—living or dead—more than 3,250 years of age. Could it be, Schulman wondered, that all the old sequoias had been wiped out about three millennia ago by some catastrophe? This question remains unanswered because scientists do not possess the tools to core very large standing trees to their centers.

In reaching for long chronologies, Schulman was hoping for continuous chronologies. His desire for continuities, long and short, reveals his focus on the pastness of the past and its presence. Schulman's climatic histories were inspired by the work of Douglass, but they were precise and concrete, not predictive. He was interested in long-range records of three to ten millennia and also focused on detailed shorter chronologies between one hundred years and a millennium.

Environmental historians have often focused on the development of cultures in arid regions. Some have defined aridity as the essential nature of the western American environment and have scrutinized the way cultures have dealt with periodic drought. When Schulman noted, almost casually, that dendrochronology contained dendroclimatology, if only it could be unlocked, he assumed climatic history was always the goal of this science he worked so hard to legitimate. He noted that the dust bowl year 1934, for instance, registered as narrow rings in many western trees, and the snowy "haylift" winter of 1948–49 registered as a very thick ring in certain regions.

Consequently, the record of periodic drought Schulman began to read in the tree-ring record was closely related to the baseline of environmental conditions that many social historians would like to possess. In many ways, he set the modern agenda for tree-ring studies in the early 1950s, before he encountered the bristlecone pine. But his work with the bristlecones in the later 1950s made him famous.

CHAPTER 2

The Calculus of Change

A World of Carbon

Willard Libby (1908–1980) was born in Colorado and educated at the University of California at Berkeley, where he taught until 1941. During World War II he worked on the Manhattan Project at Columbia University and solved the following problem. Uranium is an element with 92 protons. It appears naturally as a mixture of three so-called isotopes, with mass numbers (protons and neutrons) of 234, 235, and 238. Only the isotope 235 is valuable for making nuclear bombs, and it comprises less than one percent of the mixture. Libby helped develop a process to separate uranium isotopes by using the differences of their rates of diffusion in gaseous states.

At the University of Chicago after the war, Libby began to consider carbon and the problem of time. In 1940 two of his students had isolated the long-lived but unstable isotope carbon-14. Carbon, whose nucleus includes six protons, also normally has six neutrons and a weight of twelve. But a certain portion of the carbon in the earth's atmosphere has eight neutrons. Though it is chemically identical to carbon-12, an isotope, it is unstable and undergoes slow radioactive decay. By 1947 Libby knew that carbon-14 has a relatively long half-life of 5,668 ± 30 years. It is absorbed by all living things, and the age of carbon-bearing materials should be measurable by determining the concentration of the isotope.

Willard Libby in his chemistry lab, February 1960. This photo was taken for a lecture on peacetime uses of space. (Courtesy University Archives, University of California, Los Angeles)

Libby was able to establish this experimentally, and eventually he wrote *Radiocarbon Dating* (1955). Between 1955 and 1962 he worked for the U.S. Atomic Energy Commission (AEC); he became director of the Institute of Geophysics and Planetary Physics at the University of California, Los Angeles (UCLA) in 1962. His pioneering work in radiocarbon dating earned him the Nobel Prize for chemistry in 1960.

The ideas behind radiocarbon dating are connected by the following reasoning. (1) All living creatures absorb carbon constantly from their surroundings, plants primarily as carbon dioxide from the atmosphere. (2) A fixed and constant portion of this carbon is the carbon-14 isotope ("radiocarbon") created from nitrogen by naturally occurring cosmic radiation. (3) Carbon-14 decays spontaneously in a uniform and constant manner, measured by its half-life, the length of time required for one half of the sample to undergo radioactive decay. (4) When an organism dies, it stops absorbing carbon from its surroundings, becoming an isolated system. (5) Radiation from carbon-14 (radiocarbon) can be "heard" with a Geiger counter and accurately measured.

This straightforward, seemingly simple but perfectly abstract reasoning became, in the hands of Libby, an elegant method of measurement that seemed best suited for dating objects falling into the range of one thousand to thirty thousand years of age. His real genius shone out when he designed precise yet uncluttered laboratory procedures based upon four experimental assumptions: the half-life of radiocarbon is constant and can be accurately measured backward from the present (to avoid confusion, "present" was defined by international convention to be A.D. 1950); it is necessary and possible to obtain uncontaminated samples; radiocarbon is distributed uniformly across the world; and the proportion of radiocarbon to ordinary carbon has remained constant throughout time.

It is extremely difficult to isolate the measurement of carbon-14 radiation from background radiation. For instance, a typical carbon sample will produce about 50 counts a minute on a Geiger counter, whereas background radiation from cosmic radiation, even with the counter shielded by lead, is 600 counts a minute. At one time, or so the story goes, Libby and his colleagues considered transferring their laboratory to a deep mine. Instead, they designed an "anti-coincidence counter." The sample, contained in its own counter, is set in the middle of a ring of other counters, and as the surrounding counters record cosmic radiation, they subtract it electronically from the counts in the central chamber.

Even under perfect conditions, background radiation introduces error into radiocarbon measurements, and no matter how carefully they are made, radiocarbon measurements are statements of probability because all radioactive disintegration is a random process. Radiocarbon dates are reported, for instance, in the following form: a result of 5,000 ± 100 years B.P. (before present) indicates a 68 percent probability that the true (radiocarbon) age of a sample falls between 4,900 and 5,100 years B.P., indicates a 95 percent probability that it falls between 4,800 and 5,200 years B.P., and so on.

There is a second problem. The fourth assumption was incorrect; the creation of "natural" radiocarbon in the atmosphere has not been constant: its concentration exhibits historical change. Further, in the industrial world, humans have diluted radiocarbon through "anthropogenic" industrial uses of fossil fuels. More pertinent in the 1950s and 1960s, atmospheric testing of nuclear weapons augmented radiocarbon in the atmosphere so that it reached a peak in 1963 of near double the concentration of the recent past. Further back in history, in the pre-industrial era, the proportion of radiocarbon to ordinary carbon did not remain constant and showed systematic time-dependent variations, probably closely related to variations in solar activity.

The radiocarbon tool—as it was called—was seen by some as a great boon to European archaeology. Problems created by the assumption of constant radiocarbon in the atmosphere had not been established in the 1950s, and Libby's tool promised to extend the measurement of time backward well beyond five millennia, permitting the comparison of artifacts from various archaeological sites across Europe and Asia. When Libby began to date European artifacts his figures seemed to call into question a basic assumption held by European archaeologists, namely, that civilization began at a single site in the Near East and diffused to the north and west.

The World of Old Trees

In the automotive and nomadic American West that followed World War II, Edmund Schulman led teams of dendrochronologists from what was now a substantial but by no means burgeoning institution, the Laboratory of Tree-Ring Research at the University of Arizona. In the early 1950s, funded in part by the Office of Naval Research, he spread his search across western America for old and sensitive trees, sampling likely sites high in the mountains. His teams' data shed light on histories of the physical environment and on histories of human cultures, especially in North America. The virtue of dendrochronology was in its precision to the year, but its weakness was in applicability to a wide range of locations and a wide span of time. As Schulman wrote in 1954, "the unqualified archaeological dating to the year which tree-ring analysis makes possible under favorable circumstances is, from a world-wide point of view, of highly limited application."

In 1953, on a year's leave from Arizona, he was visiting professor of dendrochronology at the California Institute of Technology in Pasadena. There he had the good fortune to establish a working relationship with the director of the Plant Research Laboratory, Frits W. Went. Schulman was also engaged in a synthesis of material he had published in the *Tree-Ring Bulletin,* a journal he had edited since 1939. *Dendroclimatic Changes in Semiarid America* (1956) summed up this work, established his methodologies, and defended them from the criticism of other scientists. The criticism was a result of a continuing split in the discipline. Waldo S. Glock, for instance, had by the mid-1950s focused on qualitative analytic techniques and insisted on detailed anatomical and other botanical investigations. Schulman, like Douglass, was trained as an astronomer and specialized in the study of climate; he leaned toward statistical analysis and dendroclimatic correlations. Some say Douglass's naïveté toward the subtleties of botanical growth allowed him to pursue his dendroclimatology in such a single-minded way. The same could not be said of Schulman. *Dendroclimatic Changes* treated tree-rings in a more rigorous but still mechanistic way.

Schulman spent much of his 1953 summer field season near Sun Valley, Idaho, where he found a 1,650-year-old limber pine. On his journey home, following a "rumor that old trees existed there," he took a side trip to the White Mountains, where bristlecones grew in the Inyo National Forest.

It is a short if precipitous drive into the bristlecone stands of the White Mountains, stands of trees which would not have been explored had there not been a road and research facilities already established there at the White Mountain Research Station of the University of California, Berkeley. Schulman was looking not just for old but for sensitive trees, and the adverse conditions that created sensitivity also created difficulty in sampling. Yet the first season in the White Mountains convinced him to focus all his attention on the bristlecone pine. He began a survey of the species from California to Colorado.

Each summer from 1954 to 1956, Schulman cored trees in the White Mountains but still had not crossed what his team began to call "the B.C. Barrier." Long chronologies had their specific uses. When he appended some data from these early investigations to *Dendroclimatic Changes* in 1956, Schulman also acknowledged the possibility of correlating long tree-ring chronologies with radiocarbon dating techniques.

In 1956 he received a National Science Foundation grant for his research and focused exclusively on the groves in the White Mountains. In 1957 he began to bore into trees at what is now Schulman Grove. He called the first tree he could cross-date at more than 4,000 years Pine Alpha. His widening search of this small region

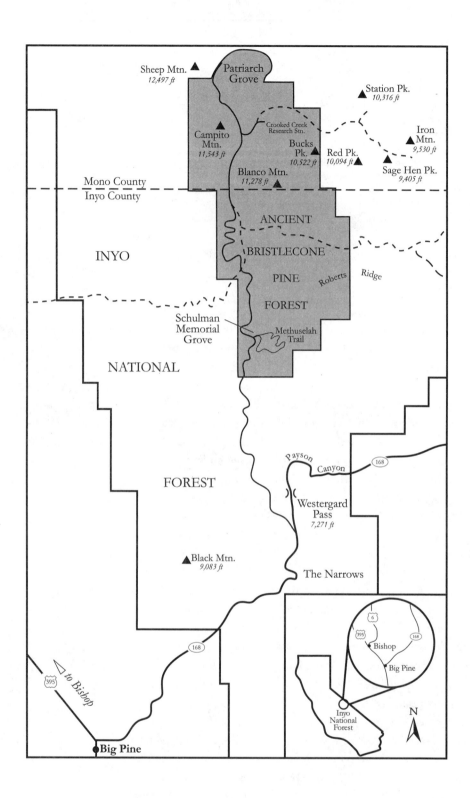

Edmund Schulman with a section of Great Basin bristlecone pine cut from the Methuselah Walk. This section is from a pickaback tree. Its surface shows an unbroken series of rings. (Courtesy Laboratory of Tree-Ring Research)

turned up a tree he could date at more than 4,600 years, growing on an especially dry slope which came to be called the Methuselah Walk. Schulman had been speaking of old trees as Methuselah trees for some time, and it was natural that he name this one THE Methuselah.

The summer of 1957 was a bizarre season for the Great Basin. In December 1956, Lewis Strauss, chairman of the Atomic Energy Commission, had received approval for twenty-five above-ground nuclear detonations, or "shots," as they were called. Some thirty tests, called Operation Plumbbob, were eventually conducted at the Nevada Test Site between April and October of 1957. At least twenty of these were dramatically visible as "second sunrises" in the predawn hours from the research stations of the White Mountains. Several of the "Plumbbob events" including "Owens," "Wheeler," "Charleston," and "Smoky" were named for geographical features of the Great Basin.

These tests were nearly coincident with the meetings of the United Nations Disarmament Commission from March to September of 1957. The U.S. Nuclear Defense Agency stated in its report of 1981, "as the PLUMBBOB series went forward, the international effort was turning toward cessation of future testing." A test ban was prevented by irreconcilable differences between United States and Soviet positions at the bargaining table, but "1957 was a year charged with controversy over the future of nuclear testing." Twenty years later, the Centers for Disease Control would begin to

(opposite) **Forest of the Ancient Bristlecone Pine, Inyo National Forest, White Mountains, California. (adapted from U.S. Forest Service map)**

Edmund Schulman (r.) and White Mountain district ranger Richard Wilson, with Pine Alpha, October 1956. (Joseph T. Radel photo, courtesy Laboratory of Tree-Ring Research)

note high rates of leukemia among populations of humans on and off the test site who had been exposed to nuclear radiation. Ranchers had immediately complained about massive die-offs of sheep and cattle, and Paiutes said the wild game animals like deer herds were decimated during this era.

Schulman was not distracted by contemporary events. People who knew him in those years believe that the story he wrote for a 1958 *National Geographic* is an accurate personal disclosure of his intense and single-minded dedication to bristlecone studies and of his pride in the craft of his work. The trees he confronted were so complex in structure that they seemed almost distorted. Because the old trees were characterized by strip growth, their narrow and sometimes partial rings could begin in one direction and then change direction by as much as ninety degrees. Boring carefully and recovering multiple but overlapping straight and complete cores from crooked wood—being able, as it were, to read around corners—Schulman used the same methods of cross-dating devised for work on the Colorado Plateau, but in this case all cores were taken from carefully chosen individual trees.

There is also something curious about Schulman's story. He suffered from heart disease, and three months before his article on the White Mountain bristlecone pines appeared in *National Geographic,* he died at the age of forty-nine. He was one of many scientists who studied the old trees and died young. His and other deaths continue to generate, among graduate students, a folklore of a strange causality between long-lived trees and men who could not live long enough to read their rings. Several years after Schulman's death, Thomas P. Harlan examined some of Schulman's samples in the tree-ring lab and discovered that a tree Schulman had cored but not cross-dated was more than 4,700 years old. Schulman had collected and cross-dated some of the data but had not read them. He was, in this sense, only the first editor of the bristlecone texts.

His quest, however, was misinterpreted in the popular press. In an influential article published in 1974, photojournalist Galen Rowell argued that impending death explained Schulman's dogged search for the Methuselah tree, a quest which damaged his health high in the thin, cold air, where he walked the steep hillsides searching the arid slopes for some fountain of youth. Rowell portrayed a double man, "who lived in a wilderness of logic, seeking patterns in what appeared random," but whose thoughts also "wandered along loosely structured mystical pathways." Rowell's version of Schulman's search for the oldest tree as a departure from the largely statistical interest of *Dendroclimatic Changes in Semiarid America* allowed him to depict "beyond the facade of a dedicated researcher . . . a doomed man hunting for an elixir." Well, that is to turn a man's complex and lifelong work into a cliché. Rowell's terrible simplification hides more than it reveals and perpetuates the perception that dendrochronologists were looking for the oldest tree and seeking longevity for its own sake.

Many images of Schulman appear in his professional writings and in the photographs of him at work during his last year of life. In the photographs, he appears a slim and vigorous middle-aged man, wearing Levis, work boots, and typically a checked flannel shirt with sleeves rolled up to the elbows, as do members of his team of investigators. His graying hair, combed straight back, leaves a wide but furrowed expanse of forehead above his dark-framed glasses. His hands are always prominent in these images, as he touches the old trees, fondling the original growth stem of the Methuselah, writing, holding borers, inspecting the shapes of trees small and large. He counts rings while sitting at a picnic table in the shade of a live bristlecone, his sight doubly augmented by glasses and a twenty-power scope, his right hand writing. In the lab, he steadies his sight by grasping the edge of a large section of tree and scrutinizes rings with a ten-power lens held in his left hand. These images dramatize the way old trees shaped his life, as presences and specimens, exteriors and interiors, objects to be felt and to be scrutinized.

Cross-dating

Schulman died with the bristlecone project only begun, and he left a complete set of cross-dating back to 780 B.C. The work fell into limbo for three years, until a new NSF grant allowed the investigation to be renewed. Charles Wesley Ferguson (1922–1986), one of the men who took over Schulman's research in the White Mountains, had lived on a shoestring there for many seasons, driving an old Model T, often working alone. Of all the investigators of bristlecone pines, he was most wide ranging and the most thoroughly comfortable in this austere working environment. Ferguson completed his doctorate at Arizona in 1960, studying the chronologies of Great Basin Big Sagebrush. During the 1960s and 1970s he surveyed countless bristlecone groves all across the Great Basin.

The center of Ferguson's work was in the Schulman Grove. He began to review Schulman's samples and in 1963 began to consider the wood of dead bristlecones. He was the first to do so with bristlecone trees, and it led down an avenue into the long past. He collected samples from standing dead trees, from snags, and even from fragments of trees that had died a long time ago. In the White Mountains, a long time ago was a very long time. He found that he could extend the bristlecone tree-ring line many millennia past the record of live trees, since dead bristlecone pines decay very slowly in their arid environment. This, says Bryant Bannister, director of the tree-ring lab from 1964 through 1981, was patient, thorough, meticulous work, "foot-slogging chronology building at its best." By 1969, after nearly a decade of work, Ferguson had established a

7,104-year chronology. Before he died he would extend his bristlecone chronology to 8,686 years.

An old grove of living and dead trees is like a long-neglected garden not planted by humans. The real work of dendrochronology begins when the investigator takes a set of cores and accurately records the location of each source. Normally the investigator records the region, locale, specific site, and precise location(s) of cores taken from individual trees, and maps the slope angles where they grow or have grown. These notes are supplemented by photographs of the sites and trees. In this way, the garden is cultivated.

In the laboratory, the cores are dried, straightened if necessary, placed in wood mounts, "surfaced" by shaving or sanding their cross section flat. Only then can they be cross-dated. Cross-dating, writes a modern worker, "is the art of dendrochronology." Douglass had cross-dated live and dead ponderosa, fir, and sequoia, but not such a long set as Ferguson faced in the bristlecone groves. Ferguson became the master of this skill.

The method of cross-dating with "skeleton plots" has not changed since Douglass established the procedures. It takes, as they say, a pencil, graph paper, and experience. The reader begins with a core that may or may not include the pith of a living tree and marks

Method of determining the date of a dwelling by cross-dating pinyon pine samples: A. Core from a living tree. B. Core from a dead tree. C. Core from a beam built into the dwelling. (Courtesy Laboratory of Tree-Ring Research)

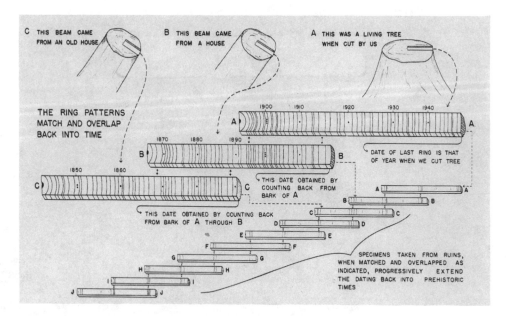

THE RING PATTERNS MATCH AND OVERLAP BACK INTO TIME

C THIS BEAM CAME FROM AN OLD HOUSE

B THIS BEAM CAME FROM A HOUSE

A THIS WAS A LIVING TREE WHEN CUT BY US

DATE OF LAST RING IS THAT OF YEAR WHEN WE CUT TREE

THIS DATE OBTAINED BY COUNTING BACK FROM BARK OF A

THIS DATE OBTAINED BY COUNTING BACK FROM BARK OF A THROUGH B

SPECIMENS TAKEN FROM RUINS, WHEN MATCHED AND OVERLAPPED AS INDICATED, PROGRESSIVELY EXTEND THE DATING BACK INTO PREHISTORIC TIMES

Method of extending a chronology between separate ruins by cross-dating ever-older pine samples: A. Core from a living tree. B. Core from a beam built into an old house C. Core from a beam built into another house. (Courtesy Laboratory of Tree-Ring Research)

on the sample core from the outside inward, with a dot for each decade, two for each fiftieth ring, and three for each century. When the reader does not have a core including either the pith or living tissue, he marks a "floating" sequence, a set of rings not anchored at its origin or in the present. A strip of graph paper is similarly marked by decade, one line for every ring.

Next, the reader looks for "signature rings" on the core. These are narrow rings surrounded by wider ones. Only the signature rings are recorded on the graph paper, according to their relative width. A line recorded on paper as ten (10) represents the narrowest ring, relative to adjacent rings. No two skeleton plots will be identical, but the patterns discerned by two or more readers should be similar. Though the width of tree-rings can be measured, these measurements are specific to the individual trees. Only the relative width or thickness matters for plotting and reading.

The reader creates skeleton plots for a number of trees in the same area, as many as possible, and these skeleton plots are visually averaged, allowing for locally absent rings, or in some cases "false" or double rings. Preferably, several composites are established by several readers and they are compared. The final and definitive composite constitutes a "master skeleton plot." Constructing one calls for patience, practice, and perseverance.

Calendar dates can be assigned to master skeleton plots by counting backward from the outermost living ring. However, in the case of cores that are not continuous from the tree's inception to the latest growth ring, or in the case of cores from trees that died in the indeterminate past, a master skeleton plot must be constructed from overlapping fragments of the whole chronology. This was the whole problem and purpose of Ferguson's enterprise. He began with, and re-established, Schulman's composite plots from living trees and matched floating skeleton plots to them, literally sliding each pattern against the composite until he found close matches. By such a process he slowly built a longer and longer composite, until it reached many millennia.

Ferguson's chronology of bristlecone tree-rings is linear, but the pattern of their widths is not. In old trees, he worked with narrow strips of wood whose rings were short, narrow embedded arcs that he counted and recorded as lines. His continuing pursuit of pattern from fragments of tree-rings became an indoor occupation, a

Charles Wesley Ferguson with a Swedish increment borer, from which he has removed a core, June 1984. (Courtesy Laboratory of Tree-Ring Research)

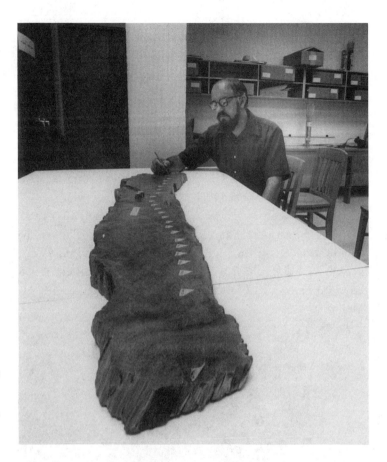

Wes Ferguson with
relic cross section from
the White Mountains.
Inside date: 2963 B.C.
Outside date: A.D. 278.
(Courtesy Laboratory
of Tree-Ring Research)

microscopic use of lumber, not trees, aimed at developing a master
abstraction of abstractions. His work was incremental and repeti-
tive as he cut core after core, took them to the laboratory, attempted
to plot their patterns, to give the set meaning by placing each fragment in a larger pattern.

Carbon and Trees: Calibration

It was probably inevitable that radiocarbon dating and dendrochronology would converge. In the late 1940s and early 1950s, Libby's
laboratory had provided a steady stream of dates for artifacts from
the Near East and Europe. Because a sample of old bristlecone
wood, precisely dated by Ferguson's dendrochronology, could also
be dated by radiocarbon methods, the two separate investigations
could be compared, with the bristlecone as the standard. This process is called calibration.

Ferguson began to submit dated bristlecone samples to radiocarbon analysis in the early 1960s, and his chronology, by 1969, corresponded to the era that included the rise of human civilization from the early Neolithic. In practice, he selected sets of 20-gram samples split radially from slabs of wood. Each sample bears a ten-year series of tree-rings. Each sample was sent, then as now, to another laboratory specializing in radiocarbon dating. Ferguson's chronology of 1969 called for the radiocarbon dating of 471 samples. His ring counts measured absolute and irrefutable dates: they tested the accuracy of radiocarbon as a tool.

Calibration was in high demand precisely because the results of Libby's radiocarbon dating were disturbing and exciting to archaeologists, precisely because they suggested a new and disruptive chronology for the rise of European civilization. History is not simply chronology, but in this case a chronological disruption altered history. A whole generation had been brought up to believe that the sequoia was the oldest living thing. The same generation had been brought up to believe that the Egyptian pyramids were the oldest human-constructed stone monuments, but the absolute chronology of Ferguson's bristlecones would make these beliefs untenable and would challenge the ideas of history they allowed.

To understand the effect of the new dates, one must imagine first the traditional structure or master plot of European prehistory before radiocarbon dating. According to the V. Gordon Childe model, named for its most articulate early proponent, European culture was imagined as a sort of tree whose roots resided in the Middle East, in Mesopotamia and Egypt, and whose branches spread out from the Aegean and Troy through Italy and eastern Europe toward central Europe and France, finally reaching Britain and northern Europe. This representation of history, known as the "diffusion model," depicts a unified but diverse flow of civilization from a single source in the east to multiple branches in the west. It appeals by a singular elegant logic and poetic beauty.

The old saying *Ex Oriente Lux* suggests this flow from the Egyptian children of the sun, from the heliolithic culture and pathway, and embodies the story of the "dawn of civilization." Within this flow, archaeology placed stories of the mother goddess and associated rites of collective burial, spreading out from the Aegean across the middle and western Mediterranean. By such a path, anthropologists imagined, the Early Bronze Age influenced the predominantly Neolithic peasantries of barbarian Europe. All of Europe was inspired and influenced by the more sophisticated world of Mycenaean Greece.

As a result of Libby's data, archaeologists reticent to submit their discipline to the nuclear physicists were forced to push back the dates of early farming cultures, and it appeared that prehistoric ruins throughout Europe were as much as a millennium older than previously thought. During this, the "first radiocarbon revolution," as it has been called, the traditional historical model was not damaged.

Disturbing History

But Libby's radiocarbon dates for Egypt, which could be compared to dates of events in texts written in Egypt, seemed incorrect. Further, the ages and relations of Egyptian and Mycenaean cultural artifacts had been confirmed by a technique archaeologists call *cross-dating,* a term which has a different technical meaning from the dendrochronologists' *cross-dating* but is similar in principle.

Several Egyptian dates, particularly one key date of 3100 B.C., could be confirmed with the written records of astronomical phenomena. Because Egypt practiced direct trade with Crete and Greece, and archaeologists could identify Cretan pottery found in a datable Egyptian context, as well as Egyptian artifacts in Aegean sites, a double link, or cross-dating, allowed an accurate chronology of the Mycenaean civilization of prehistoric Greece.

The discrepancies in Libby's Egyptian dates led to the effort to calibrate radiocarbon dating by comparing the radiocarbon dates of bristlecone samples to those calculated by dendrochronological methods. Ferguson collaborated with Hans Suess at the University of California, San Diego. By 1967 their work had been completed and documented the historical variation of radiocarbon in the atmosphere. In fact, radiocarbon had decreased sharply in the era following 1000 B.C., and its presence was generally full of variations which came to be called the "Suess wiggles," named for the appearance of a graph plotting radiocarbon and bristlecone chronologies. Nevertheless, because of the precision of Ferguson's tree-ring chronology, these variations could be corrected. Radiocarbon dates of around 3100 B.C. had to be pushed back to 1,100 years earlier. When Suess and Ferguson pushed back, corrected, or calibrated radiocarbon dates, they doubled the disturbing alterations of the first radiocarbon revolution and created the "second radiocarbon revolution."

Not all archaeological dates required revision. The traditional Egyptian and Aegean dates remained unchanged. But most other European dates were moved back so far that many chronological sequences upon which the diffusion model had been based were reversed. Now, megalithic chamber tombs in western Europe appeared to have been built earlier than the pyramids of Egypt; the impressive temples of Malta were previous to their Middle Eastern counterparts; copper metallurgy appeared in the Balkans before it did in Greece, and therefore, it must be inferred, developed independently; Stonehenge was completed before Mycenaean culture in Greece began. As archaeologist Colin Renfrew put it in 1973, an "agreeably logical picture has been completely disrupted, first by the introduction of radiocarbon dating, and more especially by its calibration through tree-ring studies."

Renfrew wrote as well, "British archaeologists have been heard to mutter, 'Why should I concern myself about this obscure California shrub?' " Libby, who first resisted the calibration of radiocarbon, knowing little of dendrochronology until 1963, visited the tree-ring laboratory in Tucson and was convinced. He answered critics of the bristlecone calibration, using what he called the "principle of simultaneity." Because radiocarbon is spread by atmospheric mixing, calibration in one location must be accurate all over the world.

Radiocarbon dating did not alter the chronologies of Troy and the Aegean cultures, but when the dates of central and northern European cultures were revised to much earlier times, major disruption was unavoidable, described sometimes as a cultural "fault" or discontinuity. The second radiocarbon revolution had destroyed three east-to-west paths of cultural diffusion. The ideas of a single source for western civilization and its consequent diffusion were no longer viable. The master plot of human history was not the same for those who pursued the discipline before the second radiocarbon revolution and those who came to it later. For those who studied history during the era beginning in the late 1960s, historical causality would be fluid, revisable, and unstable.

The implications for archaeological theory were massive. Simply put by Colin Renfrew, "The study of prehistory today is in a state of crisis." The crisis grew not from inconsistencies in dating, but because archaeology had based its models on assumptions which were no longer tenable. A new model would have to replace cultural diffusion, he said, and archaeology would have to undertake a paradigm shift in the understanding of cultural change.

As it first appeared, the new paradigm was specifically anti-diffusionist. Ethnographers would still be interested in *parallels* in cultural development, but a great deal more careful when arguing for *influence*. One warned that individual observations must not be "swamped by unitary and all-embracing explanation." They would perhaps focus more on "common human responses to similar environmental circumstances," and less on some single, total, all-embracing story of human cultural evolution.

The implications of this shift leaked out of archaeology. Perhaps fortuitously, the breakdown of a unitary chronology of civilization came at a time when some cultural historians were willing to welcome it, and when a monocular view of human culture was failing on many fronts. In those years, the United States experienced contemporary political controversies over nuclear testing, civil rights, Native American rights, and the environment. These movements all had proponents who confronted theories of unitary cultural identity and history. Tree-rings dealt a particularly precise blow to an untenable picture of human history and reinforced the efforts of some scholars to create histories and literary canons that would include multiple human cultural responses to differing environmental circumstances.

Critique

The pencil-thin core samples of Schulman's and Ferguson's live and dead bristlecones and the 20-gram samples of bristlecone wood shipped to radiocarbon labs have become standard chronological measuring sticks of not just one human civilization, but of its multiple strands, fragments which dendrochronology helped to produce. Memory is not embodied in these tree-rings, but in the way humans read them. Nevertheless, an absolute chronology paradoxically destroyed any hope of a linear plot for the development of western civilization and created perhaps a garden of forking paths, where long-held patterns of cause and effect were sometimes shattered and sometimes stood on their heads.

Partly as a direct consequence of Ferguson's bristlecone chronol-

ogy, archaeology and other disciplines depending on historical master plots were forced to expose themselves to the terrible learning
known as critique. The word crisis, in its meaning as separation and
turning point, is derived from the same Greek term, *krinein,* that
yields the term critique. This is terrible learning. A modern text like
Davis and Schliefer's *Criticism and Culture* speaks of critique as
making the familiar odd and uncomfortable, transforming the self-
evident into the questionable, and turning what seems to be natural
and universal into "quaint institutions marked by historical time."

This terrible learning refuses to stand outside the object it criticizes and calls into question the distinction between inside and
outside. It literally terrorizes received ideas and resists the illusion
of traditionlessness offered by rational positivism. "There are two
kinds of truths," Leibniz wrote in 1714, "those of *reason,* which are
necessary and of which the opposite is impossible, and those of *fact,*
which are contingent and of which the opposite is possible." Critique demolishes the boundary between two kinds of truth, of the
outside and the inside, of the observer and the observed. Its effects
are precisely illustrated in the way human reason and natural fact
cross each other in the study of tree-rings and carbon isotopes.

A change in paradigm can destroy and create. On the most basic
level, the second radiocarbon revolution created an industry in
radiocarbon dating and kept several labs in business for more than
twenty years. It also marked a revolution for tree-ring research.
Once again the discipline whose very existence depended on reading patterns of natural change had been turned toward patterns of
human change. As the anthropologist Bryant Bannister argues,
there were two dendrochronological revolutions as well. The first,
by A. E. Douglass, provided a tool for the precise dating of events
and processes in New World prehistory and consequently gave this
history a legitimacy. The second, begun by Schulman and finished
by Ferguson, reordered dates and destroyed a linear Old World
history.

Having administered the tree-ring laboratory during nearly two
decades of this era, Bannister knows that research follows financial
support. In the late 1960s and early 1970s, a research proposal which
used calibration as its rationale was likely to be funded. The work
on bristlecone dendrochronology had, by association with radiocarbon science, brought dendrochronology into the so-called hard

sciences. For those religious fundamentalists who considered radiocarbon dating the work of the devil—and there were more than a few of them— dendrochronology was found guilty by association.

In 1970, when Ferguson went to the Twelfth Nobel Symposium, an international conference on Radiocarbon Variations and Absolute Chronology, he was—and dendrochronology was by association—lionized and treated as an international icon. The Laboratory of Tree-Ring Research, tucked into a set of offices and work spaces under the University of Arizona's football stadium, was more famous internationally than it was in its home state.

Yet all of Ferguson's work created only a continuous and precise text of the story other people at the tree-ring lab wanted to read. A tree-ring chronology might be made to tell a set of stories which proliferate. As bristlecones were identified, measured, and turned into yardsticks used to measure human history, people like Schulman anticipated more elaborate and precise re-readings, aspired not just to read chronology but to assign each ring a significance, as indicators of some specific events. Like all sets of signs, patterns of tree-rings can be read only in relationship to each other, as the reader slides many fragmented skeleton plots against each other. In those re-readings, tree-rings have been made to yield converging and diverging stories of natural history.

The Ferguson style of dendrochronologist is interested in the absolute order of these signs; the Schulman style of dendroclimatologist reads tree-rings as symbols. They are symbols because they may represent a complex assortment of conditions under which the tree grew, and their meanings are not arbitrary. Nevertheless, interpreting them engages a reader in the processes of assigning their meaning by discerning continuity and discontinuity, association and analogy, syntax and paradigm.

A set of stories is, however, first recorded within the pattern of rings that the core contains. Why do I say a set? A yardstick, for instance, repeats itself, not just in small increments, but in larger measures, as microcosm to macrocosm. A yardstick's cyclical rule expresses in linear and mathematical terms an idea that can be expressed in literary terms, as Willa Cather did in *O Pioneers!*: "There are only two or three human stories, and they go on repeating themselves as fiercely as if they had never happened before." Neither humans nor trees repeat themselves precisely, and the differences matter. Fierce and perfect repetition, for instance, would make cross-dating impossible. The rings can be numbered, and their widths plotted; patterns are always complex and ring widths are often different from tree to tree, but patterns can be matched for best fit.

Tales are told of dendrochronologists who can, with a penknife, shave a section off a piece of dead wood and recognize by the pattern where its rings fit into the larger sequence. It is something like reading and remembering music, perhaps, recognizing a familiar pattern. Galen Rowell's version of the story places Schulman at a campfire. (I have also heard this story with Ferguson as the main character.) On a clear cold September evening at 10,000 feet in the White Mountains, "One man pulled a brand from the fire and examined it closely. '1277 to 1283 A.D., he said with assurance. 'This six-year ring pattern never repeats itself.'. . . He tossed the wood back into the fire. It burned hot and even and long."

Bryant Bannister notes that no good dendrochronologist would make such a statement about a six-year pattern. It is not a sound scientific or reasonable statistical assertion. Yet a great deal may be embodied in this little anecdote. As a parable it suggests the following. The fire of life burning hot and even and long, or burning short and irregular and bright. The man who looked for patterns that went on forever and repeated themselves also knew that patterns alter and often do not repeat themselves, that they can be short and distinctive. Humans come to imagine a repetition of patterns only by repeating the same patterns over and over, like a familiar piece of music. But if a pattern truly repeated itself, one could learn nothing.

Tree-rings are and are not like music. Each sequence, or phrase, fits into a larger sequence, but with a difference. And a dendrochronologist learns the sequences in the work entailed by cross-dating: counting the rings; distinguishing the rings by the degree of narrowness; determining the skeleton plot or approximate pattern by using the narrowest rings as markers. Skilled researchers have done this with thousands of cores. It is, in other words, a practice or discipline. A lab assistant may be responsible for placing a short sequence within a larger "master chronology." But a principal investigator like Ferguson must build his own master plot, a structure which precedes meaning. Douglass hoped for a larger sequence which would constitute a harmonic pattern, a repeating cycle.

Ferguson worked during an era sometimes called the dawn of the computer age. Some of his colleagues developed mathematical treatments of the problems of cyclicity, and others prepared to computerize tree-ring plots. These methods of analysis are meant to check the human recognition of pattern in tree-rings, meant to keep the perception of possible patterns from being in any sense aesthetic, meant to prevent reading from becoming an exercise in self-fulfilling prophecy. They are exercises in calibration. But a computer program cannot critique the methods of dendrochronology. At bottom, there is still a pencil, patience, practice, and perseverance.

The New West

With Schulman in the White Mountains, the proliferation of photographic representations of bristlecone pines began. Trees of little value until 1958 acquired inestimable value, labeled as the earth's oldest inhabitants, their images published widely in books on pines and on human culture, serving as frontispieces and illustrations, as measures of the times of humanity and as symbols of absolute chronology. They contrast in a frightening way to the more pervasive images of the mushroom cloud of the atmospheric test which marked for many people the possible end of the times of humanity.

When Libby's probabilistic radiocarbon techniques converged on the newly and rigorously developed but age-old craft of dendrochronology, old scientific craft met new analytical techniques and something astonishing resulted. This convergence also illustrates a great deal of the politics and economics of mid-century science, pressed by politics of extremes and limits. Libby's theory and practice were entirely of the atomic twentieth century, and he was funded by the federal government in a nuclear age. He was employed by the U.S. Atomic Energy Commission as a commissioner at the time when fellow Nobel laureate Linus Pauling, at the California Institute of Technology, vigorously opposed the policies of the AEC.

Willard Libby was engaged in selling the atomic bomb to the American public, and to the world. In 1955 he said, "People have got to learn to live with the facts of life, and part of the facts of life are [*sic*] fallout." He was also capable of writing, "We all carry in our bodies, and have in our surroundings, amounts of radioactivity very much larger than those derived from radioactive fallout." In 1954, when inhabitants of the Marshall Islands were "accidentally exposed to fallout," so were citizens of Utah and Nevada similarly "exposed." Prime Minister Nehru of India proposed a test ban.

Albert Schweitzer made an impassioned plea against any use of nuclear weapons. Responding to Schweitzer's criticism, in April of 1957 Libby wrote of a choice between "the terrible risk of abandoning the defense effort which is so essential under present conditions to the survival of the Free World" and "the small controlled risk from weapons testing." His was a singular and monocultural view of history.

In the early 1960s, when radiocarbon dating was being challenged by European archaeologists, Libby administered a large laboratory at the Institute for Geophysics at UCLA. In an environment where space travel seemed to show the way to the future, he lobbied the National Aeronautics and Space Administration (NASA) successfully for a huge new building to house his institute. A small portion of the federal funds he received was recycled to pay for my own undergraduate education in physical and geological chemistry. In the early 1960s Libby gave an inspirational speech to a class in geochemistry. He spoke of exploring the mixing of oceans by measuring the dispersion of nuclear fallout. He thought such a project would require the full-time work of a number of doctoral candidates. I, Michael Cohen, was one of that crew. I considered embarking on graduate study.

An accurate picture of the American West during this era must include not simply the open questions suggested by the landscape of the Great Basin, with its old trees and nuclear test site, its scientists and irradiated citizens, but also the laboratories in Los Angeles and in Livermore, the hierarchies of government science and of academic institutions devoted to American power. At bottom were people like me, who worked for or were worked on by these developments in American science. Some woke before dawn in Nevada to see the second sunrise of atomic bombs before walking to trees that they cored with primitive hand tools while sweating in the sun. Some squinted through low-powered lenses in laboratories in cities, recording the patterns of tree-rings.

In the mid-1960s Willard Libby was under considerable criticism from some students at UCLA because of his alliance with the Atomic Energy Commission and because he continued his vigorous support of the production and testing of nuclear weapons, which he sometimes referred to as "big fellows" and "little fellows." One year he built a bomb shelter in the backyard of his house in Brentwood. It was constructed of old wooden railroad ties, soaked with creosote, the materials costing only thirty dollars, he boasted. His shelter was, he said, inexpensive and sufficient. In the fall of that year, the bomb shelter he had constructed was incinerated by one of the many periodic brush fires for which modern Southern California is so famous.

CHAPTER 3

The Purloined Tree

A Skeleton Plot

During the summers of 1963 and 1964, Donald R. Currey, a graduate student in geography at the University of North Carolina investigating east central Nevada's Snake Range, found an ideal site on
the flank of Wheeler Peak. He was one of many people seeking
to develop chronologies of climatic change during the "Little Ice
Age," which at the time was defined in very general terms as a four-
hundred-year period when global temperatures dropped slightly,
reaching a minimum in the early 1600s. He was looking for old
bristlecones close to or on a glacial moraine which might register
climatic conditions, and he found them.

A grove of old bristlecones has grown for many millennia at
10,700 feet of elevation below the glacial cirque on the northeast
side of Wheeler Peak, precisely at timberline. They are visible upon
entering the cirque from below, bright weathered flanks of ice-
burnished wood gleaming from the talus slope along the crest of a
massive but gently sloping lateral moraine. The trees seem embedded in angular blocks of quartzite.

There, about fourteen miles from the Utah–Nevada border,
Currey found trees to suit his purpose. The apparent age of the trees
suggested that they had lived through the entire era he was studying. He chose one. According to one account, he broke a borer—

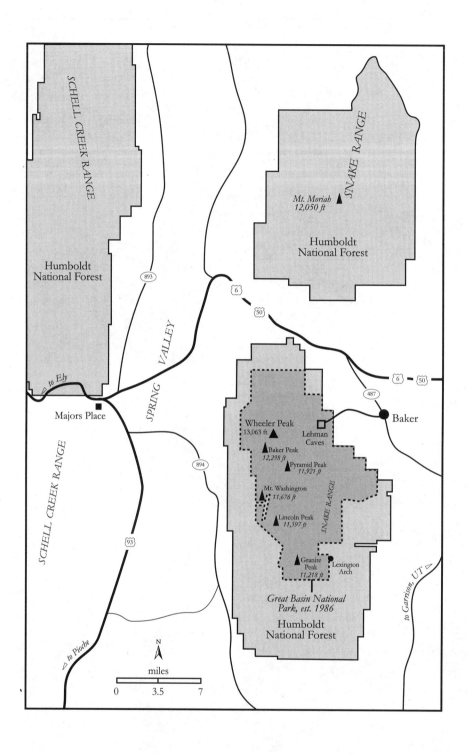

Donald Currey with the fragments of WPN-114, Wheeler Peak moraine, August 1964. (Keith Trexler photo, courtesy Darwin Lambert)

maybe on a rock embedded in the tree—and had no prospect for obtaining a new one that summer. Other accounts indicate that he did not have a long enough tool for such a massive tree. Some, including Ferguson, have said that Currey didn't know how to sample such an old tree.

Without a complete chronology, Currey could not complete his project. He decided to cut down his one representative old tree to study its rings. Donald E. Cox, the Forest Service district ranger responsible for the Snake Range, approved the task and offered assistance. As Currey wrote in an article in *Ecology,* the tree he labeled WPN-114 grew near the edge of a stand of old trees on relatively stable ground whose surface was, as a result of avalanche-transported debris, about two feet above the tree's original base. This one was chosen, as "one of the larger living bristlecone pines." It was "sectioned."

Men cut down and cut up—during the summer the United States Congress debated and passed the Wilderness Act of 1964— what turned out to be the oldest known living Great Basin bristlecone pine, found not in the White Mountains, but hundreds of miles to the east, in what is now but was not then Great Basin National Park. That tree, which Currey estimated "began growing about 4,900 years ago," has been dated by others at perhaps more than 5,100 years of age.

Because of the controversy that followed, it is best to begin with Currey's explanation. He wrote to the assistant regional forester, John Mattoon, nearly two years later, of "several factors bearing

(opposite) **Great Basin National Park. (adapted from the De-Lorme *Nevada Atlas & Gazetteer* and U.S. Department of the Interior maps)**

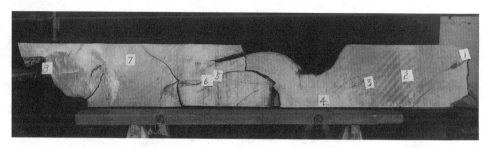

The Prometheus slab (WPN-114) in a workshop in Ely, Nevada. Number 8 indicates bark. Number 1 indicates origin of growth. (U.S. Forest Service)

on the decision to section the tree, rather than to rely solely on increment-borer cores." His summary consisted of five numbered points. (1) The massive form of the tree rendered coring "problematical." (2) A complete cross section would be the "best means of adequately tabulating incomplete growth layers." (3) A complete cross section would allow him to observe average widths of each growth layer. (4) "As complete a record as possible, from as old a living specimen as was readily available, was considered to be important as a framework around which to build a long tree-ring chronology." (5) He believed in 1966 that "there was no compelling reason in 1964, nor is there any now, to suppose that this particular tree is the oldest 'in the world,' or in the Snake Range, or on Wheeler Peak."

Currey described his specimen as having "a dead crown 17 ft high, a living shoot 11 ft high, and a 252 inch circumference 18 inches above the ground." The trunk was a massive slab. Bark grew "along a single 19-inch wide, north-facing strip. Lateral die-back had left 92 percent of the circumference devoid of bark." He noted that wind-driven ice had so deeply eroded the tree that the pith was missing below a point 76 inches above the ground, or 100 inches above the original base.

He described the sectioning of WPN-114 in this way: "A horizontal slab from the interval 18–30 inches above the ground and a smaller piece including the pith 76 inches above the ground were cut from the tree, and a smoothly finished 2-piece transverse section was prepared. Within the radius sector present in the section, the growth layers, or rings, have a rather uncomplicated concentric arrangement." Because it was written in the passive voice, Currey's article, like his letter to the assistant regional forester, created distance by erasing the actors. In the description of WPN-114, the tree appears not to be an actual growing being. In the description of the sectioning, the acts of men are narrated as if no men act. What was not asked or spoken became, as a result, the very set of issues in this story.

Currey's article in *Ecology* is also confusing because it does not focus on the main topic of his investigation, which was post-glacial history. He discussed the tree's significance as "rendering datable a sequence of Little Ice Age events," but did not do the dating and instead focused on the tree's age. The story Currey wrote seems to reveal and yet hide what this research project would most be remembered for. WPN-114 undercut a thesis developed by Schulman and Ferguson, who decided in 1956 that the oldest trees would be found only at the western edge of the Great Basin because the greatest adversity would be found there, in the rain shadow of the Sierra.

Indulging in the passive voice, which is a convention of scientific literature, Currey's article never fully discloses explicitly its central paradoxes. Local conditions and not generalized geography, multiple conditions and not simply precipitation, would determine the existence of long-lived trees. But the only known living evidence which could substantiate this thesis was destroyed. To date, nobody has found another tree of comparable age in the central or eastern Great Basin, though as a result of WPN-114, almost certainly older than 5,100 years, the U.S. Forest Service funded a substantial survey of the region.

Getting the Story Straight

Such stories are not entirely about individuals, but also of institutions and cultures. Currey had a National Science Foundation grant for two summer seasons. He was a geographer, not researching bristlecones per se, but using them for close registering of glacial events, particularly of the fifteenth to nineteenth centuries. He was, as a graduate student at a major university, an initiate into academic culture. When, as some stories claim, he broke his boring tool, he appealed to the custodial agency responsible for the use of these forests. The Forest Service became an actor in his story. It provided expertise with a chain saw, a more powerful but cruder tool than the two-man crosscut saw Schulman's team used. The story became political.

In fact, this short tale of an old tree dispatched—which is now an old story—has many versions. I cross-date five predominant stories, joined at their source like five needles bound in a fascicle, but diverging toward their ends. (1) Currey recounted a passive narrative, for a scientific journal, of the tree as WPN-114, a numbered and

The Prometheus Tree. Living portion at bottom left. (Keith Trexler photo, courtesy Darwin Lambert)

measured specimen. (2) Darwin Lambert, with other advocates of a Great Basin National Park, knew this tree by the name of "Prometheus," and he wrote of it for *Audubon* as the "oldest inhabitant of the Earth," martyred for its species. (3) Keith A. Trexler, the chief naturalist at Lehman Caves National Monument, just down the hill, witnessed the event, which he considered unnecessary, and his story dramatizes a conflict between federal agencies. (4) Galen Rowell's version of the story for the *Sierra Club Bulletin* indicts the collusion of scientists and the Forest Service. (5) Charles Hitch, President Emeritus of the University of California, attempted to respond to Rowell's attacks by recounting a story of justifiable error and defending the free inquiry of scientists. These five stories, bound together at a single event, diverge from their common source and fall into pieces which have to be put together, like the sections of WPN-114 Currey wished to study.

And there are pieces one does not know how to use. In 1996 Ronald Lanner told another story, almost as a footnote to the history of the tree. Fred Solace, a thirty-two-year-old Forest Service employee, died of a heart attack on September 20, 1965, when a second five-man crew was sent, a year after the initial cut, to take another section from the tree and transport it down the trail on a deer cart.

That Currey sectioned his oldest sample because he could not measure its age with a borer is secondary to the story he has told, but not to the stories told by others. The sectioning of WPN-114 did not, in any immediate sense, damage its scientific use for Currey or others. Indeed, the act had a precedent. Several very old trees in the White Mountains were harvested for science by Schulman and his associates at the end of the 1957 season, for detailed study of the trees' life histories. Schulman wrote about one in *National Geographic,* saying, "we hardened our hearts"—and cut a specimen similar to but somewhat younger than the Methuselah Tree. In fact, he cut three specimens. But memory is not always accurate. For instance, in 1970 Schulman's colleague Frits Went remembered that he had gone to the White Mountains twice with Schulman and wrote to Lambert, "in 1956, I believe, we again went together and at that time cut down the 4,600 year old tree." Went also believed he later saw a section of the old tree at the School of Forestry in Stockholm. Went was incorrect on both counts.

It was a major project to haul a slab from an old tree out of the forest. Schulman recalled five hours of backbreaking labor removing one from the Methuselah Walk. The finished section of WPN-114, as Currey indicated, was transported in pieces and then fitted together from sections cut at separate heights, like pieces from a three-dimensional puzzle. Provenance of some of these sections is clouded. According to Ronald Lanner's 1996 narrative, one set of pieces of Currey's tree was resawn at the East Ely shop of the Northern Nevada Railway Company and used to construct three polished specimens. These polished sections were distributed to public and private institutions. Currey took one back to North Carolina for further study, the Forest Service kept one in Ely, Nevada, and one ended up in a display case at Ely's Hotel Nevada. One small piece is now at the visitors' center at Great Basin National Park. A sample including a complete chronology of Currey's tree is stored near Schulman's sections at the Laboratory of Tree-Ring Research, where its rings were re-counted by Don Graybill at 4,862. Currey's tree, like Schulman's slabs, is available for continued study, transferred to display cases, visitors' centers, and laboratories. There is something about these sections and their fragments that suggests the obvious and the hidden, the tree turned inside out.

A Public Response

Both Currey and Schulman discovered a singular oldest individual, one of them almost by accident. Neither sought the oldest, but only the chronological and climatic record it contained. As I have been told, Schulman's oldest tree was not recognized as such by him and has no name. By the time of Currey's research, as Ferguson wrote to Darwin Lambert in 1966, finding an older tree seemed less important in academic circles than establishing a longer chronology, using bristlecone samples from dead trees for calibrating radiocarbon dates, or correlating tree-rings with climatic events. When queried in 1966, Ferguson said that wood on the ground was even more valuable to science than the living trees, and that "from a technical viewpoint, there was absolutely no need to cut the Wheeler Peak tree." According to Keith Trexler, Valmore LaMarche Jr. of the tree-ring lab was able to take a series of cores from the remains of Prometheus, and also thought it was unnecessary to have felled the 4,900-year-old tree.

The oldest old tree was less important for its scientific value than for its other uses. The controversy over Currey's tree focused on the following questions: Who owns such trees? How can their value be assessed? Were old trees being purloined, appropriated wrongfully, when they were sectioned by scientists? Was the Forest Service complicit in some breach of trust?

These questions fueled a controversy orchestrated, to a great extent, by Darwin Lambert. Lambert grew up in the Great Basin, on a small ranch. He was reporter and editor for the *Ely Daily Times* from 1955 to 1961, manager of the White Pine Chamber of Commerce, a Nevada assemblyman, and a member of the National Parks and Conservation Association's governing board from 1958 to 1983. By 1959 he had written serious and detailed proposals for making the Wheeler Peak area a national park.

"Fewer than fifty people saw Earth's oldest known living tree alive," he wrote in "Martyr for a Species," published by *Audubon* in 1968 and widely reprinted. Lambert had first approached this grove of old bristlecones in 1956. He saw, "stooped as under a burden, with roots like claws grasping the ground—a magnificent monster standing alone." Because the tree filled his sight, he grasped it.

"Four spans of my outstretched arms, six feet to the reach, were needed to encircle the misshapen trunk. Not far away were more colossi, some still larger and more grotesque." Lambert developed these trees as characters "proclaiming victory over death." They became part of a tangled story, with roles played by the writer Weldon Heald, David Brower of the Sierra Club (who "nicknamed the species 'bottlebrush tree' for those long dense clusters which distinguish its foliage"), Fred Seaton, Secretary of the Interior, and the biologist Adolph Murie, who had recommended national park status for the region including Currey's tree in 1958.

It is probable that Lambert found a precedent for his personification of trees in the writing of Murie. Unlike Currey, Murie was willing to speak of trees in the active voice. "Their weird hobgoblin shapes with arms reaching and turning at all angles, like the illustrations in the *Wizard of Oz,*" he wrote in a 1959 report, "give one a feeling of being in a strange world. Each tree is a character to meet." Following Murie's lead, park advocates, a coalition of chamber officials, conservationists, Nevada politicians, and some people in Utah had been naming the trees. "Buddha," "Socrates," "Cliff-hanger," "Storm King," and one on nearby Mount Washington called the "Money Tree" because a local photographer "sold so many portraits of it." Lambert introduced friends, neighbors, and visiting dignitaries to these denizens of the state's second-highest peak.

The tree Currey had labeled WPN-114, Lambert and his friends named Prometheus—probably in 1958 but not later than 1961— after the demigod worshiped by artisans, who stole and gave fire and the arts to humans, and who was chained to a mountain crest by Zeus, where an eagle fed each day on his liver until he was freed by Hercules. In 1968 the name seemed distinctly ironic. Lambert wrote: "Earth's oldest living thing was casually killed (yes murdered!) in the name of science."

Lambert's narrative cast Currey as a mere student, expressed incredulity at the forest supervisor's approval of Currey's plan to chain-saw the tree. "The oldest living thing had been killed in the process of discovery!" he wrote. One member of the local park association saw how the story could be exploited if told properly, saying, "Prometheus might become widely enough known as a martyr to save the other ancients." Lambert made Prometheus the central character of his narrative, the martyr whose "cross sections are to be found at the University of North Carolina, in several Forest Service offices, and on public display in a Nevada hotel,"

The Money Tree on Mt. Washington. (Edwin Fehr photo, U.S. Forest Service)

while his "stump remains unprotected and unsung on the rocky moraine of Wheeler Peak."

Lambert has retold the story several times, most prominently in *Timberline Ancients* (1972) and in his *Great Basin Drama* (1991), a history of Great Basin National Park. As he retold it, he added accurate and concrete detail and cast the narrative in more personal terms. Each of his tellings is rooted in his initial response when he read Currey's article in *Ecology* and realized that Prometheus had been cut down: "We felt that we were walking home from a loved patriarch's funeral. The wounds open every time—to this day—when memories of that ancient tree surface."

A slightly less passionate narrative is provided by Keith Trexler, the naturalist at Lehman Caves during the period, who documented the events leading up to and including the cutting of Prometheus. Not only did Trexler write his own narrative of the events, he also produced a set of photographs of the tree. In one, Donald Currey appears climbing the massive slab, which leans at about a 45-degree angle from vertical. In another photo, Trexler labeled the living portion of the tree, its pith, and the locations where it was cut, indicating these lines also with regard to the probable age of the segments. In another, Currey surveys the broken slabs of the tree arrayed on the forest floor.

Trexler's version of the story was written as reports, notes, letters, and sometimes told in interviews with Darwin Lambert. His first report, including photographs and one short summary written after the cutting, was appended to Lehman Cave superintendent Robert Jacobsen's monthly report of September 1964. Later, Trexler indicated that researchers from Arizona found the tree itself was in some sense an anomaly, as much as 2,000 years older than any of the other trees in the grove. This made it different from Schulman's Methuselah Tree, which was found in a grove containing many trees more than 4,000 years old.

As a result, Trexler reported, investigators considered it a "living freak," "decrepit," a singular phenomenon, and its discovery not likely to be followed by similar discoveries. To call the tree a "freak" suggests a great deal. A freak is something deviant. Using such a term concentrates and embodies the idea of a curiosity and speaks in turn of the beholders. Freaks are unusual, exotic, unexpected. People visit scenes of wonder and curiosity, are drawn to freaks of nature and collect curios, samples which are novel, rare, or bizarre. To be intensely curious is to be more than inquisitive, to be nosy, prying, to experience unquenchable desire.

Trexler remembered that Currey "proposed cutting down a tree, which he felt was *one* of the oldest on the mountain," not because of a broken tool, but because he "had extreme difficulty getting sufficient cores and felt he needed a full section of the tree."

Trexler's anger focused on what he believed was a lack of discretion combined with inexperience or perhaps incompetence, intensified by desire. Others, like Donald Wilcox, a district ranger in the region during the 1970s—and perhaps also Ferguson—believed that "Currey knew what he had." Humboldt National Forest district ranger Donald Cox granted permission to cut the tree on August 3,

1964. But he did not do so on his own authority. He consulted W. L. "Slim" Hansen, his supervisor, who worked at Elko, 250 miles away. Slim Hansen was responsible for forest management in seven separate mountain ranges spread across the eastern edge of Nevada. Slim told him to look at the tree. Cox apparently found the tree "very common." "No one," he is reported to have said, "would have walked more than a hundred yards to see it." So it could be used for science. Hansen casually responded, "Cut 'er down."

Bob Jacobsen, superintendent at Lehman Caves, attempted to intervene across bureaucratic boundaries, as he wrote in his monthly report, because cutting the tree "would be a loss to the world." One Forest Service sawyer refused to cut the tree on August 6, 1964. The next day, Cox and several Forest Service crew members took turns at the saw.

There was a scandal and a cover-up. Later, when questioned by Senator Alan Bible of Nevada, the Forest Service chief Richard McArdle said that there would be no more cutting of old bristlecones, but he also said "We have a lot that are the same age or older." This is what Currey believed.

Stories of premeditation and refusal, of shared guilt and casual assent, of callousness and caring, of curiosity and lack of concern, of value and lack of evaluation, of arrogance and ignorance, led to pointed arguments about the Forest Service's ability to combine custodial responsibilities with a scientific and utilitarian mandate. As anyone might guess, a lot of men—each with his own political allegiance—got to calling each other bad names as a result of killing that tree, and the language escalated to terms indicating blame and bitterness, rape and murder. George Kell, a director of the Nevada Outdoor Recreation Association, said that the Forest Service allowed Prometheus to be cut "apparently because it does not wish to surrender jurisdiction of the land in question to a rival government agency." This, then, was the extreme rhetoric of the politics of timberline.

An Argument Conducted near San Francisco

So the stories of WPN-114, or Prometheus, diverged, depending on the allegiances of the tellers and the audiences to which they appealed. For instance, Galen Rowell wrote his version of the tale for the September 1974 *Sierra Club Bulletin,* introducing it with a well-known quip from Governor Reagan of California, who "may have gotten away in some circles with saying, 'If you've seen one red-wood, you've seen them all,' but could never say that about a bristlecone pine."

A decade after the act, Rowell spoke of Currey in the present tense, saying, "In his scientific report" Currey "offers no remorse or compassion," and the tree "which he fondly calls WPN-114" is reduced to a set of statistics. Further, wrote Rowell, "subsequent literature has been purposely obscure," which he found understandable with the Forest Service, "which would wish to conceal this fact." Rowell accounted for "half truths in the writings of scientists" by the fact that "most all dendrochronologists have cut down certain trees in their time."

Rowell's distance from the story allowed him a certain creative latitude, and yet the central fact—the central fact of all these narratives—is the tree itself, "sliced by a chainsaw to see how old it was." For Rowell, "a stump of the oldest living thing, cut by man, the tool user, is one of the most repugnant sights I've seen." He threw a blanket of condemnation over scientists, Forest Service rangers, any humans who failed to understand that "the wood belonged in the mountains." He broadcast his condemnations so widely that they confused all the issues.

Dendrochronology begins with craft but uses a statistical methodology. Calibration of radiocarbon dates requires more than pencil-thin cores. The ownership or utilization of wood cannot be resolved by saying it belongs to the mountains.

Rowell was answered by Charles Hitch, a student of A. E. Douglass who later became a professor of economics at the University of California at Berkeley, and in 1981 was president emeritus of the university. Hitch felt called upon to answer the versions of the story promulgated by wilderness advocates. He did so in an address to the Kosmos Club in Berkeley, and a version of the talk was published in *American Scientist* in 1982.

Hitch refers to Donald Currey as a "young research scientist," who planned to use a Swedish increment borer. "Actually," Hitch wrote, "cutting down a tree to examine the rings in the stump seemed unlikely to be necessary." Then "the borer stuck—irretrievably. This was a tragedy, for the borers were available only in Sweden" and waiting for replacement was impossible, or "summer would be over and his expedition a failure."

Now, when Currey selected a suitable bristlecone pine for establishing his climatic record of the era under investigation, Hitch reports, "the selection was rather arbitrary," since other similar trees might have served. But—and here is a crux of the story—the selection was made before Currey stuck his borer, because he had already obtained permission to cut a tree if he wished. A ranger, "having verified his permit and anxious to help the cause of science, offered Currey a saw and offered to help him take down the tree." "Actually," Hitch concludes, "in my opinion, both Currey and the ranger acted reasonably and responsibly. They just had incredibly bad luck."

Two repeated terms in Hitch's narrative, "actually" and "incredibly," suggest the extent to which acts or credible intentions of people might be believed or not, depending on the way the story is told. What does it mean to cut down a tree? It depends on which tree was actually cut, on the intentions, credible or not, and on the results of the act. For what? we ask, why? how? and according to whom? Why might such an act, carried out in the practice of "normal science," be important? Who were the actors? Were they truly active, or passive participants? Can one take all these pieces of the story, the fragments or segments, and put them together like the pieces of a crossword puzzle? Can they be put together into one history, or do they constitute a puzzle whose single picture, both obvious and hidden, has an inside and an outside, like a glove which can be turned inside out and worn upon either hand?

Hitch titled the narrative in which the tale of the Prometheus tree is embedded "Dendrochronology and Serendipity." The word serendipity is derived from a Persian tale, *The Three Princes of Serendip,* and comes from the ability possessed by the heroes of the tale to find valuable or agreeable things not sought for. So, Hitch illustrates this plot within a larger narrative of the history of science, wherein "even Libby died happy" with the fruits of the marriage of radiocarbon dating and dendrochronology, and "A. E. Douglass can turn over in his grave and smile."

The Scientist and the Public

All this talk of smiling dead scientists because someone cut a single tree. It is a particular feature of old bristlecone forests that they are made of discrete individual trees. And this tree became an ethical touchstone. Methods matter to the living. The Swedish increment borer and the chain saw: most investigators of bristlecones use both. The borer was designed to investigate the growth of cultivated trees in orchards, or, if etymology matters, in gardens. It multiplies human vision and allows the investigator to see inside the tree without injuring it. The chain saw was designed to harvest wood efficiently. It multiplies power and allows a user to get the lumber out. It is confusing when someone uses one tool when he meant to use the other, but the uses of these tools are linked. In this particular incident, science gave the public the oldest tree and then seemed to take it away. Science gave old trees value and then seemed not to value them sufficiently. The tree as object of study yielded the tree as object of reverence, but one of those engaged in the study seemed not to respect the value science had created for a larger public.

Wes Ferguson recognized the problem immediately. As he wrote to Lambert in April 1966, "I have advised the Inyo National Forest in California, where we do our research, that under no conditions should a living bristlecone pine tree be cut for determination, display or radiocarbon analysis." On the other hand, he also told Lambert that his opinions on the ethics and technical need to cut the WPN-114 tree were "personal opinion privately expressed." "I do not wish to be quoted in any manner in regard to the tree that was cut."

Scientists had made bristlecone pines valuable, and scientists had created needs. Ferguson had assisted Schulman in assembling his collection of bristlecone samples in 1956. By the 1960s, when radiocarbon dating and dendrochronology converged, the Laboratory of Tree-Ring Research found itself besieged by requests from researchers all over the world for samples of dated bristlecone wood for laboratory purposes.

A team of scientists had established "standardized techniques for specimen preparation and dating control." These scientists were engaged not only in providing and shipping their "product," they also had adapted a master tree-ring chronology to standard computer programs, had developed techniques of statistical analysis, and had begun to develop the theory of dendrochronology and its allied fields dendroclimatology, dendroclimatography, dendroecology, dendrohydrology, and dendrogeomorphology.

In 1968 Ferguson wrote an article entitled "Bristlecone Pine: Science and Aesthetics." He reported that after Schulman's *National Geographic* article, "visits to bristlecone-pine localities took on the nature of pilgrimages." By the mid-1960s, Ferguson observed, nearly 20,000 visitors were coming to the Schulman Grove each year, a number which seems small now, but some of them collected "ornamental wood," even where such activities were restricted. Which meant, wrote Ferguson, "I must compete with the public for my basic research material." Surely, he thought, the highest use of old wood was not as "personal memento" nor as decorative wood—was not aesthetic, but scientific. He concluded, with characteristic understated, passive voice, "Concern is expressed for the preservation of this ancient wood."

Rowell too saw the need for concern, writing, "Today the oldest living thing by default is the Methuselah Tree in the White Mountains; its exact location is kept a secret for fear that tourists will desecrate it or carry off souvenirs." Rowell did not know that the oldest tree was anonymous and consequently twice removed from the public, but, like Ferguson, he saw that trees would have to be protected from the attention of those who competed for them.

As Ferguson argued, it is not clear that the tree's being alive had by 1968 as much value to the dendrochronologist as its being mostly dead, since his study of its already dead wood was directed toward extending what was at that time a 7,100-year chronology. But Ferguson misunderstood or at least simplified the aesthetic impulse by narrowing it to the act of collecting for interior decoration. He understood that the public followed the scientists into the Schulman Grove but did not acknowledge the reciprocal debt of scientists to the readers of *National Geographic* and the funders of federal programs.

He failed to understand that an overwhelming proportion of artists, even amateur photographic tourists who took snapshots, were interested in confronting these trees in place and responding with their own forms of expression to the forms of the weathered snags. He did not consider the artists who did not presume as much as scientists do about the importance of their activity. Might an artist cut a tree down or collect ancient wood? Some have asked to do so. But artists, interested in the outward form of the trees, have less need, perhaps, to possess them materially. Yet the artist, like the scientist, also abstracts something from the tree and is interested in some law, harmony, or form which can be used in an aesthetic representation.

If the historian steps back from the foci of serious tree research on time lines and climate change, or from the frivolous rights of tourists to collect decorative wood, or from fanciful representations of trees as personages, the qualities of trees themselves remain. The oldest trees still seem important because of what comes together in them.

Scientists found the old trees themselves neither all dead nor all alive, but both, and the record of their growing—the rings—was also the record of their dying. In this sense, even a living tree was both present and absent, because it had a surface and an interior, which in a young tree consisted of the live wood encasing the dead part. But in the old tree, such as the one cut by Currey, less than 8 percent of its surface was alive. A dead surface and a solid but inert substance created most of the body of the tree, sought by scientist and artist alike.

The dead wood, which makes a tree so scenic and historic, is not absent from the life processes of the tree. Some represent the dead wood as protecting the live wood, as necessary to the survival of the tree itself, an adaptation which makes the structure of an old bristlecone seem almost like an inside-out version of the structure of a "normal" or "healthy" pine, whose living cambium protects its largely inert interior.

As it turns out, the longevity of these trees revealed only the beginning of their value. Their value came not only from their age, but from how they aged, what their aging revealed, how their aging was related to the environment in which they lived. As writer Stephen Trimble puts it in a somewhat metaphorical way, their value comes from what humans imagine these trees to have witnessed. Why they live so long, what aspects of time and what changes they have inhabited; these questions make them interesting to humans because they are questions about humans too.

CHAPTER 4

Capturing a Cloud: On the Stability and Movement of Bristlecone Forests

On an early summer evening in the foothills of the eastern Sierra, one's eye is drawn eastward across the valley to the high rolling country of the White Mountains. On the high slopes, great weathered surfaces hold snow and light late into the evening. They glisten. As the top tier of an island in the sky reaching 14,000 feet, an unbroken undulating sky mountain, these alpine slopes are sometimes known as barrens. Later, at sunset, the White Mountains seem to recede across the Owens Valley, as fading light hovers over the wrinkled and furrowed, reddish-tinted lower desert slopes. Between the cold snow and the dry desert a double band of forests floats, cloudlike. The bottom band of piñon and juniper is relatively recent in this place and has only been on these mountains for a few thousand years. The top band continues a history begun millions of years ago in this region, perhaps begun when the range of mountains did not exist, a history punctuated by a series of glacial eras. Like the humans who study them, these forests live now in an interglacial period, as they have before, and will, presumably, again.

In the 1960s, faced with the collection of old trees in old forests, a scientific community composed of botanists, geologists, and dendrochronologists began to ask what these remarkable trees are doing and where they have been going. In 1953 the Forest Service designated a Patriarch Grove Reserve, surrounding Alvin Noren's Patriarch Tree, and in 1958 enlarged the reserve so that it was a total of 27,160 acres, adding a "Botanical Area" around the sites of Schulman's studies. Most of the oldest bristlecone groves grew in this area and were accessible from a twelve-mile stretch of narrow gravel road.

Those engaged in studying these trees came from diverse disciplines. They subdivided the subalpine forest—a life zone that falls between the Piñon-Juniper Woodland Zone (at 6,500 to 9,500 feet) and the Alpine Zone (at 11,500 to 14,246 feet) in order to know it in detail. Some studied the forest's lowest limits, some the upper limits, and some sought typical forests not subject to limiting conditions. Their studies became more specialized at the same time they became increasingly dependent on each other.

Dissecting a forest is as problematic as dissecting a cloud, because the forest itself obeys no simple geometric rules. Recognizing that forests are not static and do not constitute a simple laminar flow over the earth, the botanists, geologists, ecologists, and dendrochronologists tried to understand the shapes of these forests, the way they changed, and what forces changed their shapes. Always uppermost in their studies was the desire to read the rings of these trees, use them as tools for monitoring conditions in the mountains, and construct a history of those conditions.

In the nineteenth century, Clarence Dutton described the ranges of the Great Basin as armies of caterpillars crawling toward Mexico. Such an orderly but now unscientific comparison predates theories of plate tectonics. A more modern conception of the region's long geological history depicts a sequence of abysses opening and closing beneath islands of upturned stone. This model replaces the growth of individual mountain ranges with the compression and expansion of huge irregular plates that migrate great distances. When these plates rub along each other, they generate great heat and flows of molten rock. Once the crust of the earth stretched here, creating the basins and ranges, where tremendous stresses continue to create a jigsaw system of faults. To think, like Dutton, that many north- and south-tending ranges are going somewhere is to entertain an illusion born of light and space, or an illusion created by the sparse flow of life upon them.

On a much shorter time scale, changes in weather and changes in the patterns of life make these mountains seem to move. The naked eye cannot see mountains that move, but sees forests that float like clouds. The naked eye cannot see forests capturing the clouds and clothing the mountains, moving ever so subtlely up and down the slopes of Great Basin ranges over many centuries, following the march of climatic fluctuations. But humans can construct stories. Dead bristlecone and limber pines can be found above the present stands and forests, their presence (or recent absence) suggesting that these upper tree lines have migrated. Forests of live trees are sometimes bracketed above by phantom or ghost forests of standing dead trees. On the ground, beneath the picturesque but skeletal remains of ancient forests, fresh seedlings have germinated in the last century.

Many kinds of change can create a ghost forest. Some are gradual, and some, like insect infestation, geological catastrophe, volcanic eruption, and fire are sudden disturbances. Archaeologists of forests can only say for certain that old dead trees were once alive, that a dead forest once flourished, that newer seedlings reveal limits of life that are now different: changing patterns mean that these limits will change again. The causes and rates of the changes may be read, perhaps, from the rings of living and dead trees. Those who desire to read these changes transform dendrochronology into dendroclimatology and dendroecology. Such investigators must connect trees to their places, must know when the trees grow, why in certain regions, and how they are connected to their environments: these connections ground all readings of tree-rings.

Tree Lines

A tree-ring connects the life of a tree to its environment and represents, in the present, the traces of an individual tree's growth and past life. A ring is made of wood, which grows as concentric surfaces. So-called rings are really surfaces cut transversely, originating from the cambium, a layer of formative cells only one cell thick, which sheaths the living surface of stems and roots. The cambium of a bristlecone pine, for instance, manufactures cells from midsummer until frost, a period of forty or fifty days, beginning in late June and ending near mid-August, and increases the diameter of the woody stem. Located between the mature wood and bark, cambium generates both.

When the tree grows, it is making wood, a vascular tissue which stores and distributes nutrients and water. Made of elongated vessels, of very long thin cells called tracheids, and soft tissue made up of nonspecialized, thin-walled cells called parenchyma, xylem or

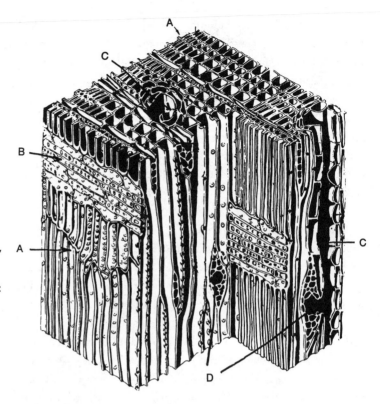

Structure of pine wood, showing different tissues. *A.* Tracheids, the cells which conduct water. Notice pits. *B.* Radial rays. *C.* Vertical resin canals. *D.* Horizontal resin canals. At right, horizontal and vertical canals merge. (U.S. Forest Service)

wood is the chief substance of plant stems. It also serves as the tree's skeleton. Wood cells are thickened with lignin, which constitutes about 25 percent of the cell volume. The tree's rings are also known as its grain. Those who cut the material of trees with hand-powered tools feel its differences through plane, chisel, gouge, crosscut, or ripsaw. Each piece of wood has a distinct feel and imparts a rhythm to the hand when it is cut. A tree-ring is a discontinuous entity, a surface and a boundary, and trees contain surfaces within surfaces.

The differences between so-called early wood and late wood allow the observer to see a distinct ring. However, there is a continuous transition between these layers. Nicholas Mirov was Al Noren's friend and in the 1960s the world's preeminent expert on pines. He told Schulman about the old trees and suggested that Schulman might wish to investigate the White Mountain groves. As Mirov explained in his definitive study *The Genus Pinus,* "the annual ring pattern is caused by formation of vigorously grown, thin walled cells in the early wood; as the season progresses, the growth slows down and in the late wood the cell walls become thicker." The rings are themselves made of rings, down to the cellular level, each microscopic concentric layer potentially different.

All trees have rings, but some are not distinct or readily readable. A pronounced ring can be found only in some species of trees and only where the seasons are themselves well defined by sharp differences: the rings of trees will differ according to conditions under which the trees grow. Rings may not always be annual, and they may not be annular. For instance, the shape of a ring of an old bristlecone is regular with regard to years, but maybe a strip or small arc rather than a circle. And because abnormalities in rings are commonly caused by adverse climatic conditions, rings may be anomalous. To read a ring with absolute certainty, the dendrochronologist would ideally like to have a complete surface, which in a young pine would be shaped like a tall thin cone. This is not possible, so trees are often sampled in several places at different heights.

Common anomalies in these trees include missing rings, which suggests no annual growth for a year; discontinuous rings, extremely narrow rings, asymmetrical or lopsided rings, multiple rings, "reaction wood," which is the result of tension or compression when a tree leans, damaged rings like frost rings or fire rings. These anomalies, though rare in old bristlecones, may reveal specific singular events in a tree's history.

An investigator who samples tree-rings inadequately may be trying to read what literary editors call a corrupt text. In the trees Ferguson and others before him called "complacent," trees growing in slightly less adverse positions, the rings appear less sensitive to changes in environmental conditions. Because they are more uniform, their chronologies are more easily read but harder to cross-date. In the trees he called "sensitive," the chronologies are more difficult to date with precision, but the rings themselves reveal more completely the conditions under which they grew. In the bristlecone, these sets of rings are highly condensed. One might say they are written in small print. A slow-growing White Mountains specimen at 10,500 feet grows one inch in radius for every 140 years of growth. Tree-rings are most difficult to read when they are most accurate and complete texts. As Mirov explained: "[B]y its living processes the tree 'writes' on its tree ring calendar whatever environmental conditions prevailed during each year of its life." But in what language? And how can one infer the conditions, or distinguish them from each other? In practice, reading tree-rings is not a straightforward task.

Imagine that every individual tree writes its own text. Every tree, one might say, writes what is important to it, but what is important to the tree may not be what is important to the investigator. A tree absorbs parts of its environment which are not immediately relevant to its growth, such as nuclear radiation from atom bomb tests and other trace elements that come from atmospheric sources. When a tree literally embodies the world it lives in, it does not necessarily record what scientists want to read. So, too, some trees may produce very idiosyncratic records.

To decode and read the forest's history, investigators collect a set of samples, each a separate text. Some, on the one hand, are judiciously chosen from areas where bristlecone pines grow under less stress. Their chronologies provide a time line with all the rings present. Some, chosen even more carefully from what appear to be sensitive trees, allow a close reading of the difficult texts, but are perhaps missing some rings seen in the time line. Reading rings became, in the 1960s, close reading indeed, and was pursued with great caution. Reading rings sometimes called for microscopic and cosmic perspectives, a highly specialized understanding of cellular biology and meteorology. Reading tree-rings went far beyond chronology.

A chronology has no plot, but a story does. Dendrochronologists began to assign causes for the events in the lives of forests they could see in the tree-ring record, and when they continued to discuss those causes they were contending over the meaning of those stories. Whatever a tree-ring embodies is not obvious and does not speak directly of causes, but can be made—through correlation—to represent certain events. Bristlecone rings may reveal many things happening at the same time. An investigator may determine that some of those things should be correlated with other data and developed as "signals," that other things should be treated as "noise" and filtered out of the reading. The scientist who reads tree-rings seeks to depict actual conditions at particular times as patterns by linking the actual pattern of tree-rings to changing environmental conditions. Scientists create and defend their readings. They imply that some causes or changes are more important than others and arrange rings and environmental conditions in a certain cause-and-effect order.

Rather than assuming some single cause of change, dendroclimatologists develop a set of questions about the landscape, hoping to produce accurate records of changes in the environment. A study cannot be grounded in a pattern alone; a pattern is only readable by reference to the conditions related to its engendering. Consequently, a simple tree-ring must suggest a complex system of historical causes. Each obvious line of chronology may reveal subtle changes in the environment of the tree. What kinds of changes?

A tree is connected to everything in its world: to light, water, air, earth. Botanists first make initial distinctions between the kinds of connections trees have to the world, speaking of climatic (solar and atmospheric) and edaphic (soil) causes. They also recognize general and local causes. Dendroclimatology must have a clear sense of such causes to read them into the rings. If changes in climate produce changes in trees, these changes can be correlated.

Substrate and Pattern

Any serious discipline must investigate its own methodological grounding, and so it has been with the sciences investigating bristlecones. Grounding became particularly crucial when bristlecone samples were used to calibrate radiocarbon dating, because the readings that were drawn out of bristlecone pines assumed a role as the primary foundation for many inferences about time and change.

The bristlecone forests of the White Mountains, viewed as a static entity existing in the present, occupy a certain region, dry and cold, commonly from 10,000 to 11,650 feet in elevation, and occasionally grow as low as 8,500 feet, where they intermingle with piñon pine. From the perspective of the tree, elevation is a set of conditions of air and light, of temperature and precipitation, as they change through the solar year. In the White Mountains average temperatures are below freezing from November through April; annual precipitation is 12–13 inches. These kinds of statistics can and have been elaborated, revealing in detail the climatic perspective: that each bristlecone pine grows not so much in a place as in a set of conditions.

Neither the same conditions nor the same forest are found equally everywhere in the present mountains of the Great Basin. Quite the contrary. The distribution of organisms across the Great Basin varies, even under similar conditions. (Trees do not read maps or altimeters.) Ecologists began early in the 1960s to describe the bristlecone forests as part of a static mosaic, a pattern species seem to create as they inhabit the White Mountains. The mosaic can be mapped. It consists of patches of limber-bristlecone forest, sagebrush, and sometimes mountain mahogany. The pattern is

Harold Mooney, September 1996. (Courtesy of Harold Mooney)

pronounced and dramatic, with very distinct boundaries between some species, determined primarily by soil, moisture, and topography. Such boundary lines are semi-permeable but not illusory, and they do not appear to be the result of disturbances like fire, flood, earthquake, or volcanism. They suggest that species only inhabit certain sites, but not all available sites, as if laid out on a chessboard. To depict these patterns on a map as a set of patches, as seemingly static patterns of ground cover, is to delineate not just spatial relations but possibly causal relations between site and species.

In the early 1960s, Harold A. Mooney (1932–   ) of the White Mountain Research Station, and later of Stanford University, and R. D. Wright of UCLA began to survey the present relations between plants and environmental variables. The possible causes for a mosaic-like pattern are many. Mooney and Wright contemplated the substrate. They analyzed the constituents of soil, its color, temperature, and moisture content; they listed available species that might dominate a plot of particular soil, and they mapped the way all of them, but especially sagebrush and bristlecone, were distributed. To identify what grew where, and in what densities, they plotted transepts with 50-meter steel tapes, on grids which were laid out according to the cardinal points and according to elevation belts. Then they identified and counted plants along each line and—since a line has no width—close to it.

Sage, they found, grows minimally on north and west slopes, bristlecone populations thin toward the opposite directions. Both species can grow on quartzite, dolomite, sandstone, or granite, but bristlecone seems most dominant on a light-colored soil made of Reed dolomite, a limestone rich in magnesium. Sagebrush is most dominant on darker-hued sandstone. Why?

Because they were looking for a characteristic and generalized pattern, Mooney and Wright eliminated sites influenced by local causes like wind deposition of snow in certain areas or temperature inversions in valleys where cold air settles. Then they constructed a set of experiments to define the boundaries between patches of species. They subjected bristlecone and sage to a variety of conditions, and measured photosynthesis and respiration of these species as a function of temperature and soil moisture. They considered the competition for natural minerals and moisture in the soil, finding that bristlecones were more tolerant than sage of low mineral and nutrient content in dolomite soils but less tolerant of drought. Most important, from the perspective of bristlecones, "it seems . . . that small site differences in soil moisture could cause large differences in productivity of bristlecone pine, and that such small moisture differences do exist between dolomite and sandstone soils in the field."

In large part, a heightened sensitivity of trees to environment produced these patterns, so dramatic when viewed from above, whose boundaries amplified or magnified small differences in conditions. Sensitive dependence on small gradients of moisture drew bristlecones to sites on dolomite. The grounding of such a study is double and problematic. Mooney and Wright recognized presences and absences of species as relative, but tried to see the changes in a forest by depicting its present state. Their work is basic to bristlecone science and is used unquestioningly by those who study patterns of bristlecone distribution in the distant past. Yet it provides an essentially static and unhistoric picture of forest dynamics, a slice of life and not a story of change.

A Disappearing Substrate

The substrate in the White Mountains is not a stable foundation for old growth. Unlike the quartzite blocks of the moraine burying

Valmore LaMarche Jr., late 1960s or early 1970s, White Mountains. (Courtesy Laboratory of Tree-Ring Research)

the bases of old trees on Wheeler Peak, the dolomite of the White Mountains erodes—degrades, as geologists say. In the early 1960s, Valmore C. LaMarche Jr. (1937–1988) began to study the bristlecones. He was perhaps ahead of his time, a long-haired youth with a leather headband, an undergraduate at the University of California, Berkeley, studying geology. LaMarche was so fascinated with the White Mountains that he continued his investigations as a graduate student at Harvard, wondering how the bristlecones could be used to measure erosional rates of the dolomite on which they grew.

LaMarche had a fertile and imaginative approach to understanding the tree's relation to its environment. During his twenty-five-year career working with the bristlecones, his work was characterized by great scrupulousness in reading the geological, biological, and climatological record the trees suggested. He contributed to a series of methodological innovations instituted at the Laboratory of Tree-Ring Research during the 1960s. Douglass had established cross-dating, and Schulman developed precise sampling techniques; Ferguson did the foot-slogging work in creating long chronologies for the White Mountain bristlecone groves. Harold Fritts would come from Ohio to develop theories of tree growth. Val LaMarche, because he did not come out of the program in Arizona, would bring a distinctive set of methods which produced new and intriguing perspectives. In his Harvard doctoral dissertation of 1964, he described the ways in which root exposure of the trees could be used to measure rates of erosion in the White Mountains.

He thought of these erosional processes as uniform. "Degradation," as he wrote in his classic analysis of 1968, was for his purposes "the gradual lowering of the surface of the land by erosive processes."

Though he was not interested primarily in the oldest growing trees, he was interested in one of the qualities of the older trees. "Living bristlecones," he observed, "are rarely overturned." And dead ones may stand for more than a thousand years, "falling only after supporting roots have decayed or been undermined by deep erosion." Like other observers, he was struck by the "extensively exposed root systems of certain individual trees, as well as the deeply exposed roots of large numbers of old trees in large tracts." Root exposure, he concluded in 1968, must be a result of "degradational processes operating uniformly over large areas for long periods of time."

The trees themselves, he noted in an interesting inversion of substrate and tree, could be perceived as "static features in a changing landscape," and used as measuring devices. Since trees could also induce pronounced local topographic changes, he needed to create a model of the trees' root growth, an architecture of their foundations.

To establish a model of the trees' root growth under erosional conditions, he began by noting examples of symmetrical and asymmetrical exposure of roots with a series of photographs and detailed drawings, maps which portrayed individual trees and the actual spread of their roots on slopes of various profiles. The model, a composite of these individual maps, demonstrated the complex dynamic between the ways roots were uncovered and the ways trees dammed erosional debris, creating terraces on their upslope sides and hollows downslope.

The real work, however, was in determining a quantitative relationship between root exposure and slope degradation. This was where tree-ring dating came into LaMarche's work. First of all, he had the chronologies of Schulman and Ferguson, largely unpublished as late as 1968. He was writing for geologists, who would be surprised to find geological maps with trees in them and who would probably be ignorant of the procedures of dendrochronology, especially the craft of cross-dating. He needed to ground his geology in the biology of bristlecones, as he turned to the roots themselves.

The root systems of bristlecones are shallow, more than 75 percent concentrated in the uppermost foot of soil. Vertical taproot development is rare. The internal and physiological structure of

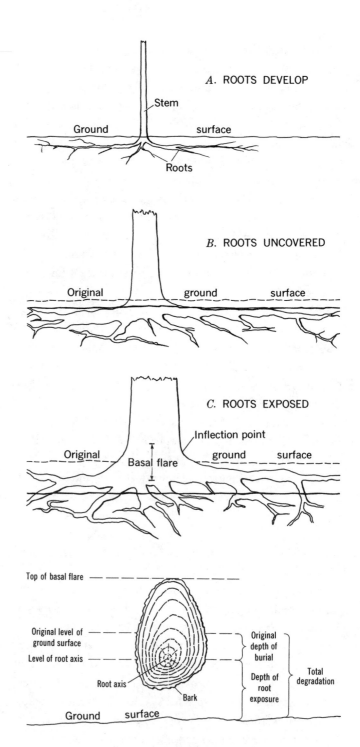

A. ROOTS DEVELOP

Stem

Ground   surface

Roots

B. ROOTS UNCOVERED

Original   ground   surface

C. ROOTS EXPOSED

Inflection point

Original   ground   surface

Basal flare

Top of basal flare

Original level of
ground surface

Level of root axis

Root axis

Bark

Ground   surface

Original
depth of
burial

Depth of
root
exposure

Total
degradation

**Root exposure.
(LaMarche, *Rates of
Slope Degradation*,
1968)**

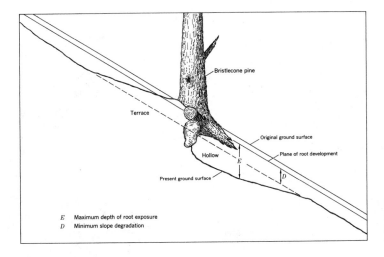

Bristlecone pine

Terrace

Original ground surface

Plane of root development

Hollow

E

Present ground surface

D

E   Maximum depth of root exposure
D   Minimum slope degradation

**Slope profile.
(LaMarche, *Rates of
Slope Degradation*,
1968)**

mature roots, LaMarche assumed, is created by a growth pattern
essentially the same as that of the stems. Though it is difficult to
estimate the time taken to expose roots initially, once roots are
exposed they begin to grow in a form called "buttress roots." Imagine a tree seen from above. Most of the exposed roots spread downhill, covering the ground with a weblike pattern. Several major
roots buttress the tree. As they are exposed by erosion, the bark on
the upper surface dies and the roots grow radially downward as if to
stay in contact with the ground along their length. In essence, a
kind of strip growth begins as roots assume asymmetrical cross
sections. Growth continues radially downward from an exposed
root's axis. So a precise discontinuity emerges in the form of the
growth layers and indicates approximately the inception of root
exposure.

A straightforward model—illustrated by line drawings of root
patterns and slope profiles—allowed LaMarche to convert measurements of root exposure to estimates of slope degradation rates. His
model included maps of the slopes, detailed drawings of root forms,
patterns of trees shown on maps of hillsides, and data from trees
cored and measured according to discrete individual buttress roots
and trunks.

When LaMarche measured the distance from the center or axis
of radial growth to the ground and also counted the rings subsequent to exposure, he could plot the length of time indicated by the
rings against the quantity of exposure during this period. He did
this with a great many individual trees, on various slopes of differing exposures and slope aspects.

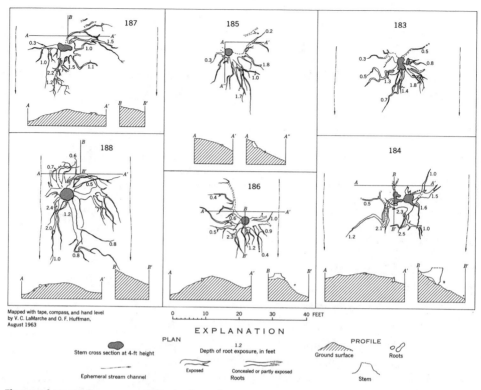

Figures of exposed roots, from above and from slope profile. The numbers refer to individual trees. Mapped with tape, compass, and hand level by V. C. LaMarche and O. F. Huffman, August 1963. (LaMarche, *Rates of Slope Degradation*, 1968)

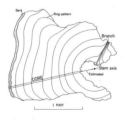

The problem of coring eroded stems. (LaMarche, *Rates of Slope Degradation*, 1968)

If he had used only the oldest trees—for him, ancient meant more than 4,000 years old—he would have biased his results toward the particular topography where they grew. So he investigated primarily trees of about 3,000 years of age, which he could sample in a random fashion. What he found was that degradation rates seemed not to have fluctuated greatly in the last 3,000 years; they had been consistently as great as 3 to 4 feet per 1,000 years on steep banks adjacent to channels now being incised, and more than 1 foot per 1,000 years even on the rocky crests.

A characteristic doubleness of attention marks LaMarche's process of investigation, and his method became characteristic of the kind of reading used by investigators following him. I will describe this doubleness in terms of hands and feet. When he mapped and drew diagrams, bored and counted tree-rings (hands), he was engaged in shaping the bristlecone forests as tools for measuring an elementary geological process: rates of slope degradation, as determined from botanical evidence. He used the tools of dendrochronology to measure erosion directly. His direct botanical evidence extended dendrochronology to the roots. To provide a firm footing for his theory, he had to create a model of the bristlecone's root develop-

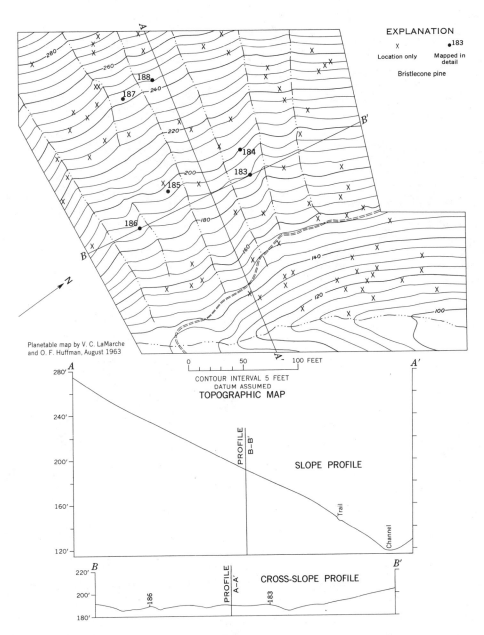

EXPLANATION

X — Location only   •183 — Mapped in detail

Bristlecone pine

Planetable map by V. C. LaMarche
and O. F. Huffman, August 1963

0   50   100 FEET

CONTOUR INTERVAL 5 FEET
DATUM ASSUMED
TOPOGRAPHIC MAP

SLOPE PROFILE

PROFILE B–B'

Trail

Channel

CROSS-SLOPE PROFILE

PROFILE A–A'

ment and its adaptation to erosion as a foundation on which his measurements could stand. Consider that a 4,000-year-old tree, three-quarters of whose initial root depth developed in the top foot of soil, has remained standing while the slope on which it grows has degraded more than four feet. This is not developed as the main thesis of LaMarche's work, and yet the way the trees do this constitutes a striking feature of the forests upon which his data depended.

A crude map of tree location and slope profiles. Planetable map by LaMarche and O. F. Huffman, August 1963. (Lamarche, *Rates of Slope Degradation*, 1968)

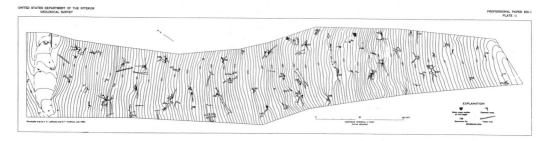

UNITED STATES DEPARTMENT OF THE INTERIOR
GEOLOGICAL SURVEY

PROFESSIONAL PAPER 352-I
PLATE II

Topographic map of area 2 showing standing and fallen trees and exposed roots, White Mountains, Calif. Numbers refer to individual trees. Planetable map by LaMarche and O. F. Huffman, July 1963. (LaMarche, *Rates of Slope Degradation*, 1968)

Researchers using his methods in Utah to gauge expected erosion and consequent siltation into a reservoir found some trees near Cedar Breaks National Monument which had stayed upright for nearly 3,000 years by adjusting their contact with the more easily eroded, and therefore more rapidly degraded, soil. Over that period, in which there has been at least forty inches of erosion, the trees have come to look as if they stand on stilts—as they will until they eventually fall over.

It is a conventional joke among dendrochronologists that the methodological grounding of the discipline is linked to the literal grounding of a tree's roots in a substrate. The relationship between the two groundings, as Mooney, Wright, and LaMarche demonstrated, is by no means trivial.

Tree Growth and Environmental Change

Another set of basic questions was framed by Harold C. Fritts (1928–   ). Just how sensitive to their climatic environment are bristlecone pines? In graduate school at the University of Ohio, Fritts had studied the growth of forest trees and developed a "dendrograph," a sensitive device which could record daily variations in stem size and the radial growth of trees. He was recruited by the Laboratory of Tree-Ring Research in 1960, five years after he completed his doctorate in 1956, to pick up a strand of Schulman's unfinished investigation. Someone like Ferguson, who gained a Ph.D. from the Department of Watershed Management at Arizona in 1959, was not prepared to develop a model of tree growth.

As he has written in *Tree Rings and Climate* (1976), Fritts was at first "skeptical of tree ring dating and of the possibility for climatic inference." He saw the complexity of the problem because he was thoroughly grounded in plant physiology and ecology. Consequently, his work emphasizes the botanical basis for the principles and concepts which allow scientists to, as he puts it, "analyze both the spatial and temporal variations in growth and to use them to infer variations in climate." He explains that "the juxtaposition of the biological and statistical discussions is a result of my firm belief that biological insight is essential for obtaining the most meaningful statistics and that statistical methods are similarly important for the accurate quantifying and testing of biological results." Space and time, biology and statistics: these coordinates formed the matrix of his thought and grounded his readings of climate from tree rings.

When he began a study of White Mountain bristlecone trees in 1962—a study leading to his definitive monograph of 1969—Fritts realized that he was studying not a homogeneous forest but a set of groves living under significantly different conditions. By applying a general theory of the growth of trees, he was able to compare these communities, producing a kind of sociology of these small groves. To gain reliable indices of their growth, he began with a conclusion of Wright and Mooney (1965), who recognized that the bristlecone, in gross terms, responds primarily to the moisture gradient in the area, which explained to Fritts "how its distribution runs counter to

Topographic map of area 1 showing standing and fallen trees and exposed roots, White Mountains, Calif. Planetable map by LaMarche and O. F. Huffman, June 1963. (LaMarche, *Rates of Slope Degradation*, 1968)

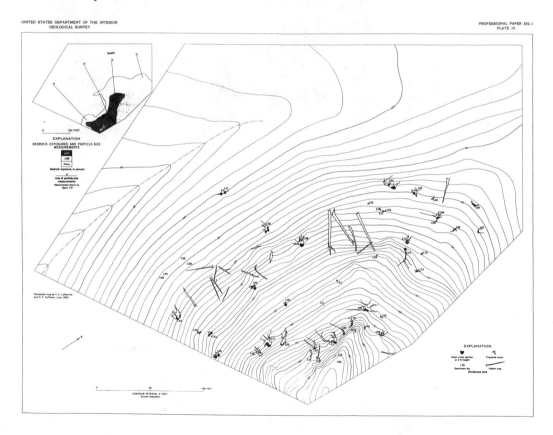

Harold Fritts (l.) installing a dendrograph on a ponderosa pine, spring 1962. (Courtesy Laboratory of Tree-Ring Research)

most of the subalpine herb and shrub components which seem to be controlled essentially by temperature gradients."

Fritts focused on the forest *in medias res,* developing seven study areas at about 10,000 feet, at various positions and exposures. He equipped many of his trees with dendrographs and measured for three years (1962 to 1964) their wood densities, growth, soils, and various environmental parameters, especially with regard to precipitation, soil moisture, and moisture evaporation. He was particularly interested in the "water budget" of trees.

He measured individual stems: they expand at night and on cloudy days according to "environmental parameters." He called this response to patterns of moisture their "daily march." Other measurements revealed weekly, monthly, and yearly changes. He could date many of the most important events in the trees' annual lives: initial bud swelling began as early as June 20, buds elongated around July 10, new needles emerged at the end of July, pollination started after the first week in August, and the trees ceased to grow for the year by mid-August at most sites.

This schedule allowed Fritts to understand better what tree-rings represented. There were variations in the dates of events in a tree's season according to the slope, aspect, elevation, and substrate on which it grew, but he was most interested in variations of rings associated with sensitive old trees, which were found widely spaced on rocky crests.

He correlated the narrow rings of these trees with particular climatic conditions, determining that "the climate for April through June, as measured by calculated evapotranspiration deficits, is most highly correlated with ring-width growth." This was also true with regard to elongation of needles, climate prior to but not during the growth season being "statistically related" to growth. More recently, using foxtail pines, Louis A. Scuderi and others have correlated climatic conditions two years or more prior to a growth season with the tree-ring widths.

Fritts sorted what he would later call signal from noise, testing for "factors which directly or indirectly limit the rates of growth processes." He considered the possibility that these were limiting factors:

1. Immediate internal and external conditions, inside and outside the trees. Cell water balance, temperature, day length, and damage to cambial tissue were found *not* to be limiting factors.

2. Larger rhythms of the tree's growth and reproduction defined by biotic factors. Bud swelling, which precedes cambial growth, might compete for internal resources as female cones compete for food. Bristlecone and foxtail pines flower later in the season than any other North American pine. Biotic factors, genetic potential, and competition within the forest might play a role in growth, but Fritts did not believe they were measurable.

3. The histories of a tree's changing internal and external environment. Moisture and temperature conditions of the previous summer, autumn, winter, and especially during the spring before growth for the year commenced, were primary factors limiting tree growth.

The physical condition and structure of a tree, he determined, integrated several central biotic factors; especially the so-called strip-bark tree, he wrote, "*apparently reaches a quasi-equilibrium with its environment*" (italics mine). His central finding in 1969: the width of strip-bark of a tree correlated precisely with so-called die-back in foliage he—and Schulman before him—observed in older trees. These biotic factors had allowed the internal trees to adjust to historical conditions under which they lived and made them precisely sensitive to those conditions.

He found that "rings from old, semiarid-site bristlecone pine provide uniquely homogeneous, millennia-long time series," highly correlated to climate. By homogeneous, he meant these widths were relatively independent of long-term changes associated with the ages of trees. Site mattered, especially where locally higher moisture or wind deposition of snow resulted in environmental conditions which were *not* limiting and allowed the maximal growth each year.

These were not surprising observations, but they had previously been intuitive. Fritts grounded them in actual observations and expressed them precisely and mathematically, depicting trees sharply and elaborately linked to their surroundings in ways that could be partially but not completely quantified. A tree's growth measured its connection to its environment, made it a meter, a dendrograph in itself.

No single tree could tell the whole story of a forest. Fritts related the data from his various sites in an interesting way. As he pointed out, "dendrochronology is a precise tool, in that every ring is identified (cross-dated) as to the year in which it was formed," but this is accomplished in the process of cross-dating "not by ring counts but by matching patterns of wide and narrow rings." Sensitive trees, on exposed, low-elevation rocky dolomitic sites provide a great deal of information but are difficult to read and not easily dated. Data from these trees must be put in the context of the lives of other groves "to reconstruct and analyze the climatic fluctuations of the past." The dendrochronologist builds a chronology from what Ferguson called less complacent sites, and the dendroclimatologist superimposes the information from sensitive sites.

Dominance and Submission

What the tree does in each of its rings is extracted, read out by scientists from separate disciplines for its structure and detail, which are then recombined by the dendroclimatologist. The climatologist is dependent on the chronologist, as Fritts's work depended on the chronology established by Ferguson. The climatologist is also indebted to the tree physiologist, who consults with the ecologist. These sciences began to form networks and hierarchies in the bristlecone investigations.

Trained as a botanist, Fritts was prepared to observe the consequences of conifers' own special genetic characteristics, so-called xeromorphic structures favorable to bright light, resistant to cold and drought—such as needles with a small surface-to-volume ratio and a tough skin which allows them to resist harsh and variable environments. Yet there are strange paradoxes between the characteristics of trees and their survival. The largest trees often grow near the upper limit of their range where the precipitation is highest, but do not grow remarkably old because they develop "heart rot," as it is somewhat anthropomorphically named; the oldest trees usually develop in conditions of most austere drought.

The bristlecone forests "predominate," as some say, where there is no running water, the most sensitive ones in the driest places, on rocky ridges, flourishing on dolomite because they have little or no competition on this surface, in particular because of the rock's low nutrient content and high reflective qualities. Sagebrush will dominate sandstones nearby, because it is, in fact, more drought resistant. Limber pine will dominate granitic soils. One must be attentive to this language of dominance and submission. In the White Mountains, plants seem to grow not so much where they are best adapted as where nothing else does so readily; their presences or absences are determined less by patterns of dominance than by patterns of submission. Fritts inferred that variations in ring widths he found in the lowest reach of these forests indicated the trees' submission to variations in precipitation.

A Book of the Bristlecone

It took Fritts nearly a decade to pursue and analyze the biological ground for Schulman's trees of longevity under adversity. In 1969 the Laboratory of Tree-Ring Research published his *Bristlecone Pine in the White Mountains of California: Growth and Ring-Width Characteristics,* which summed up and condensed this era of research on the Great Basin bristlecone. The book measured the cyclical pattern of the bristlecone's everyday life.

Fritts's team sampled trees and environment with an elaborate array of instruments and monitored environmental variables simultaneously, calculating soil moisture, evaporation, and tree growth in order to produce such accounts as a tree's water budget to explain its characteristics. The text of Fritts's report is filled with charts and graphs; it is highly mathematical in its organization of perceptions. This kind of work can be called grounding because it detailed the way the bristlecone pines acted in the present and provides a foundation for inferring the meaning of tree-rings which grew in the past. It is, however, a reduction of the tree to an abstraction, a generalized tree made of quantifiable factors. By harnessing the trees to machines, these men proposed to turn the tree of long life into the tree of profound historical knowledge. Their portrait of the bristlecone in the present was a just and lively representation, but dehistoricized and despatialized, which allowed them to read a story. Their portrait was of the tree as a tool, mechanically accurate but highly selective in its choice of detail.

It was the work of no single person. A team from the Laboratory of Tree-Ring Research at the University of Arizona was supported by National Science Foundation grants, received equipment and data from the U.S. Weather Bureau and the Department of the Navy. Researchers used facilities provided by the White Mountain Research Station of the University of California, Berkeley, and were helped by personnel of the Inyo National Forest; they obtained time on the digital computer at the Numerical Analysis Laboratory of their own university. In its literature cited, the report includes about seventy references to a wide range of subjects, from statistics to the microbiology of soil. Only three or four of these titles were published before 1950.

In sum, Fritts's volume reports upon an expedition of a diverse group into the life of a single species growing in a single region, work supported by a diverse group of social institutions. Such an elaborate and expensive project indicates how important the Great Basin bristlecone had become because of its ability to embody completely, and consequently represent in its growth rings, many changes in its environment, primarily with regard to temperature and moisture.

The way they determined where this tree lives, why, and how it lives there can be read also as a kind of portrait of the people who sought knowledge. What did Fritts, Mooney, and LaMarche want to measure, if not the very strategy of life facing adversity in the form of drought, erosion, and limited choices of substrate? Fritts in particular wanted to know how long each year inert wood became live, when it quickened, when it grew dormant, what marks of its passing resurrections it left, how its being in the world, growing, flourishing, and suffering, was reflected in the patterns of its body and what that body could tell about the conditions of life to which it had been subjected. And this inquiry, too, was subject to generalization.

The Culture of Bristlecone Studies

While bristlecone forests were cultivated for data, the bristlecone pines also created human communities and scientific institutions. This two-sided transaction reveals ways in which people are altered by the shapes of their studies. As an immensely valuable tool, the bristlecone groves convened an interdisciplinary study that correlated the past and present, attempted to reconcile various versions of the past, and linked mathematical models and biological research.

At bottom, a new science engages in its birth in what Michel Foucault, in *Discipline and Punish,* has called "small techniques of notation, of registration, of constituting files, of arranging facts in columns and tables that are so familiar to us now." Knowledge is found in these "ignoble archives." These techniques are not trivial, and they do not create knowledge alone. They also create "a new type of power over bodies," power over the bodies of trees and over the bodies of researchers.

The crafts of dendrochronology and dendroclimatology grew up in the White Mountains and under the bleachers of a football stadium in Tucson. They preceded and then joined radiocarbon dating, and the bristlecone pine became an international species when Hans Suess used Ferguson's data to calibrate the radiocarbon scale. The procedures used for sampling bristlecones, treating the samples, visually analyzing them, and sorting their characteristics by statistical and computerized methods became the subjects for a series of standardized textbooks. The textbooks, in turn, allowed the science to universalize its methods and to standardize discourse among researchers. Courses on dendrochronology were taught at universities. Individual researchers went forth across the globe, using these standard techniques, extending them to other continents and to a total world view.

An influential textbook, *Tree Rings and Climate,* published by Harold Fritts in 1976, set out the "climate-growth system" he devel-

Harold Fritts at the Laboratory of Tree-Ring Research, November 1985. (Courtesy Laboratory of Tree-Ring Research)

oped in great part from his work with bristlecones. He wrote it for "at least a third year college student with some experience and background in at least one science," to establish the basic terminology of the discipline, review essential basic botany, introduce basic principles of statistics, survey methods of analysis pursued first in the White Mountains, and extend the applications of the craft to problems involving the history of climate. The text's organizational structure is precisely empirical and inductive.

A Guggenheim Foundation grant allowed Fritts to write the textbook. Because he wished it to have practical value, he kept close to the basic procedures. Dendrochronological study was, first of all, work. Fritts tallied the average work time required to collect and process a 200–400-year ring-width chronology, which had a mean time of 215 person-hours, including a time-budget of 13 percent for collection and preparation, 69 percent for dating and measuring samples, and 18 percent for supervising and processing data. In other words, workers spent more than two-thirds of their time in laboratories. If they imagined they worked in the forests, it is because forests were on their minds.

Bristlecone pines were especially on some people's minds after the 1960s. A brief review of the examples in Fritts's text demonstrates that the mid-1960s were banner years in bristlecone studies, and these early studies created the foundation for dendroclimatic methodology. Terms like sensitivity, cross-dating, and calibration took on universal meaning. The dendro- words proliferated, among them dendroclimatology, dendrogeomorphology, dendroecology, and dendrohydrology. At the bottom of all these growing sub-fields—which might better be called superfields—were the trees, particularly those of the White Mountains, and their rings.

Cross-dating was possible not only because there were communities of trees responding to similar environmental conditions, but also because there were scientific communities with shared methods, discourse, and procedures used in their investigations. Fritts's text was devoted to standardization of data and to replication. Most of all, he taught methods of reliable close reading and correlation. At the bottom of these standards, a very large mass of data from bristlecone and ponderosa pine created a foundation, largely a set or matrix of computer-stored measurements upon which theoretical models could be built.

Fritts, for instance, was particularly concerned with what he called, by analogy to electronic systems, the signal to noise ratio, variations in tree-rings expressing meaningful information versus variations which provide no useful information on the trees and their environment. He defined a signal as "a detectable quality, pattern, or variation in a time series." It can be argued that the signal-to-noise ratio was constantly shifting, depending on what an investigator considered meaningful.

Fritts's textbook is also a participant's autobiography combined with a history of his community, not so much a story of individual

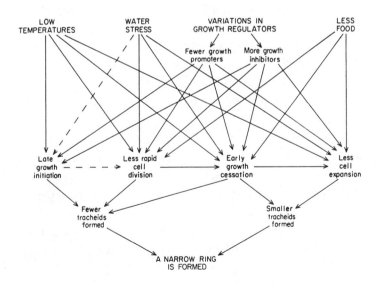

A general diagram of the climate-growth system. (Fritts, 1976)

heroes as of the cooperation of scientists from many disciplines who agree upon what is meaningful. It is designed to regulate or police a community's findings and the shapes these findings can take, in order that investigators might be urbane and understand each other.

Information has an economic cost too and requires institutional structure for its dissemination. Who was interested enough to fund this work? American citizens through state universities, the U.S. Navy, the National Air and Space Administration, the National Science Foundation, the Atomic Energy Commission, the Guggenheim and Ford Foundations, among others. Sometimes wealthy sources funded very strange studies. NASA, in the mid-1960s, was worried that astronauts might be endangered by solar flares (sunspots) and wondered, as Douglass had wondered, whether dendrochronologists could predict solar flares by analyzing tree-rings. Can you find cycles? these sources asked, with their checkbooks open. This investigation, funded by NASA, done by Fritts and LaMarche, answered no. Astronauts would have to chance it.

Institutions have boom times and bust times. There will probably never again be such financial support as was obtained for the kind of attention the bristlecone pines received in the late 1950s and early 1960s. Much of the support came from the boom in radiocarbon dating. But information is often turned to topical problems like global climate change because of the prospect of future financial support.

Individual people advanced dendrochronology by devoting their careers to study. Dendrochronology had seemed in 1950 a somewhat frivolous occupation, but it was self-consciously serious and truly interdisciplinary. At a time when botanists, geologists, and ecologists had no fear of finding good traditional jobs, a small number took the risk of coming to the tree-ring lab in Tucson, which was small, isolated, and hot in the summer. They worked for the cause of dendrochronology, to turn a tool into a hard scientific enterprise.

In the 1960s, the bristlecone samples were reason for a small number of men to undertake a certain kind of travel akin to the concurrent exploration of outer space. Some, like Ferguson and LaMarche, were wanderers, and others were homebodies who spent their time indoors. Because of the present distribution of bristlecones, in islands, men traveled a great deal in the Great Basin, from range to range, shuttling between the island groves. These men's lives were shaped by their travels, by their work, and by their mental journeys.

They had common desires to see beyond the present and they had some common values. Like others of their generation, they acquired a certain discipline in the intensive study of one place. And most researchers were engaged in filling out the picture, doing what has come to be called "normal science," until that picture broke into multiple images. Yet they also went forth with their techniques to other places across the world.

Almost all of the bristlecone pine trees these scientists studied, cored, and tagged, still live in the groves of the Great Basin, as reserves. Some were killed, and with others, already dead, were transported to Tucson and archived. The storage archive under the football stadium in Tucson contains cartons of samples labeled with the names of the principal investigators—most of them gone now. Douglass collected great slabs of sequoia wood and old, sometimes charred beams from ancient cities. Schulman and Ferguson left many cross sections of older bristlecones. Cardboard cartons marked with LaMarche's name line the dusty shelves as part of the collected data of several generations of dendrochronologists. Most of all, the basement smells good because it is a room full of wood.

CHAPTER 5

The Upper Edge

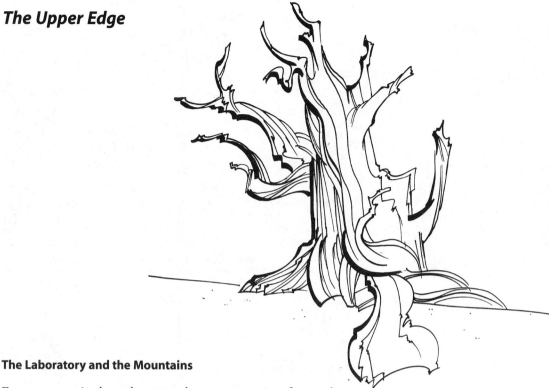

The Laboratory and the Mountains

Every summer in the early 1960s a loose community of researchers entered the mountains and worked simultaneously on different projects in the ancient bristlecone botanical reserve established in 1958. They occupied several stations of the White Mountain research facility and walked into the old groves each day from gravel roads that improved access. In some places, every tree had been cored several times and clearly labeled with the small numbered aluminum tags used by the Laboratory of Tree-Ring Research. The forest of this region was no wilderness: it was, by the middle of the 1960s, surveyed, mapped, and cultivated to produce climatic data. Ferguson estimated that a summer's field data would take a year to study in the lab. Most of the data gathered each summer flowed out of the mountains to feed the steady but modest growth of the urban and indoor laboratory at the University of Arizona in Tucson.

In Tucson, Harold Fritts endorsed bringing Valmore LaMarche from the U.S. Geological Survey. First LaMarche worked on a NASA project and later, with Thomas Harlan, he reestablished Ferguson's bristlecone chronology. Not that anyone at the lab doubted Ferguson's accuracy, but establishing an independent chronology would confirm the radiocarbon calibration. LaMarche and Harlan treated data from timberline trees on Sheep and Campito Mountains, near the Patriarch Grove at the northern and upper end of the reserve, developing it independently from the data in the Schulman Grove, at the bottom and southern end. Their results, apart from two missing rings, at 2142 and 2681 B.P., confirmed Ferguson's work and established an independent chronology over five millennia.

Although confirmation was important, Fritts, LaMarche, and others chose particular portions of the forest where they pursued histories of climate. Unlike those who worked with the longest-lived trees, LaMarche began to investigate the upper edge of the forest where trees did not live so long as the ones below. Researchers shared data, but because each investigation was independent and LaMarche was working at the outer edge of the forest, he found it necessary to engage in much of his own groundwork. He reevaluated and mapped the distributions of the highest bristlecones according to substrate, or soil.

LaMarche wished to read the trees at the upper edge of the forest and use them to measure changes in climate. By 1973 he could define what he called, in an article title, "Holocene Climatic Variations Inferred from Treeline Fluctuations in the White Mountains, California." What did that mean? It meant he was engaged in a relatively narrow special study of a line on the vegetative map of the White Mountains. And yet the line he drew would, in the next decades, extend outward to encompass climatic events across the globe.

LaMarche refined and doubled the hypothesis of sensitivity by showing that the width of a tree-ring at the top of the forest belt revealed a "limiting" variation in temperature during the short six-week growing season. This meant that there were two ways of reading a series of bristlecone rings, depending upon one's position in the forest. Ring width was limited most strongly by variation in temperature at the upper edge of the forest, by variation in precipitation at the bottom edge. Adversity took two different forms that crossed at the middle-elevation forests but could be read independently at the upper and lower edges. Both kinds of reading required that the investigator think of correlation, or relationship between the tree and its environment.

Survival at the Upper Edge

LaMarche correlated the changing spatial patterns of the forest and historical patterns of temperature change at timberline. In a series of articles appearing regularly from the mid-1960s into the 1970s, he read these patterns against each other. Because LaMarche had studied geology, his language for describing change was geological. "Paleo-" means early, primitive, archaic in all earth sciences. He was studying paleoclimatology and especially paleoecology, the history of ancient environments and the relationships between them and ancient plants and animals. The most recent era of climate and ecology begins about ten thousand years ago at the end of the glacial era called the Pleistocene. The bristlecone tree-ring record comes very close to the edge of the Pleistocene epoch. It covers nearly the full range of modern or recent geological history called the Holocene, an era which includes events since about ten thousand years ago.

He had studied the extent of Pleistocene glaciation in the White Mountains in 1965, the recent or Holocene rates of erosion in the range in 1968, and focused especially on the changes in climate during the Holocene. Now, like Fritts, LaMarche was following the idea implicit in the work of Schulman, that the tree-ring record can be re-read according to the methods employed by an investigator.

During the mid-1930s, Ernst Antevs, a Swedish paleoclimatologist, established the idea that a period of global warming and reduced precipitation occurred between seven thousand and forty-five hundred years ago, during the middle of the Holocene. He called this the "altithermal." As LaMarche established, aged bristlecone pines, dead and alive, can be used to read a detailed record of the climate changes of the entire Holocene, and especially of the "altithermal." Unlike glacial moraines and other geological signs of this era, the bristlecones provided direct evidence for investigating changes in the modern environment over a range of time corresponding approximately with the eras of intense human habitation on the North American continent.

The starkest relationship between external climatic conditions and the internal growth of trees can be measured by their survival. Survival correlates the extreme minima of temperature or precipitation, or both, with the presence or absence of a forest. LaMarche focused on the ways trees responded to stress; though he was not primarily interested in their strategies of survival, his correlations define the limits of strategies and how limits have changed with time.

In the White Mountains, as elsewhere, relations or associations between bristlecones and other species are complex at the bottom of the forest. In other mountain ranges, bristlecones are found in mixed forests with a wide variety of other conifers, including limber pine, white pine, Engelmann spruce, and Jeffrey pine, and these associations each have their own patterns and causes, none of which are so decisive or so easily analyzed as the association between bristlecone pines and sage. At the top of their range, the bristlecones are more likely to appear in nearly pure stands, but there are usually a few limber pines, right up to timberline.

Because a nearly pure bristlecone forest is readily accessible high in the White Mountains, the trees provide a special opportunity. LaMarche worked there not simply because of the extreme limiting conditions to be found, or the great number of old trees that register those limits. He worked there because those limiting conditions could be isolated. There, along accessible roads, LaMarche could examine a very long and complex pattern or edge at the top of the forest.

Some writers less closely tied to the scientific culture grow poetic about individual trees in this region because, in many senses, they seem to take such dramatic shapes at timberline, shapes that seem beyond conceptualization. LaMarche's work, however, is not poetic. Individual trees at timberline appear to test the limits of life under adversity, as adversity takes the form of temperature. LaMarche did not focus on individual trees. He developed some broad concepts about the way these forests responded to extreme conditions. Yet his correlations between bristlecone forests and environmental conditions relate, as he recognized, to a very hazy understanding of the somewhat poetic idea of strategies of survival. Survival depends on a tree's responses to stress. LaMarche studied the bristlecones by positioning himself precisely between their life and death.

Signs of Stress and Change

Dead trees stand on slopes above live trees because the line between life and death has descended, but not in one fell swoop. Stress does not strike a tree in a uniform way. A set of discontinuities may appear in the rings and in the structure of a tree when it loses— periodically or suddenly—some of the basic conditions necessary to its survival. This is especially true when the tree is growing near its biological limit.

When LaMarche drew what he called the "climatic" upper tree line on the large pattern of the forest in 1973, he depicted it as tied to topography and soil, and as a result as "very irregular" in its large scale and its smaller scale. His detailed topographical maps of actual stands marked individual living and dead trees. He measured each tree's radius, since these older pines, because of past strip growth, had produced "stems that are very asymmetrical in transverse section."

"If the treeline is defined on the basis of the altitude of the oldest living trees at any point in time," he reasoned, "the precise delineation of past treeline levels requires knowledge of the location and of the dates of establishment and death of all the trees in the area under study." LaMarche drew this line by mapping individual trees. He hypothesized that climate has consistently been the exterior limiting factor in tree survival. This hypothesis could not be paired with a theory of internal or genetic limiting factors. As LaMarche indicated, "unfortunately, little is known of conditions promoting cone production, seed viability, germination, and survival of bristlecone seedlings."

In 1973 general ignorance of the detailed habits of reproduction in bristlecones was paired with a very general theory of past changes in climate. No researcher could witness detailed climate change of the past. The roles of long-term temperature fluctuations at tree line could be complex and irregular. In the shorter term, complexities proliferated. Photosynthesis in any tree could be limited by lower daytime temperature, later occurrence of spring, or earlier onset of winter. The tree could run through its food store, called photosynthates, and in a devastating way if its winter dormancy lasted too long. The shape of annual climate change altered the timing of a tree's phenological events like bud swelling, initiation of cambial activity, or growth in height. Low temperatures at crucial times could devastate bristlecone seedlings, though they are particularly resistant to winterkilling by desiccation.

Consequently, reading a forest's history by the presence and absence of living trees is a crude procedure. As far as dead trees went, LaMarche distinguished dead bristlecones from dead limber pines on the basis of "color, odor, and appearance of the wood." He sampled living stands immediately below tree line. He created skeleton plots from the rings of dead trees and remnants and combined them to produce a master plot, then compared them to the rings of living trees in order to extend his master plot to the present. He examined man-made stumps and estimated that bark persists for about ten to twenty years after the death of the tree, and that sapwood probably is removed in one or two hundred years. He made a "moving" set of topographical maps which depicted separate maximum altitudes of tree survival, drawn as altithermal lines. Above these lines the forest did not simply end; above were graveyards of past forests. The lines defined moving boundaries of temperature, or from the tree's perspective, limiting conditions of heat supply. They defined a set of moving edges between life and death.

Correlations

Because investigators shared data to multiply the way tree rings could be used to read the trees' lives, inferences of a variety of kinds poured out of LaMarche's maps and ring counts. Harold Fritts constructed one statistical map of the threshold between active and inactive periods in tree life by correlating elevation with approximate dates when maximum, minimum, and mean air temperatures set the beginning and end of growing seasons. Fritts also mapped LaMarche's data to test differences in what he called "generating processes," contrasting the patterns of ring widths between high-elevation and low-elevation stands of bristlecones.

LaMarche's study revealed important short-range trends in climate change. He noted first of all a "large number of bristlecone pines . . . established in the upper treeline area since 1850, a high reproduction rate at and above tree line for the past hundred years," which confirmed a well-documented warming trend since the middle of the nineteenth century. It was hard to predict the extent of tree-line advance in the future or guess about the persistence of the changes that encouraged that advance, since the transition, from the tree's perspective, would take several hundred years. But from the human perspective, LaMarche knew, "the biological and cultural impact" of this trend had already produced what he called a "lively discussion." The magnitude and direction of this very recent change suggests an anthropogenic cause because it correlates with the industrial revolution.

Correlation of data sometimes reveals key differences, as anomalies can also be made to reveal patterns. LaMarche compared ring-width chronologies from low arid sites in the White Mountains, sampled by Schulman and analyzed by Fritts in 1965, with his own chronologies from high timberline sites. He attempted to correlate precipitation as a limiting factor for the low-elevation tree growth with temperatures that limited growth in his high-elevation trees by plotting mean ring widths from the two sets of data for a twenty-

year period against each other. Reading the anomalies as differences, he linked the temperature-precipitation data to inferred features of contemporary patterns of weather circulation, which typically alternate between cold-moist and warm-dry regimes.

Fritts mapped these patterns on the continent of North America
as barometrical regimes producing warm-dry conditions (a low-
pressure trough over the North Pacific Ocean associated with a
high-pressure ridge over the Rockies) and cool-moist regimes (an
upper-level trough which allows cool, moist air to flow from the
ocean inland). The result was a set of tentative weather maps of
the past.

Fritts elaborated LaMarche's weather model by linking it to his
climate-growth system. Other scientists, including Fritts, investigated changes in global biological systems by making correlations
which would have seemed whimsical a decade earlier. For instance,
one investigator correlated tree ring-data from forty-nine sites in
western North America with the albacore tuna catch north of San
Francisco during the years 1938–61 to produce a history of ocean
surface temperatures along the west coast of North America.

One section of Fritts's *Tree Rings and Climate* reconstructs spatial
variations for the climate of the United States during most of the
eighteenth and nineteenth centuries, producing weather maps of
immense value for American historians. In 1991 he produced a historical atlas of North American climate patterns from 1602 to 1963.

In longer historical terms, LaMarche found his separate sites did
not produce identical patterns of tree lines over the approximately
six-thousand-year history he studied. The maps agreed in their
gross features, especially indicating a relatively high tree line until a
few centuries ago. He decided that differences among his study
areas were due to their varying exposure to solar energy. He suggested that "the period 5400–2000 B.C. was one of relatively high
summer temperatures." This era, the altithermal, is known also as
the "mid-Holocene warming." The death of large numbers of trees
that had lived as high as 200 meters above the modern tree line until
about 1500 A.D. suggested an "abrupt climatic deterioration" a "few
centuries" ago. This is a version of the Little Ice Age. LaMarche was
confirming precisely, with a separate set of data or a separate text,
general patterns which had been derived by other means.

In separate studies, he plotted tree-growth fluctuations at tree
line with Holocene glacier fluctuations constructed by glaciologists.
These showed what Fritts believed was "good comparison between

periods of inferred low summer temperatures and periods of growth and advance of glaciers."

The altithermal was not a simple problem. In 1972, LaMarche and Harold Mooney correlated his study of the mid-Holocene warming period in the White Mountains by studying changes on Mount Washington in Nevada's Snake Range, where timberline had descended in an era between 4,000 and 2,000 years ago. Climate was not the only focus of their work there, and the tree line was also more complex, because it included a *krummholz* zone. But they found that climatic cooling might be responsible for the shift in vegetational zones on Mount Washington and believed the shift was also associated with increased precipitation. Consequently, LaMarche and Mooney suggested that the most probable long-term climatic shift over the past 4,000 years was of decreased temperatures and increased precipitation.

A casual visitor who drives past the Schulman Grove and continues north up the rough dirt road for another twelve miles to the Patriarch Grove, near timberline at 11,000 feet in elevation, will be tempted to describe the whole forest as living way up high in an indifferent sky, in sight of vague edges, surrounded by a cold desert. People come to the Patriarch Grove and speak of the region as a "moonscape," a place where life is a miracle. They are describing limits, and as LaMarche measured them, those limits change. Their changes indicate a complex dynamic. Because it is an edge, because it is sensitive to change, the timberline reveals the invisible flux of conditions that support lower-elevation terrestrial life, like humans.

The Frontier

The abrupt and jagged edge LaMarche studied and mapped is usually called a "cold" timberline, to distinguish it from the "dry" timberline one sometimes finds at the bottom of Great Basin forest belts. This moving line marks a set of places where changing conditions have created a temperature-sensitive biological boundary. Stephen F. Arno defines this upper line in *Timberline: Mountain and Arctic Forest Frontiers*. Timberline is created by cold but shaped by other conditions. It is the sharpest temperature-dependent boundary in nature, but is also carved by wind, especially because of desiccation and snow deposition, etched by the precipitation and abrasion of frozen water, dependent on soil chemistry, emphasized and held in place by frozen ground, by rarefied atmosphere, polished by intense light, and shaped by other factors as well. Because timberlines occur high in the isolated ranges of the Great Basin, they delineate islands of forest, which are often separated from one another by "an ocean of desert or sagebrush-grass." Because they are islands, the forests are sharply varied across the Great Basin. LaMarche's version of this frontier is particularly austere and abstract, partly because it is mapped using only one species of tree.

A visitor at the Patriarch Grove might step out of his auto and walk to the highest living tree on Campito Mountain in twenty minutes. It has a great canopy of foliage spread out like a lenticular cloud. Here a single bristlecone—a remarkable tree—seems to call attention to timberline, to its own dilemma, caught at the edge of possibility. In a single tree's story of change, the rules may seem simple and unwavering. A tree seems to speak of its life and reveal the nature of timberline, which is a real boundary. LaMarche wanted to know what this boundary was, what it meant, and how it changed.

Described in such figures as I have permitted myself in the last paragraph, using language unlike that of scientists but quite frequent in the more popular literature, timberline seems like something achieved by individuals, trees that climb the slopes until they are too high to survive, and trees that go too high, and perish. In *Timberline Ancients,* Lambert and Muench's popular book on these forests published while LaMarche was completing his own studies, Lambert accompanies one photograph with the text: "They will appear to be climbing the slopes or even vertical rock, into which they thrust their pitons of living wood." To the paleoecologist, such an anthropomorphic narrative misapprehends a process. Expressive language seems to fail by making forests appear to be made, designed, or built by an act or set of conscious acts.

If I were to write that timberline is the roof of the forest, I would be wrong, because I would be giving it an architectural permanence. In *Landscape and Memory,* Simon Schama writes: "There never yet has been a nature writer who, confronted with a primitive forest, has not resorted to the vocabulary of architecture . . . since it has been impossible to visualize or verbalize nature in terms free of cultural association." "Landscapes," Schama believes, "are culture before they are nature."

Schama is right and wrong. The White Mountains became a place where scientific culture converged and read, according to its cultural assumptions, the biotic "nature" of survival and death in the Great Basin's subalpine forests. Individual investigators then wrote essays describing those landscapes. LaMarche, a principal "nature writer" for this community of scientists, had good reason to embrace the premise that these trees lived in these regions before humans conceptualized them, though not always in the same places, and that changes in their lives could be investigated as nature. Their stations could be assigned reasons, but not volition. Trees could, or could not, live at the edges of their possibilities. There would be no point in the investigation of this stark distinction if the bristlecone was not first of all "nature." As for the idea of a frontier: that is a conception about human history.

Life Zones

When botanists or ecologists interrogate the relations in a bristlecone forest, they begin with geology, move to climate but scarcely rest there, being drawn into a labyrinth of possible ways to describe these relations as patterns. When they speak of timberlines as frontiers they suggest something beyond physical conditions. LaMarche's maps can be used to recount a narrative of conditions for life in mountains: their lines depict shapes of migrations by bristlecones and hide the means of their survival in isolated extreme conditions. A map can explain why young forests are found primarily on the leeward sides of the White Mountains, shielded from cold and exposure, away from the wind, and why older forests barely survive in more exposed positions. But conditions do not explain the strategy of these trees, how they established such strange forms while keeping their living parts away from the wind.

Life under adversity is interesting partly because it seems to fall into relatively simple patterns. And in the austere writings of Schulman, Fritts, and LaMarche, the pattern is defined by a single species. The White Mountains are austere, sustaining few representative species in the subalpine zone, where the bristlecone flourishes: three species of tree, nine shrubs, sixteen herbs, few mammals, no fish, birds that come and go but rarely nest. It is a "simplified" system, the Great Basin with a vengeance. But there is more living there than bristlecone pines. People are surprised by a pantomime of mountain bluebirds in the Patriarch Grove, the lush growth of penstemon in the Schulman Grove, gregarious inflections of Clark's nutcrackers, innuendos of the ravens, and when a golden eagle disappears behind the next ridge it seems to mark the edge of one of many invisible circles. People walk in these mountains during the seasons when life flows through these forests. In the winter the trees seem more like static entities.

In 1973 Harold Mooney used the traditional concept of life zone to portray the forests of the White Mountains, but he was careful to indicate the limitations of such portraits. Speaking of plant communities, he presented a set of plant zones, because "recognition of these zones is a convenient means of partitioning the total vegetation into manageable units for discussion." The subalpine forest, for instance, was distinguished by the presence of bristlecone or limber pine, or both.

Mooney was cautious because the life zone is one of the earliest conceptions of ecological pattern. C. Hart Merriam is generally credited with developing the pattern as a temperature-dominant biogeography while studying the San Francisco Mountains of northern Arizona in the late 1880s. As its name suggests, a life zone is a belt, zone, or lamina of life apparent as one climbs up a mountain or travels north or south toward the earth's poles. Life zones contain groups of species within their boundaries, perhaps even as self-contained systems wherein certain biological processes can be studied. Whether life zones constitute habitats from which communities emerge is a more difficult question.

When the ecologist Ronald Lanner, for instance, characterizes the subalpine woodland by the name Limber Pine–Bristlecone Pine Zone, he is following the tradition of discourse established by Merriam and used, for convenience, by Mooney. Lanner characterizes this pattern as a system, a "simple arboreal flora," which not only "bespeaks aridity" but also includes dynamic interactions between species. Sometimes the interaction consists of the relative presence or absence of interchangeable species, including the limber pine dominant in the northern ranges and bristlecone pine in the southern ranges. Sometimes these seemingly linked species are replaced by other components, like Engelmann spruce in wetter ranges, and in an anomalous island of the Pine Forest Range (in the northwest corner of Nevada, thirty miles from the Oregon border), whitebark pine replaces both species. Viewed as a life zone, the dynamic but continuous relationships of a forest's species constitute its essential aspect. What if the dynamic process is disturbed?

The Frost Ring

In 1970 LaMarche observed, especially in trees near timberline, a kind of discontinuity called the frost ring. The frost ring is made of distorted tissue damaged by frost during the growing season and had been noticed in other species as early as the 1930s. These rings are more likely to be found in small stems, presumably because thicker bark and larger mass protect larger stems. He could associate the damage along inner portions of bristlecone tree-rings with rare early-season frosts, and damage near the outer boundary with the more frequent but still rare late-season frosts.

He used these rings as temporal markers, aiding the dating of dead trees at high elevations, extending back 2,500 years. He noticed late frost rings in the Snake Range occurring in 1884, 1912, and 1965. The frost ring, however, is more than a marker and reveals

Valmore LaMarche Jr., fall 1984. (Courtesy Laboratory of Tree-Ring Research)

A.D.   1883   1884   1885

Frost damage (marked by arrow) in latewood of a White Mountain bristlecone pine, following and correlating to the eruption of Krakatoa in August 1883. (Courtesy Laboratory of Tree-Ring Research)

more than climatic fluctuation. It suggests a major discontinuity in the rhythm or timing of the seasons under which forests have grown. Trees in the White Mountains might record worldwide climatic phenomena as slow to come but dramatic when they appeared. Or climatic events, as suggested by the frost rings, might be short and swift.

As early as 1970 LaMarche recognized that some frost rings coincided with major volcanic events—those of Krakatoa, Indonesia, in 1883, Katmai, Alaska, in 1912, and Agung, Bali, in 1963. Other investigators, using ice cores drawn from glaciers in Greenland in the late 1970s, were able to find evidence of major volcanic eruptions as far back as six centuries, and then longer. But ice-core dates were only accurate within about a 2 percent range. Of particular interest was the eruption of Santorini on the island of Thera in the Aegean, dated by ice cores at 1390±50 B.C. The Santorini eruption buried a town, but its effects were also global.

In 1984 LaMarche could reevaluate this correlation because he had acquired a colleague, Katherine Hirschboeck, a graduate student in geosciences at Arizona who possessed a thorough grasp of volcanic history. She had published a new "Worldwide Chronology of Volcanic Eruptions" in 1980 and had studied geography at the University of Wisconsin before coming to Arizona. She was especially interested in global climate change, and between them LaMarche and Hirschboeck correlated volcanic events and tree-rings, constructing a vigorous argument that correlated frost rings in White Mountain and Rocky Mountain bristlecones to sharp and

Frost ring, 1626 B.C., correlated to the eruption of Santorini. (Courtesy Laboratory of Tree-Ring Research)

significant global cooling consequent to the volcanic dust veils created by major volcanic eruptions. These dust veils could produce climatic conditions in July that seemed like those to be expected in mid-May. In particular researchers found a severe frost event at 1626 B.C., which they believed, as a result of comparisons with other archaeological evidence, correlated well with the eruption of Santorini and gave a major Bronze Age event—and a whole set of archaeological data toward the end of Minoan civilization—a precise date. By the mid-1980s this date had been confirmed by independently obtained Irish, German, and English oak chronologies.

Frost rings seemed to record climatic disturbances of global proportions and could be used to date these disturbances to the year.

Santorini was only one of more than twenty possible correlations. M. G. L. Baillie has created a long Irish oak chronology and has correlated frost rings in North America with low growth rates in European oaks. He believes that it was not all that important to identify the volcanoes or other forces responsible for the effects on trees; "what was important was the specification of precise dates for some potentially major environmental events."

So climatic events are distinct, but their causes are often clouded. Investigators have correlated tree-ring patterns from across the northern hemisphere and have established the existence of abrupt climatic changes they call events. Interpreting these events depends on what the investigator wants to know, since a set of questions determines what data will be used to correlate them. Reading these events also depends on the audience to which they are presented. For instance, such phenomena as the frost ring, because they neither follow a pattern nor fit into any uniform or regular variation in a timed series, might be capable of deconstructing Fritts's signal-to-noise ratio, the relationship between what is meaningful and what is not.

When LaMarche published the results of his climate studies in 1973, he acknowledged "lively discussion" about global climate change but could not predict the extent to which his work on a localized climate revealed a singular global change in the last century. Nor could he anticipate how much the century-long warming period would become part of an international political controversy. By the late 1980s popular conceptions of the earth were poised, as Yaakov Garb has written, on the "cusp between modernity and postmodernity." Americans were highly conscious of the whole-earth image, which seemed embodied in a ubiquitous and well-known photograph borrowed by Stewart Brand from NASA files to decorate the cover of his *Whole Earth Catalogue*. From the perspective of the timberline, global warming would reduce the extent of the moonscape. But for some of the American public, global warming seemed a real, gradual, and uniformly worsening human threat to a stable history of life on Earth that would slowly transform the human environment into a moonscape. For the public, the specter of a moonscape contrasted to the whole-earth image as an apocalyptic possibility. Irregularly spaced natural disturbances of the magnitude suggested by frost rings opened more dramatic, catastrophic, and apocalyptic possibilities.

The Shared Language of Tree-Rings

To a single investigator, the rings of trees constitute a set of indicators arrayed in space but created sequentially in time by living organic beings. The indicators may be interpreted as signs of climatic change. Paleoclimatologists do not believe that trees express themselves. Yet the indicators are not arbitrary, but document real events in the past lives of trees. They are recognized by their differences, and their differences suggest to the investigator distinct and unique events for each individual tree. Many of these events influence more than a few trees and can be cross-dated to corresponding patterns of rings in many trees.

Reading the language of trees requires an absolute uniformity of sequence in the record. Absolute sequence allows ordering of the indicators correctly and connecting or correlating them to the (possible) events they signify. The events may be multiple and their causes may be unknown, so there are many possible readings of indicators. But there is no syntax of tree-rings.

The investigator trusts the individual events, in the same way that people are often taught in literature classes to trust the tale, not the teller. However disordered the events may seem, their meaning depends upon correlating them within a sequential order, or syntax of other indicators of events perceived from other sources. Correlation grows more difficult with historical distance and with the infrequency of recoverable signifiers.

If, however, several investigators, using different sources, see similar sets of events, these must be taken as more real because they are more than just local anomalies. The events are more real, by this method of reasoning, precisely because they are global in scale. By 1990 dendrochronologists were working across the globe and were comparing their records with investigators using other sources for their data.

Correlating the events read out of tree-rings with records of other natural events, and with events recorded in human records, allows a certain kind of "reading out" of meaning from tree-rings, particularly of changes in environmental conditions which have affected human history. These days, investigators routinely compare three or more sets of records. For instance, frost rings can be made to correlate well with some volcanic eruptions—but not others—and sometimes with certain historical changes in human society.

Reading actual events out of tree-rings is a disciplined kind of

decoding, pursued with great skepticism. Reading "into" or inscribing human events upon tree-rings—as for instance by marking the
birth of Jesus on a slab of wood—has been an arbitrary activity until
very recently, but it may not be in the future.

An Event of Unknown Cause

M. G. L. Baillie of Dublin, Ireland, is an investigator of old-world
tree chronologies. When LaMarche died at the age of fifty in 1988,
and Hirschboeck pursued correlations between flooding and climate change, Baillie inherited the frost rings, the kind of environmental discontinuity they suggested, and especially the kind of
thinking they led to. In 1995 he made a strong case for the following
possible event, dated approximately at A.D. 536–45. It is, as he says,
a Dark Age event which could not have been properly discerned
before 1980, when a pronounced acid layer was found in an ice core
from Greenland. No known volcanic event fits this date precisely.

From written records there is ample evidence of the densest and
most persistent dry fog in European history during a period of
eighteen months in A.D. 536–37. The sun was without brightness
in much of the northern hemisphere. Written chronicles indicate
that "fruits did not ripen and the wine tasted like sour grapes."
An "Irish failure of bread" in 536 and 539, and anomalous reports
of two "eclipses," are reinforced by records from China of summer snows and frosts, drought, and severe famine. The "Justinian
Plague" in Europe, maybe as severe as the later Black Death, began
in A.D. 542. Why should the plague not be taken as a result of
famine, death, and population disruption brought on by the fog of
A.D. 536–37, asks Baillie?

There is no distinct set of frost rings. But reconstructions of
climatic regimes from Finland and Scandinavia show a drop of
temperature for the period A.D. 536–45. Tree-rings are narrow for a
decade in chronologies from European oaks, bristlecones in the
White Mountains, and foxtails in the Sierra. Although these ring-
width patterns do not match perfectly—and nobody would expect
them to—their trend records what is almost certainly a massive
decrease in plant growth and a corresponding decrease of the so-
called biomass produced by plants through photosynthesis in the
northern hemisphere. How great this might be—10 percent, 30
percent?—would be difficult to estimate. Baillie says, "The real
message from the trees and the famine is that, when the biomass is
sufficiently reduced, humans are merely one part of the biomass

reduction." When he makes this categorical statement and translates the limiting factors for trees into the limiting factors for humans, when he follows a model of strict environmental determinism, he brings up all the problems of cause-and-effect reasoning.

Unlike the Santorini "event" which could be correlated to disruptions of Irish kingships, changes in Chinese dynasties, and the collapse of Mediterranean civilization, the event beginning in A.D. 536 has not been linked to social or cultural change. It is one of many floating events—and there are many of them—that suggest a natural history punctuated by disturbances of the environment great enough to disrupt the course of human societies. Something happened, produced major consequences, but nobody knows for sure what caused the climate change that disrupted life.

Disturbance and Dendrochronology

In 1982 LaMarche co-edited (with M. K. Hughes and others) and contributed to a book called *Climate from Tree Rings*. That text does not deal with the idea of abrupt climatic disturbance. Dendrochronology was, after all, a uniformitarian science devoted to continuity, seeking connected, unbroken, logical sequences of change. Investigators created a foundation of complacent records upon which they inscribed the records of sensitive trees. But the frost ring was a wedge in the idea of stately environmental change. It was a discontinuity, but as first reported it did not suggest a disturbance or any tumult breaking the settled pattern of environmental change into turbulent forms.

When LaMarche and Hirschboeck showed that volcanic eruptions disrupted *global* climate and plant growth, they introduced disruptive environmental forces quite beyond human control, forces capable of swerving the course of human civilizations. All the "dis-" words came into play and suggest, as the etymology of this prefix indicates, the breaking in twain, and the doubleness of possibility.

In 1986, at an international symposium on the ecological aspects of tree-ring analysis, participants spoke of disturbance at great length, dramatizing a major reshaping of dendrochronology, perhaps a new paradigm, because investigators were looking for disturbance. What is a disturbance? Linda B. Brubaker of the University of Washington cited Pickett and White's *The Ecology of Natural Disturbance and Patch Dynamics* (1985), which defines disturbance as "any relatively discrete event in time that disrupts ecosystem, community, or population structure and changes resources, substrate availability, or the physical environment." As Pickett and White wrote, previously ecologists had focused on "successional development of equilibrium communities," but recently "many workers have turned their attention to processes of disturbance themselves and to the evolutionary significance of such events."

A cascade of dendrochronological studies of disturbance was appearing. LaMarche, Fritts, and others published "Increasing Atmospheric Carbon Dioxide: Tree Ring Evidence for Growth Enhancement in Natural Vegetation" (1984), using Great Basin bristlecones for part of their data. LaMarche also collaborated on a study of the movement of the San Andreas Fault that used dendrochronology on local trees. Much of the early data for reading global anthropogenic climate change came from those collected in the 1960s in the bristlecone groves of the White Mountains, because the records were long in duration and sensitive to change, and because the trees had been intensively studied.

The Laboratory of Tree-Ring Research began to produce case studies which linked disturbance, forest structure, and forest dynamics. Articles spoke specifically of "disturbance chronologies." Articles flowing out of the lab in the early to mid-1980s analyzed fire histories of forests, air pollution, defoliation of trees by insect infestations, ozone and tree growth, carbon dioxide and tree growth. By the late 1980s and early 1990s, issues of biosphere and climate were prominent in the literature of dendrochronology and in public discourse. Harold Fritts collaborated with Tom W. Swetnam in 1989 in a long review of research, "Dendroecology: A Tool for Evaluating Variations in Past and Present Forest Environments." Increasingly, tree-ring evidence—especially distinctive changes of ring widths and evidence of injuries in the rings—was being used to date damaging ecological events and forest disturbances.

By 1988 there was a United States Committee on Global Change, issuing reports and participating in international conferences, charged with creating plans for action. The Arizona Research Laboratories, part of the University of Arizona system, had a Division of Global Change. Its published prospectus was introduced with three images: Hurricane Gladys photographed by the Apollo astronauts, a close-up of circular tree-rings, and the spherical whole earth photographed from space. As the prospectus explained, "the arid and semiarid portions of the Earth's land surface are particularly sensitive to changes in the behavior of the dynamic atmosphere, whether they occur on a year-to-year basis or over hundreds of years." One of many tools for investigating these changes was tree-ring studies.

While models from arid sites in the White Mountains were being globalized in the late 1980s, investigators also found that life zones seemed to change in a disturbingly urgent and nonuniform way. The same data that had been collected by those who sought a uniform pattern of climate change created a foundation for seeing the present as a disruption from the past. And scientists were being pressed by their governments to predict the future at exactly the moment their studies of change suggested no continuous fluctuations, but rather regimes of discontinuity and disturbance.

Did dendrochronology establish a new paradigm for paleoclimatology and paleoecology? A recent text on paleoclimatology devotes only an eighth of its pages to dendrochronology and a tenth of its pages to dating methods using radioactive isotopes. But the bristlecone data are at the bottom of almost all methods of analyzing climatological change. Looking in this direction, toward the source of data, one might ask, Did dendrochronology create the bristlecone in the Laboratory of Tree-Ring Research, or vice versa? The frost ring seems a case in point: it is in a tree but has been read only by elaborate correlations with other data and interpreted according to modern theories of ecology. The answer is, both.

CHAPTER 6

Recovering the Forest

What Is a Healthy Bristlecone Forest?

Modern Americans inherit this idea from John Muir: what a forest does must be good for itself. In 1878 Muir entered what was called the Troy Range, ninety miles south of the boom town of Hamilton, Nevada. On the south ridge of Troy Peak he found his idea of a healthy, young, and flourishing forest—straight trees, as he wrote, "the tallest and most evenly planted I had yet seen." For him, they were like a garden planted by God. Some, he apparently exaggerated, were more than eighty feet tall, "feathered with radiant tail tassels down to the ground, forming slender, tapering towers of shining verdure." He compared their sound in the wind to the sound of harps. Young forests, he noticed, are shady, with species intermixed, and are homes for wildlife.

When Muir arrived, the settlement for which the Troy Range was named had already emptied. Hamilton, the nearest town, was in decline and has now been a heap of stone and brick for a century. Muir's forest, more than a hundred years after his visit, is still essentially unaltered by humans, although only a fragment or island of the bristlecone pine forests of the deeper past.

The Troy Range, now known as the Grant Range, contains old and weathered snags on some rocky ridges, but Muir deliberately eschewed these trees for the thicker growth of younger trees. In this

he reveals the type of forest he preferred over a landscape of picturesque ancients. And Muir's forest is one in which students of bristlecones should, perhaps, be interested, one which evokes a litany of
qualities associated with a perspective defined now—and sometimes deprecated—as "organic ecology." Muir's articles, written for
the *San Francisco Evening Bulletin,* suggested stasis within change, a
natural system balancing order and heterogeneity, and creating ho-
meostasis within a vigorous community. Muir found a diversity of
life tending toward its maximum potential, but he did not speak of
the forest in ecological terms.

He used his articles to argue about the uses of Nevada's forests,
conceding that the most valuable tree in Nevada is, no doubt, the
single-leaf piñon pine, because its seeds are a source of food. "The
Indians alone," he wrote, "appreciate this portion of Nature's
bounty." As for marketable timber, the mountains of Nevada paled
in comparison to California. Of the trees that grew there, the bristlecone pine—which Muir called the foxtail pine—was the hardiest
and most picturesque and made a "thick spicy forest," but he
seemed to prefer the fertile Engelmann spruce groves and the rav-
ishing splendor of the aspen groves.

Muir's subalpine forest was an aesthetic resource. He reveled in
the pleasing variety of limber pine, bristlecone pine, Douglas fir,
Engelmann spruce, and aspen. He listed the few wildflowers he
recognized and noted the wildlife he encountered: jays, Clark's
nutcrackers, grouse, chickadees, grasshoppers, and squirrels. He
reported that wild sheep, antelope, deer, and wolverine lived in
these mountains. (Modern commentators stress that a band of 60
to 100 desert bighorn sheep inhabit the Grant Range, as do mountain lions, goshawks, and a couple of sensitive or endangered species of grass and primrose.) But Muir was unable to advance beyond
iteration or establish a coherent picture of the Nevada subalpine
forest as an ecological system.

With Muir, as with any writer, it is hard to separate interest from
self. From the perspective of gross human interest, the bristlecone
forest offers no significant quantity of food or fiber, does not provide much watershed, and imagining a healthy bristlecone forest in
conventional terms as a system which maximizes biomass, stores
water, prevents erosion, and provides habitat seems not a perspective immediately useful. The "healthy" forest regime used to be
called "climax." Now some conservationists speak of "old growth,"
by which they do not mean the oldest trees but the forest regime

least disturbed by humans, containing the greatest variety of life and especially containing stands of mature trees. It is hard to know how to use this phrase for bristlecone forests. They are not, as western American forests go, places of great biotic variety. Places where 4,000-year-old trees persist must be, by some definition, old growth, but old bristlecone pines are not, as far as can be understood, "mature," nor do the places where they grow constitute representative bristlecone forests.

The bristlecone forest has been valued chiefly because it offers a fascinating record, because it can be read and re-read as a text. The record embodies a human idea, of some ripeness of possibility living in the present and in danger of being lost. A great deal of modern interest in forests as endangered places arose at precisely the time Schulman began to study old trees. His study ran counter to the general interest of ecologists who sought to understand systems of species, as associations or assemblages.

Chris Maser argues in *The Redesigned Forest* that "motives determine what we look at and how we look at it." As a forest, the bristlecones are problematic precisely because they always reveal the motives of their observers. Few of the criteria used to define a healthy forest seem to apply to them. Indeed, the very criteria for health seem difficult to ascertain from the literature of forestry. By healthy, I mean something relative. Muir had no problem saying a healthy forest is vigorous, sound, and whole. He could do this by evading issues of use. Many modern observers do not wish to repeat this evasion.

Anyone interested in the way a bristlecone forest maximizes its own potential and flourishes would not necessarily be interested, as the students of tree-rings have been, in old trees growing under extreme conditions. Nor would an investigation of healthy forests depend on sampling and measuring a set of exceptional trees' responses to environmental conditions with regard to ring production and the record produced. The dendrochronologist isolates and pays attention to one species of tree in a forest and hones that attention in certain ways which allow precise but specialized uses that also limit the field of his perspective. The bristlecone forest calls for a wider, but consequently more general, perspective.

There are many places in the Great Basin where trees seem to grow comfortably—one might say naturally—in diverse biotic systems, producing their maxima of fiber and seeds, reproducing vigorously, making the most of limited possibilities. These systems

Distribution of bristlecone pine (*Pinus longaeva*) in Nevada. (from Charlet, *Atlas of Nevada Conifers*, 1996)

might be taken to be healthy or representative forests. In them, one might say, a set of narratives can be read concurrently but not independently. According to the relations among species, these narratives will cross each other and affect each other. Only one of these narratives will be that of the bristlecone pine.

Reconstructing an Unplanned Experiment

The forests in the Grant Range, White Mountains, and Snake Range are of special interest to paleoecologists, who wonder about the history of their distribution. Bristlecones seem to move in slow motion; even in favorable surroundings they reproduce slowly and have done so in largely undisturbed regions. As always, they seem to embody an extreme version of some rule of forests. "Many seeds, few seedlings" is a law of tree life, but very few seedlings are necessary for a forest whose individuals live thousands of years. The bristlecone's seed, smaller than that of piñon pines growing on slopes below and smaller than that of the limber pine, makes the bristlecone less likely to attract human consumers, birds, or animals whose caches often become nurseries for new seedlings.

At present, as LaMarche observed, many bristlecone seedlings

Great Basin mountain ranges. (from Trimble, *Sagebrush Ocean*, 1989)

sprout through the dolomite gravel, looking unlikely to survive, even within the forests of the White Mountains. Yet there *are* many seedlings and a significant number cross the forest's boundaries. Some investigators speak of this diaspora of trees as "recruitment." In the Schulman Grove, the trees reproduce one seedling at a time, the young trees scattered widely. Very old trees fall here and there—especially on steeper slopes—and dam up occasional drifts of cones in dry gullies, giving a sense of austerity and possibility.

High altitude, low oxygen levels, sparse ground cover, and scarcity of litter lessen the fire danger in these forests of the White Mountains, once again permitting sparse reproduction to suffice. But fire is a clear and present agent of change in the Grant Range. Muir noticed that young tall trees tended to be evenly planted. Close inspection reveals this to be not so true of the more widely and unevenly distributed old trees of the Methuselah Walk. Fire rarely thins the old groves, but scarcity of resources does. Anthropogenic fire has been nearly nonexistent in the old groves; fire has shaped Muir's forest. A century after he visited, the Bordoli burn of 1977 (in the Bordoli Creek drainage area) altered the mosaic of trees. It was probably set by lightning. Split and shattered trunks and fragments of new wood on the forest floor bear witness to the recent effects of lightning.

Young forests like those in the Grant Range offer a kind of baseline of bristlecone life, attracting the interest of paleoecologists. This is because paleoecology must use the present as a point of departure. Writing in "Long-Term Records of Growth and Distribution of Conifers," Lisa Graumlich and Linda Brubaker say, "Paleoecology offers insights in the nature of climate-vegetation interactions that derive from the well-documented response of plant communities to environmental changes of the past—a record that is equivalent to natural, if unplanned experiments." From their intriguing point of view, the past is a laboratory and investigators are engaged in recovering the data from these paleo-experiments. All paleo-reconstructions are constructed with reference to present data, but by noting differences—because, as Graumlich and Brubaker also say, "these natural experiments typically include conditions not observed in the twentieth century" and "offer a broader range of biotic responses to environmental variations." Investigating the receding past calls for grasping every scrap of information, advancing backward knowing less and less about more and more. Knowing the past seems opposite to knowing the present, where myriad data demand selection, but the past is only knowable if one has a firm grasp on the present.

It seems no accident that bristlecone pines would flourish in the Great Basin, I might say, before realizing I have created the very tautology history is supposed to open. If there is a characteristic Great Basin bristlecone forest, if there is an order to these forests—and it is human to seek order—that order escapes any static description, as it escaped Muir. No location or set of conditions seems the same as any other. When viewed historically, even in the short period including the last thirteen thousand years, the shapes of the bristlecone forests seem contingent and particular. Forests have waxed and waned greatly, and in no single direction. Yet the old trees, and the fragments of wood that surround them, contain a record of bristlecone forests that date from the edge of times when the forests themselves were vastly different from what they are now.

Observers seek some symmetry or relation between individual trees, looking for order by comparing the chaos and disorder of the ancient trees and the relatively youthful and symmetrical bristlecone forests. Traveling through the groves of the White Mountains, up and down, north and south, across the actual topography, visiting the study sites, they have experienced what appear to be very different forests, depending on position. The forms and shapes of these groves depend radically and variably on location, and these differences speak obscurely of history.

The Grant Range is about 150 miles due east of the White Mountains. About a hundred miles to its northwest, on Mount Moriah in the Snake Range, just north of Wheeler Peak and Mount Washington, is the characteristic pattern produced by slightly heavier snow deposition. Stephen Arno calls this pattern a "ridgetop ribbon forest" and shows how it is a result of interacting forces of snow and wind. This particular pattern is a reminder.

It reminds, by a small but marked difference in local conditions, that no factor in the shaping of these forests is of more universal consequence than the position of the Great Basin ranges in the rain shadow of the Sierra Nevada—in the cold desert. Above all, as Schulman observed, and Fritts and LaMarche explored, the bristlecone forest is found in conditions of aridity and cold. It is hard not to call this austerity. Harsh, arid, grave surroundings. Few neighbors, least of all humans. It is a place of last resort.

Unpacking the Assemblages

Even in austerity, many ecologists look for past evidence of plants living in relations. Relations always extend beyond individual trees to patterns among species, but the desire to find these patterns may cause them to appear in the mind. One danger of this sort comes when an investigation focuses or centers on a specific species and clusters knowledge of the world around it. No matter how much they deal with relations and correlations, bristlecone studies center on bristlecones and create a constellation of species with the bristlecone at the center.

Bristlecones have probably never grown entirely alone. Near my home on the eastern edge of the Great Basin, where the Markagunt Plateau in Southern Utah marks the beginning of the Colorado Plateau, bristlecones grow next to manzanita on southern exposures. Relatively young, many of them have been uprooted over the years and fallen down the loose limestone slopes. On Mount Charleston to the southwest, they flourish in a mixed forest including Engelmann spruce. The tree growing at the top of the forest on Troy Peak is, surprisingly, a limber pine.

Shall one describe these sets of patterns as "associations," or "assemblages"? This is no trivial distinction. When paleoecologists speak of assemblages they treat separate populations of separate species as independent variables, with separable narratives. In what follows, I use the term assemblage to reveal how paleoecologists tell stories of change.

Which is more important, long-term or short-term relations among assembled species? Even the pattern called a mosaic seems to make a static picture, with sage the contrast for the bristlecone, the darkness behind the light. Harold Mooney wrote of the subalpine forests (in the 1973 introduction to Lloyd and Mitchell's *A Flora of the White Mountains*), "sagebrush forms the groundmass upon which other communities are superimposed." Sage, he continued, "separates" piñon woodland from the subalpine forests, which rarely contact each other. Sage, in Mooney's figurative description, is the fabric upon which the mosaic is drawn. Following Mooney's figure to its conclusion, Stephen Trimble makes sage the center of all Great Basin patterns in *The Sagebrush Ocean*.

Ronald Lanner has spent more than a decade exploring the relationship between Clark's nutcrackers and the Limber Pine–Bristlecone Pine Zone. Limber pine are planted, albeit inadvertently, by the nutcracker, as seed caches under rocky ledges. Since the limber pine has a large wingless seed, this is highly advantageous for the tree. The process of dispersion by nutcrackers centers Lanner's attention in an interesting way. It is probable also, Lanner thinks, that the nutcracker distributes the winged seeds of the bristlecone as well, but only when the limber pine is not available.

When Lanner looks at the Patriarch Tree, springing out of the earth as a great bundle of seven or more stems in a clump twelve and a half feet in diameter, he sees it as an example of those multiple-boled trees, common in the timberline forests, which germinate from a single seed cache. Genetic testing of the Patriarch revealed that all the stems came from a single seed, but it could have been a cache of one seed. Perhaps, as Lanner argues, high-altitude stands of bristlecones were planted by nutcrackers, the birds a means by which the tree "has fortuitously become a high-elevation species perpetuated by germination from seed caches." Limber-bristlecone. Bristlecone-limber. The order and clustering of information shapes perceptions of it. Surely the "pine-corvid seed dispersal mutualism" of Lanner's work hints at a great number of other unrecoverable relations between species in the past. And because it suggests the human activity of planting a garden, it has immense appeal.

Order and disorder are related to the historical position of the perceiver. In the last decade, paleoclimatic attention has shifted in a complex way from long histories of uniform change and stately cycles to short-term histories illustrating disturbance. LaMarche's frost rings illustrate a desire to uncover distinct disturbances in the recent past. Those who study tree-rings revealing fire scars seek patterns of disturbance in the more recent past. Lanner has followed the very recent dispersal of the piñon pine in the Great Basin, a diaspora so sudden that it marks a dramatic and possibly irreversible change.

Scientific approaches toward the bristlecone have always been driven, not by ideas of the past alone, but by anticipated uses of data, uses which are utilitarian and political because they are carried on by humans who live in cities. It is no accident that the correlation of precipitation and tree-rings would be carried out in metropolitan southern Arizona where water is the most valuable resource. And urban dwellers desire stately rates of change in their societies, over long stretches of time.

But driven by the urgency of sudden global climate change, in the last decade paleoclimatologists have shaped data abstracted from bristlecones to form a backbone of material to measure short-term changes, and then have fleshed the body of information with data gathered from other sources. These other sources of information have in turn often provided background useful in filling out the longer history of bristlecone pine forests.

The most dramatic example of this recycling of information has come from the uses to which radiocarbon dating has been put. A handful of more recent and sophisticated dating techniques depend on reading other radioactive isotopes. But in practical terms, radiocarbon dating continues to be central to the study of the Great Basin's history. Recently the tool has allowed investigators to date the assemblages of vegetative matter found in the packrat middens of the southwest and especially of the Great Basin, which are as old as twenty thousand to forty thousand years.

In 1960 Phil Wells and Clive Jorgensen, two researchers in their late twenties, visited the Nevada Test Site. They discovered fragments of junipers in a packrat midden high on a peak where no junipers presently lived and used Libby's laboratory to date their materials. Packrat middens have been studied intensively since then. They appear to be assemblages of fragmented plants and animals, accumulated locally by packrats and woodrats, quite often held in place and protected by a matrix of amberlike crystalline urine called "amberat." They are like assemblages of fossils preserved in crevices and caves throughout the arid West. Some of them are quite massive, filling small caves, covering hundreds of square feet and reaching four or five feet in depth, their strata deposited over the millennia by many generations of rodents.

Analysis of these middens depends on knowledge of the ecology and behavior of the rodents and upon radiocarbon dating. People who unpack the middens have come to believe, from watching present-day animals, that packrats gather their materials from an area of relatively small radius, about 50 to perhaps 100 meters surrounding their houses. Some investigators have mapped contemporary packrat dwellings and have established criteria for identifying their contents. Packrats do not dig through and recycle these materials, but other animals (including deer mice) and insects sometimes do. A recent concern of researchers is the hanta virus which can be contracted from the feces of deer mice. Packrats are selective in the materials they collect, and the geography surrounding their middens can influence the sources of collection.

A woodrat midden from the Pahranagat Range of southeastern Nevada. Photographed in 1988 by Peter Wigand. The tape is 19 inches long. Analysis revealed that the lower portion is 6700 years old and the upper half is 5800 years old. It contained juniper in an area where none occurs today.

Investigators date the materials by separating them into layers, like sediments, washing the samples from each layer, sorting and identifying vegetative fragments by species, recording presence and absence, and submitting them to radiocarbon dating. Working with packrat middens is not an aesthetically pleasing activity, although the beauty of amberat is apparently in the mind of the beholder. In a particularly strange set of events, members of the William Lewis Manly Party of 1849 came across some middens in southern Nevada. Manly described the substance as "looking like pieces of variegated candy stuck together" and wrote that some of the party, being hungry, took it for "sweet but sickish" food, and were later "a little troubled with nausea."

In intellectual terms, digesting the material is also problematic. After researchers process the samples by dissolving the urine in water, they screen the fragments in a soil sieve and sometimes separate fecal pellets from the vegetable matter. They sort out the fragmented materials by species and sometimes record their proportion by weight. The significance of these proportions is unclear and not standardized at present.

In some of those middens, bristlecone pine fragments are prominent in places where bristlecones are not found now. Fragments of bristlecone pines are common in middens found across Nevada

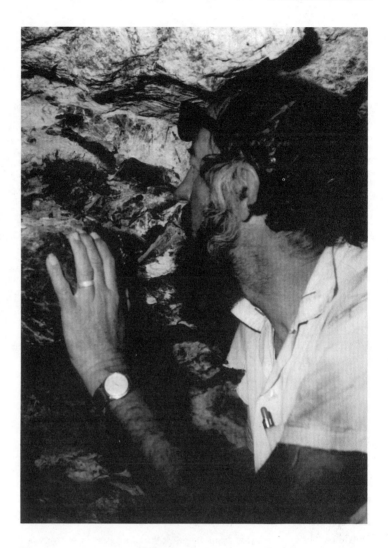

Wes Ferguson inspecting a packrat midden. (Edwin C. Rockwell photo)

between the latitudes of 38 and 40 degrees. More detail always makes the story more interesting but also gives the story new twists. The past is not as smooth and uniform a process as it used to be.

Paleoecologists collect fragments and date the assemblages. They mark the middens on a map of the Great Basin so they can say the bristlecone was here ten thousand years ago, and here fifteen thousand years ago. The midden record has its own gaps: as of 1990, there was a complete lack of samples for the period corresponding to the era of mid-Holocene warming.

The presence of tree fragments in a specific packrat midden presents a complex natural and cultural abstraction to a paleoecologist, who uses it as a simple point to plot a line or set of lines, some pattern that suggests but does not depict struggle, time, and change, or the limits of adversity and survival, beginning and end, birth and death, creation and destruction. Sometimes fragments of the bristlecone pines are found with fragments of other species. For instance, in the south end of the Egan Mountains, near Ely, Nevada, they are found in sections of middens mixed with fragments of rabbitbrush, fernbrush, snowberry, and horsebrush, and dated between twenty thousand and sixteen thousand years ago. In Silver Canyon in the White Mountains, packrats collected bristlecone, piñon, and juniper fragments only three or four thousand years ago, in a site where piñon and juniper grow now. It is hard to know precisely what these associations mean, beyond such statements as "the pines grew with a suite of montane and steppe shrubs." Bristlecone forests do not ask questions. People do, and they answer only the questions they ask themselves. At present, paleoecologists who work with packrat middens consider their work to be a kind of archaeology, because they have very limited evidence of what they call synecology.

Going Back in History by Climbing a Mountain

As dendrochronologists look at and through the trees, the concrete aspect of their close and resinous grained wood reveals a wealth of detail, but also curious gaps in history are revealed by the methods used to investigate their past. This too depends on perspective. From above, trees appear as a subalpine forest, from below as timberline forest. One observer dates trees that express a last extravagant gesture of life before the barrens, and another examines the patterns of growing trees, asking about associations with other species and about their exterior shapes.

One thing is certain. Standing in a flourishing forest like the one Muir observed, you are standing in a remnant. You are stuck in the present of the forest. To make a virtue of a necessity, you would like to subscribe to the principle of uniformitarianism, assuming that the relationships of the present have not been different during the period you are studying. There are two parts to this principle, and they are not easily separated: The past is like the present, and rates of change in the past were slow and uniform, as they appear in the present. Neither is, strictly speaking, true.

The old trees Schulman, Ferguson, Fritts, and LaMarche studied seem like monuments from some bygone geological era. In some ways, this is true. Before the Sierra arose and even very recently, the whole Great Basin became, during several eras, a mosaic of bristle-cone woodland, or perhaps a forest. Bristlecone needles and stems have been found in packrat middens in the Mojave Desert, dated at 25,000 years ago. Now, to see living trees you must, in most Great Basin ranges, reach them as Muir did, on foot.

Park your car at the head of an alluvial fan at the bottom of a watercourse in some unnamed range in the middle of the Great Basin, and walk uphill about four thousand vertical feet into what seems like the past, onto cold ridges, moraines, cirques on the high peaks. Going up those mountains will seem like hard work and like going back in history. You may find an old grove growing on naked rock, sense not only naked biology but naked geology, and the trees may seem to have almost archaeological significance. Indeed these forests have been isolated for a period longer than that of the isolated monuments of bygone civilizations, for nearly ten thousand years.

Go where there are roads. Some trees on Wheeler Peak grow several feet deep in accumulated avalanche detritus and talus. The dead and dying trees on neighboring Mount Washington: these too are for the paleoclimatologists valuable primarily as monuments to some past climatic conditions. A photograph of an isolated tree near the top of Mount Washington has been printed frequently in books and articles on pines. This tree, called the Money Tree by Darwin Lambert and his colleagues, led Nicholas Mirov to comment, "Bristlecones once formed vigorous forests but now exist in only a few remote areas." In Hall's *Natural History of the White-Inyo Range,* Deborah L. Elliott-Fisk tells the same story with the same conclusion: "[M]ost tree stands in the White-Inyo Range are relicts of the more extensive woodlands and possibly forests that inhabited the area."

Forests and individual trees sometimes seem to be relict, but that is only according to one of three contemporary models of vegetative response to climate change. Some species remain in place during high-magnitude oscillations in climate and are called "orthoselective." Some migrate. Those relic species, referred to as "relict" populations by paleobotanists, have remained constant in place because climate changes have not been sufficient to force their migration. Separate species may move or stay in regions for different reasons. A large portion of the shrubs of the Great Basin have acted in accordance with the orthoselective model, while subalpine conifers like the bristlecone pine have been migrational.

So how did these groves come to be seen as remnants at the end of a story, and when did people decide to see the present as the end of the past? Trees on the Methuselah Walk, exposed by the inexorable erosion of the slopes to which they are rooted, seem weathered yardsticks for erosion whose wood does not rot but is eroded. Trees on Mount Washington seem remnants of some distant past, but which past? Why, ask some paleoecologists, should these forests—and perhaps their historical associations—not be seen as preludes to some near future?

Pieces of Some Puzzle

The forests of the Great Basin are simple and complex, whole healthy units, but they are also fragments. So too theories of their histories, like the forests, are made of fragments and remnants, mapped as presences and absences. Knowing the problem of bristlecone history requires thinking in a set of time scales appropriate to the histories uncovered by these historical investigations.

Until recently a broad and general version of this history started twenty-five million years ago, in the mid-Tertiary period, when western North America began to experience a cooler and drier regime, which was later reinforced in the Great Basin by mountain building to the west as the Sierra Nevada arose and a rain shadow slowly formed.

For how long have bristlecone forests been able to persist only as islands in higher-altitude regions? In 1976 the standard history of California and Nevada forests characterized populations of bristlecone and limber pines as Tertiary relicts confined to high elevations for at least the last two million years in places of natural inaccessibility. Six years later, in 1982, as a result of research using materials unearthed and dated from packrat middens, the most recent upward migration of bristlecones was imagined to have been far more recent. In fact, downright modern.

Very little is known about the tree in the preglacial era, forty thousand to twenty thousand years ago. But in the full glacial era, between about twenty-two and fourteen thousand years ago, subalpine species dominated the Great Basin. The Snake and Egan Ranges to the north were dominated by the bristlecone pine.

The story of their island isolation, as told now, begins only after the late Pleistocene epoch, between fourteen thousand and ten thousand years ago. At the beginning of this era, the lower edge of bristlecone forests came down about four thousand vertical feet below their present boundary. On the east side of the Great Basin, within two hours of driving from my home in Cedar City, they flourished in the foothills of the Snake and Wah Wah Ranges, at 5,500 feet in elevation, until fewer than twelve thousand years ago. At about that time bristlecone pines disappeared off the top of the nearby Confusion Range. A walk in the Wah Wahs now takes me from grass and sage into piñon and juniper, and I find a small but vigorous stand of bristlecone pine at the very summit, at about 8,900 feet in elevation. At one place, I find a ponderosa pine, a juniper, and a bristlecone pine growing next to each other.

So a map of the vegetation in the Great Basin, during a period lasting at least as long as nine thousand years and ending only about thirteen or twelve thousand years ago, shows the entire central Great Basin as subalpine woodland dominated by the bristlecone forest. They inhabited the lower slopes of the mountains, and perhaps even the valleys of the Great Basin, until the early Holocene epoch.

The density of these forests is still a matter of disagreement. One estimate says that very recently—scarcely longer ago than ten thousand years—these forests were growing not just where you left your car, but across the valleys, too, in a massive continuous single zone. A more conservative estimate projects Wright and Mooney's studies upon the past, drawing open woodlands as a mosaic determined by substrate, scattered across the map, mostly on rocky areas. These forests frequently came down to fringe the shores of huge freshwater lakes of the so-called pluvial period of the Great Basin, during the time called late Pleistocene, which ended around ten thousand years ago.

The world of the very recent past is almost unimaginably different from our own, but it is possible to visualize its changes as slow and gradual. The present fragments of forests have been recently, but gradually, broken from a whole forest—possibly one inhabited by people. The specific shapes of these woodlands in the past, the causes of their changes, and the meanings of their history are intriguing, partly because one can conceive that humans lived in them.

Absences seem to inhabit all maps of the Great Basin, past and present. The ponderosa pine, white fir, Douglas fir, and lodgepole pine cannot be found in Great Basin packrat middens of thirteen thousand years ago. As Robert Thompson puts it, "the full-glacial flora of the Great Basin was apparently impoverished." The region during this period may be best imagined as a set of latitudinal zones, of vegetative bands, distributed south to north. Such a model calls for imagining a robust and nearly homogeneous bristlecone forest between 38 and 40 degrees north, especially in the eastern Great Basin, a forest flowing east to west, and more likely to contain species endemic to the region or shared with the Rocky Mountain region. The northern portion of this band is bisected now by U.S. Highway 50. Why did these Great Basin forests, probably inhabited during the human history of this region, shatter?

Those who have recorded the massive climate changes which accompanied the bristlecone's transition from its dominance in the Great Basin during the most recent major ice age to its island existence in the Holocene, have used climate to explain these changes and also have framed many questions. First, and most obviously, these species have experienced climatic variables of overwhelming magnitude which cannot be read out of records of recent history. Long-term dynamics of these populations are almost certainly more complex than those measurable by humans. Did these climate changes shatter important relations between species?

Following a methodological model set out by Herbert Gleason, paleoecologists think of the populations of the past as assemblages of separate species. According to this model, species responded to the changes of the late Pleistocene as if their histories were separable, in "individualistic fashion," and they flourished or dwindled not as communities but as individual populations. If one asks whether this has been a theoretical decision or a decision required by the methods of investigation available to the discipline, the answer is that paleoecology has no theory, but concerns itself with accurate presentation of data on real temporal and spatial scales. If one is to think of communities, according to this model they are, say Graumlich and Brubaker, "relatively short-lived, temporary assemblages characterized by continuous flux." For these historians the changes in biotic systems were forced by climate change, and their present shapes are neither random nor communal, but caused when individual species faced specific crisis events and sought to advance their own interests, so to speak.

The Effects of Fragmentation

Major transitions of climate are interesting also because they produce eras of prolific biotic change, sometimes multiply biodiversity, and seem to be periods of swift evolutionary change. The transition from the Pleistocene to the Holocene between twelve thousand and nine thousand years ago may have been just such an era. A related but distinct community of researchers who call themselves conservation biologists has been far more concerned than paleoecologists with consequences of such changes that result in the proliferation and fragmentation of populations of species, and has been especially engaged in an analysis of the effects of fragmentation. Conservation biology is, as Michael Soulé (one of its chief theoreticians) explicitly states, a "crisis discipline." It creates models in order to distinguish between kinds of fragments, especially between the fragments created by past biotic history and those created by modern humans. The models, in turn, can be used to establish guidelines for the design of nature reserves. In these two approaches by different communities of scientists, two perspectives reveal motives and goals and a split focus between those who pursue the causes of the past and those who wish to mitigate adverse effects of present and future fragmentation.

The transformation from the last glacial to the modern era, from the Pleistocene to the Holocene, has been for both disciplines a compelling turn of history, especially in the Great Basin where "species-area relationships are similar to those of oceanic islands," and where, according to Robert Thompson, "extinction without subsequent replacement has guided the development of these floras."

What has happened to the bristlecone during that transition is especially relevant to both communities of researchers, and both depict this transition in the form of a changing mosaic. The bristlecone was the predominant forest tree of the region 16,500 years ago. It began what might be called its most recent retreat with the end of the glacial era and disappeared from the drier sites around 10,500 years ago, while it continued to grow on relatively wet low-elevation sites with limber pine until about 9,600 years ago. Part of the picture includes the following phenomenon. Around 9,600 years ago, limber pine began to grow more dominant in many areas, but species from the Sierra and the Rockies were unable to colonize the Great Basin during this era. Bristlecones may have lived under different conditions before this era than they do now and may have been, along with the whitebark pine in a few places, the dominant tree near the upper tree line in every range west of the Ruby Mountains of extreme northeastern Nevada.

Dead Wood and Live Wood: Change in the Bristlecone's Present

The present is, by a somewhat arbitrary definition, the last 10,000 years—the Holocene—and known in the Great Basin by its absences. The glaciers, widespread woodlands, and lakes of the pluvial era are gone from the map. Donald Grayson, who has integrated studies of the human and natural histories of this epoch, divides the Holocene into three eras: the early (10,000 to 7,500 years ago), the middle (7,500 to 4,500 years ago), and the late (4,500 years ago to the present).

During the early Holocene the region was no longer filled with pluvial lakes, but was marshy in valley bottoms. Summer temperatures may have been 7 to 9 degrees Fahrenheit cooler than they are now. During this warm, moist era, the bristlecone, and then the limber pine, became island populations in the mountains.

The middle Holocene—Antevs's altithermal—has been conceived as hot and dry. This era, studied by LaMarche, was associated with elevated timberlines. LaMarche found that it was not the long drought Antevs proposed, but a highly varied era. During this era, piñon (*Pinus monophylla*) colonized much of the central Great Basin from the south. During the warming, beginning about ten thousand years ago, the piñon enacted the Great Basin's most rapid recent recorded change in vegetation, which may still be going on. Ronald Lanner has demonstrated that the advent of the piñon pine is a distinctive story because it includes dispersion of this migrating species by the agency of corvids—nutcrackers and jays.

What if the junipers are added to this narrative? The Utah juniper (*Juniperus osteosperma*) now covers more acres of the Great Basin than any other tree. Presently, it often provides shelter for new seedlings of piñon pines, and it has been in the Great Basin for the past thirty-five thousand years. Twelve thousand years ago it occurred along the western shoreline of the pluvial Lake Lahontan on the western edge of the Great Basin. On the eastern side of the lake, the western juniper (*Juniperus occidentalis*) apparently followed the retreating shoreline of the pluvial lake during the late glacial era and may have formed mixed forests with bristlecone pines. The western juniper is a picturesque species found now primarily on the eastern edge of the Sierra, and has gestures sometimes compared to the bristlecone pine's. If paleo-migrations led to associations between western junipers and bristlecone pines, the complex relations and their historical development are not understood.

The late Holocene has been a cooler and moister era, and conditions are normally taken to constitute the onset of the climates of the past few hundred years. Now, even after these changes in climatic conditions, bristlecone pines are all over the place, growing in at least twenty-five mountain ranges of the Great Basin. They have been more widely distributed in the recent past, and they are absent in some places where one might expect them, which requires explanation in the future. But the wood of dead bristlecones has rings whose chronology covers almost the entire Holocene. How did they come to be so stable in these places where long chronologies can be created from their wood?

Sooner or later one must return to the trees' present lives, confront the fact that not one or two, but many individual trees in the Great Basin exist for many millennia, some of them for about half the era we call the modern. Trees constitute discrete entities or discrete quanta in the history of these forests; the eras of change are comparable to the eras of individual trees. The stands in which they live have existed throughout the entire Holocene, and these high stands may have existed when bristlecone pines also created a woodland in the valleys. Trees have grown while climate changed, for time out of mind, and most recently for thousands of years under often highly restrictive and widely varied circumstances. They were more widespread; they grew through a wider range; they were, as some suggest, nearly weedy in their Pleistocene diaspora across the Great Basin. Forests are more and less fluid than one might suppose. Trees make wider journeys than their stability suggests. Old bristlecone pines seem to be falling in slow motion, but a few generations of this species have inhabited their sites since the glaciers retreated.

Dead and alive, individual trees contain more information than investigators have learned to elicit, though the process of unlocking this knowledge continues in the laboratory. For instance, Xiahong Feng and Samuel Epstein have recently analyzed the content of stable hydrogen isotopes—deuterium-to-hydrogen ratios—in dated tree-rings from bristlecones. The higher the ratio, the higher the temperatures. They found "presence of a postglacial climate optimum 6,800 years ago and a continuous cooling since then." Steven W. Leavitt has measured the ratio between carbon-13 and carbon-12 in the cellulose of old bristlecones. This yields a record of changes which he has linked to higher and lower moisture regimes. He found a dramatic event from A.D. 1080 to 1129. He calls this wettest period in the White Mountains over the last thousand years a "brief but pronounced wet excursion" during the medieval warm period.

Each factual detail is abstracted from the trees. They seem an unending source of climatic data. Because bristlecone pines have inhabited the Great Basin for so long and so pervasively, even the modern forests are themselves assemblages of the past. But in terms of their own history, the readable past they offer is largely recent.

The Inner Lives of Trees

What follows is a discourse my son would call "going off." It is a personal response to the tales of real and virtual forests I have attempted to recount.

Do we only imagine that bristlecone pines know something or that they possess some secret of life? Knowing *from* them is not the same as knowing *of* them. It is never possible to separate the way a tree responds to change from the information one can acquire from it. One must, finally, know the habits of an individual tree to learn what information it has stored. We are inexorably drawn back to the qualities of old bristlecones.

The questions advanced about these trees, meant first of all to allow scientists to retreat back into human history, have been re-employed to read beyond human history, back into deeper time in the lives of trees. What has been learned about ourselves by boring into bristlecones does apply to what the tree seems to be in itself. One would like to be able to speak of the ecology of the timberline, but one is drawn over and over again to individual trees and di-verted by aesthetic criteria, as were Schulman and Muir before him. And yet one cannot know individuals without knowing something of their relations to the larger systems in which they are embedded.

The old bristlecone is a character. It seems to struggle, and so we may even call it picturesque as Muir did, suggesting an aesthetic use. It is, perhaps, a philosopher's tree, the plot of its growth being its aesthetic, its record striving with its knowledge in some way made concrete by its physical form, which insinuates, even if it does not answer, questions of being and knowing, of life and death, beginning and end. Most of all, it is a historian's tree, speaking of time's cunning passages and contrived corridors.

And so the question Emerson asked in "Nature," "What is it good for?" continues to reside to a great extent in the individual trees and the way they are linked to the landscape they alter, inform, and inhabit. The line of rings abstracted from the tree seems, when compared to an actual living old tree, or to the history paleoecologists attempt to reconstruct, a pitifully linear and abstract measure of a more complex history embodied in the craggy and rugged form. Perhaps paleoclimatologists, like dendrochronologists, are themselves engaged in replacing the thing in itself with a record, in the way archaeologists might focus on skeletons or skulls in the absence of the culture of ancient humans with whom they will never communicate. The tree is constantly becoming an abstraction, and it is not our fault. But it is valuable because it is an actor in a history we have not created or abstracted completely.

Humans do not simply create abstractions *ab nihilo*. When one looks at the oldest representatives of this species, one recognizes that the trees themselves are neither all dead nor all alive, but both, neither interior nor exterior, but both. Their tree-rings can be read as records of growing and records of dying, records of dispersion and migration. Further, the dead wood which makes so many scenic snags and repositories of history, which is etched by the winds of time—or so we like to say—also protects that live strip of individual trees through which metabolism transpires. We imagine that the dead portion of these specimens is necessary to their survival, as a kind of shelter that protects live wood, which is one effect of strip growth. Foliage of exposed bristlecones seems sculpted in the lee of the old trees; bristlecones hide in their own shadows.

As the protagonists of their own story, the bristlecones are, even according to the paleoecologists, first of all good for themselves. Surprisingly, the aesthetic perspectives of John Muir and of the individualist paleoecologists who follow Gleason in speaking of assemblages are similar. The trees may also be participants in a community of life and good for it in some way we would like to understand, according to the perspective of so-called organic ecology. They are individual and as players in history have been parts of many collectives. They have been more widespread, and no doubt have engaged in associations we cannot uncover. Their isolation at present may be brief. A conservative estimate of the climate of the last two million years indicates that a transition like that between the Pleistocene and the Holocene has occurred many times over those years, and that 90 percent of the two million years constituted glacial ages, when the bristlecones inhabited the valleys of the Great Basin.

To speak of community is to say that the bristlecone's reality is social or sociological, though perhaps statistical or stochastic. This is hard to establish in old-growth forests, but easier to establish in forests of younger trees. To speak of individual trees is to say their reality is single, chronological, discrete. Trees provide separate discrete histories not entirely associated with each other. Each has a separate record of its encounters with its conditions. But in a large history of many millions of years, the real individual that we call the bristlecone pine is a breeding population, which changes. For instance, those trees growing in most austere sites seem least linked to others yet most driven by local conditions of absence and most revealing of larger environmental changes. They seem individual, exposed, and isolated, and for that reason most and—paradoxically—least essentially bristlecone pines. Consider the longevity of downed trees as they hold detritus from sliding down slopes, or the way the roots of live trees dam materials that allow them to retard erosion for millennia. In these processes, dead wood and live trees are part of the same system where organic material accumulates, where bristlecone seedlings and other plants take root.

The dead part is the live part too, as the past is part of the present, not only because of the way it contains and releases itself in the present, which is not the way humans contain and release their histories. Wherever dead beings affect the lives of present beings, there can be no extreme separation of individuals from each other. A tree is concentric and eccentric, containing circles and, as it grows older, fragments of circles, but because it seems to practice a discipline of solid geometry, of embedding surfaces, embedding cones of life within itself, a tree seems remarkably self-contained, but it is not.

Bristlecone pines are, of course, where conditions allow them to be. They inhabit places also as a result of particular genetic qualities. Trying to imagine the ways a species of tree has grown to become itself makes an interesting story of a still deeper past.

CHAPTER 7

How Bristlecones Came to the Great Basin

Climate, Pines, and Mountains

Changing trends in the earth's climate, the evolution of pines, and the record of the modern geological earth are three stories which cross, analytically separable but linked as causes and key events in the life of the bristlecone pine. It may be that some large master narrative could integrate these. They are linked, as I will tell this story, by the ways humans untangle them.

One modest aim of paleoclimatology has been to acquire a reasonably accurate record of the climate of the last three-quarters of a million years, of the late Quaternary period. Before that period the story of climate as it changes through geological time becomes very vague. As Ray Bradley explains in his modern text *Quaternary Paleoclimatology: Methods of Paleoclimatic Reconstruction,* "studying the proxy record of paleoclimate is rather like looking through a telescope held the wrong way around; for recent periods there is evidence of short-term climatic variations, but these cannot be resolved in earlier periods." There is a great deal of arm waving and consequent painting with a broad brush, and talk of relative changes between dry and wet and cold and warm global regimes. This makes for round numbers, as they are called, and does not allow precise storytelling.

Dendroclimatologists use trees to tell stories linking time and

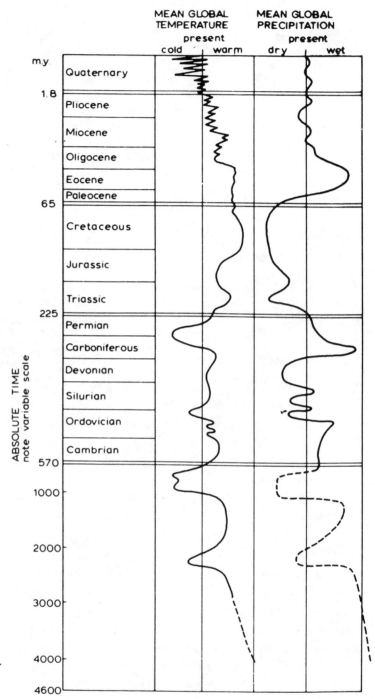

Generalized temperature and precipitation history of the earth. (from Bradley, *Quaternary Paleoclimatology*, 1985)

climate, but tree-rings are now only one source for what are called proxy data, defined by Bradley as a set of information obtained by "the study of natural phenomena which are climate-dependent, and which incorporate into their structure a measure of this dependency." Though bristlecone pines are nearly invisible in these data, they are at the bottom of it, as a standard of measurement.

Yet history never escapes the present. Any long story about trees is still based on the evidence in the present revealing traces of the life and reproduction of species in the past. In the absence of living or dead trees subject to the methods of dendrochronology, over the last thirty years paleobotanists have studied any datable evidence of trees in the past: fossils, remnants of pollen in lake basins, fragments of trees cemented into packrat middens. When they speak of this material as proxy data, they mean proxy as from *procuracy,* data appointed to represent the past, authorized to substitute for testimony of those who are not here to speak for themselves. By proliferating their sources for proxy data, paleobotanists and paleoclimatologists have created a network of complex relations among information drawn from diverse sources.

The record of pines—as reconstructed from macrofossils—establishes them as inhabitants of the northern hemisphere from about 180 million years ago. Properly speaking, there was no North America at this time, but only a single land mass known now as *Pangaea.* Presumably, pines originated in the northern reaches of this supercontinent at about this time. This would appear to have been a very warm and dry era, but there is no reason to believe it did not include variations of climate as great as those measured in the more recent past. Paleoclimatologists are fond of the term "quasi-periodic," because there is at present no way of knowing what those variations looked like.

The earth wobbles on its axis and its orbit around the sun is not circular. In theory, these eccentricities should result in quasi-periodic climatic changes on schedules of twenty thousand and forty thousand years. There may be longer periods too. This would be a very long story if I devoted one paragraph to each quasi-period of about a couple of million years, leading up to the main story. Let me say that time passed slowly, it got warmer and dryer on occasions and colder and wetter on others. Major disturbances surely punctuated this long history.

Paleobotanists know largely from fossils that pines flowed first across what we now think of as the Bering land bridge and then

EONS	ERAS	PERIODS	EPOCHS	Years Ago (in millions)
Phanerozoic	Cenozoic	Quaternary	Holocene	
			Pleistocene	
				3
		Tertiary	Pliocene	
				7.5
			Miocene	
				26
			Oligocene	
				37
			Eocene	
				54
			Paleocene	
				67
	Mesozoic	Cretaceous		
				130
		Jurassic		
				200
		Triassic		
				237
	Paleozoic	Permian		
				293
		Pennsylvanian Carboniferous		
				320
		Mississippian Carboniferous		
				356
		Devonian		400
		Silurian		
				431
		Ordovician		
				495
		Cambrian		
				586
Cryptozoic	Prepaleozoic			
				3,500
	Azoic			
				4,500

Geological time scale. (from Fiero, *Geology of the Great Basin*, 1986)

southward, during the Jurassic but chiefly during the Cretaceous period, between 140 and 65 million years ago. The leap probably followed very closely the breakup of Pangaea. In other words, they immigrated to the New World taking advantage of the same path humans utilized more recently. The Cretaceous saw the demise of dinosaurs, the spread of flowering plants, the origin of the Rocky Mountains and of the great sandstone layers of southern Nevada. Climatic and geographical conditions changed radically during this period, during which a Cretaceous epeiric sea divided North America all the way from the Arctic to the Gulf of Mexico. This sea separated the migrating populations of pines in the West from those of eastern North America. In this history, the American West where I live is distinguishable by its biotic history. It has not been like the East for a hundred million years. It has been nearly a different continent.

Some detailed climatic data exist for the time when our main character, the bristlecone pine or its close relatives, arrived in the Great Basin, perhaps as early as about fifty million years ago. Something happened to lower global precipitation after the middle of the Tertiary period, about twenty-five million years ago, perhaps a catastrophic event like the impact of an asteroid with the earth. As one consequence, the world of pines in southwestern North America was shattered into fragmented populations which evolved separately and diversely.

This event or set of events scores of millions of years ago is not an academic issue. Paleoclimatologists want to establish a record of natural climate change in the distant past, partly so they can recognize human effects of more recent times. Paleoecologists and evolutionary botanists want to follow the migrations of pines and their evolution during this set of eras to know something of the variability of natural populations. They too want to know about anthropogenic effects on plants in the more recent past.

To recover the bristlecone as a species, the historian of evolution must grasp changes beginning scores of millions of years ago and consider geological and climatological history from the perspective of changing species. Evolution is not a story whose details come from anyone's experience: it is a composite, and an abstraction. Those who tell such stories must take advice, precisely because their stories take dominion everywhere.

The Bristlecone as a Character

The bristlecone is a dynamic character. It changes, alters, evolves in subtle ways. When evolutionary botanists characterize pine trees by a set of differences which identify separate species, they do not imagine that taxonomies are unchanging in the longer term. Trees are dynamic actors in the drama of life, evolving from times out of mind. Crudely put, one can distinguish accidental aspects of the bodies of pines, including roots, limbs, and bark, from their true or essential natures, revealed by visible lineaments of life: seeds, cones, and foliage.

Most trees commonly referred to as evergreens are gymnosperms. Gymnosperms, unlike angiosperms, are plants bearing seeds on open scales, usually in cones. *Gymno-* means bare, naked, or uncovered, as opposed to *angio-,* which indicates a vessel.

Pines produce a dry compound fruit, called a cone, consisting of overlapping scales. These first appear as male and female tufts, conelets, or strobili, on the same tree. The male tuft, or catkin, produces pollen from two sacs packed with airy sperm, released as sulfur-yellow clouds, which in the random flow of summer wind drift into female tufts or conelets on the same or different trees. The receptor of a small portion of this grand diaspora, the female conelet, is larger than the male but of similar structure, evolved into a scaled receptacle. Typically, at the end of the second summer of the reproductive cycle it releases its seeds, which are again dispersed by various agents, including wind and fellow creatures.

Each seed carries genetic material which has been subject to essentially random mutations, of which only 0.1 percent are likely to be beneficial in the process of dispersing viable populations. Pines are uniform in the form and structure of their chromosomes, and these structures resist attempts to change their orderly behavior. Pines are consequently resistant to mutation by environmental disruption. Their evolution is caused chiefly by gene mutations, not by rearrangement of chromosomes. The uniformity in the number and structure of chromosomes in all pines makes genetic study difficult, but genetic changes appear to be additive and linear, by accumulation of, or single-gene, "point" mutations. Hybridization of pines is irregular for both external, geographic reasons—they live in diverse and separate places—and for internal reasons: they reproduce by different schedules, according to internal timing of reproduction, pollination, and growth.

There is no such literal thing as an evergreen. All trees are deciduous, and it is only a question of how long they hold their leaves before they shed them. Bristlecones take twenty or thirty and sometimes as long as forty-five years to shed their needles, making them more evergreen than other pines. Alpine and boreal species—*Boreas*: the north wind—bear the shortest-length needles. As one would expect, timberline species have very short needles, some barely over an inch long.

Each needle, writes Nicholas Mirov, "is the uppermost terminus of a strand of water coming without interruption from the tree's roots." This striking image of a tree standing on the geological earth and exposed to a changing climate presents the whole tree as a conduit of life, striving to couple light and water in the service of metabolism and reproduction. Its monumental effort is grounded in a fungus-root association called *mycorrhizae,* which aids absorption of water and nutrients, and is crowned with photosynthesis and reproduction at the ends of stems, where conifers generate cones and needle-shaped foliage.

Any story of the year-to-year endeavor of an individual pine is cyclical in a complex way: the rate of a tree's growth in its season is influenced by the nutrients it stored at the completion of growth in the previous fall, and the growth of any year may be influenced by the previous several years. But the life story of pines, including the origin and development of a genus, is chronological and branched. Humans can assign such stories no precise beginning. Nobody knows why the pine, as a form of life, appeared on earth about 180 million years ago. There is no etymological or biological relation between the terms *pine* and *alpine,* or between *pine* as noun and verb. Pines, as characters in the life story that follows, are populations, not individuals. Their changes have been genetic, but for the most part their genetic code has been only partially unraveled or mapped. Genetic changes are still investigated in pines primarily by changes in the physical features of individual trees.

Early in the Cretaceous period, sometime before about 105 million years ago, cones and needles of pines acquired certain distinguishable features. Botanists have, since the late nineteenth century, spoken of two groups of pines as *diploxylon* and *haploxylon,* hard and soft pines that branched from common ancestors. This distinction has been confirmed by DNA analysis. The bristlecone is the soft pine nearest to that divergence of species. Soft pines normally bundle five needles in each fascicle.

Slice a razor through the needle of a soft pine like the bristlecone and you reveal the cross section of the organ, little changed over 140 million years, the site of photosynthesis and respiration so essential to the life of the tree. Seeing its single vein or fibrovascular bundle is easier with a ten-power hand lens. This single vein, which is the source of the name haploxylon, is central to the axis of the larger triangular cross section and is surrounded by several resin ducts or canals. In soft pines a fascicle or sheath binds the needles together at their base and is frequently shed when needles are full grown.

Soft pines usually do not have prickles on the scales of their cones. As the prickles on bristlecone suggest, the sharp distinctions of structures associated with hard and soft pines were not necessarily complete or permanent.

Trees in a Dynamic Landscape

All pines can be characterized by their capacities to respond to major alterations of environment, to survive difficult conditions. The paleozoic ancestors of pines—if ancestors is the right word—responded to aridity by developing xeromorphic structures: narrow rigid leaves, with small surface-to-volume ratios, sunken stomata, leathery cuticles, and waxy bloom. Pines themselves, especially the soft pines, became *xerophytes,* lovers of relentless sunlight and little moisture, adaptable to high mountains because drought resistance also enhances resistance to cold. Their reproductive cycles adapted to limited growing seasons. Bristlecone pines are among the most xerophytic species.

At the dawn of the bristlecone pine's modern history, in the early Tertiary, about 65 million years ago, the mountain slopes and uplands of the Great Basin bore sparse cover of the same species of pines that grew on the western slopes of the Cascade Mountains and the Sierra Nevada. The Sierra was, at the time, a low range of hills. Their capacities were not created by the rise of the Sierra Nevada, but their xerophytic dexterity was tested and reshaped.

Until around 5 million years ago there were no mountains between the present region called the Great Basin and the Pacific Ocean, whose mild moist air flowed west to east over the land. Fifty million years ago the Great Basin, barely above sea level, sloped gently to the west. Even 13 million years ago the Sierra was only three hundred feet high. Globally, this era first saw increased precipitation 55 to 38 million years ago, with a general cooling in temperature. At the beginning of the Tertiary a generally warm, wet climate in western North America supported a forest across the Great Basin like that present now on the northern coast of California. This was a quiet period in the Great Basin's geological history, with little volcanism and mountain building. In the Great Basin, global increases in precipitation did not seem to dominate the weather. Indeed, some believe a localized drought began 60 million years ago and ended 30 million years ago. No doubt the local weather patterns were more varied than this. It was an era of vast erosion, and erosion in dry climates is usually greater than in wet climates. Eras of erosion also remove their own evidence. Whatever happened brought about a drastic rearrangement of flora. Drought preceded the earliest evidence of the bristlecone's forebears, and the Great Basin's flora underwent a simplification: many species disappeared. Also, around 50 million years ago, the North American tectonic plate was shifting south 10 degrees in latitude, into warmer climes.

Between 40 and 20 million years ago, volcanism was widespread in what are now northern Nevada and the Snake River Plain in southern Idaho, and volcanism spread toward the southeast. A map of the Great Basin reveals that the whole region is, by and large, igneous. Volcanic tuff is now a dominant type of rock in the central and southern ranges. These huge layers of ash-flow tuffs erupted across the surface of the region. As Bill Fiero writes in *Geology of the Great Basin,* instead of becoming the intrusive interior of another Sierra Nevada, the magmas belched out, searing and burying the land's surface. The guts of what would have been lofty mountains blanketed the whole region with incandescent white-hot ash falls, covering thousands of square miles, sometimes in single layers six hundred feet deep, pouring down valleys, filling basins, until the magma chambers collapsed, leaving calderas which themselves filled. Many calderas have been recognized only recently from photographs taken from satellites. The ranges and canyons of the volcanic southeastern Great Basin are a catastrophic landscape; their violent history is enough to evoke imagery from Dante.

Sometime in the middle of the Tertiary, in the mid-Oligocene epoch, about 30 million years ago, after the time the bristlecone arrived on the scene, the flora of the Great Basin was rapidly "modernized." It became largely what it is today. It is hard to know what role volcanism played in climatic conditions associated with modernization, but surely this was a significant factor. The region began to rise and its topography became more diverse. About 17 million years ago the basin and range topography we know evolved as the crust was pulled apart for reasons not entirely clear—"like taffy," as Fiero writes. Around 7 to 5 million years ago, in the late Miocene and early Pliocene epochs, when the modern Sierra was still in its infancy, the Great Basin climate was dry enough to be less favorable for the widespread northern forests. During the driest portion of the Tertiary a process began that paleobotanists think of as thinning the species of the region.

The ancestors of the modern bristlecone were like it; they were western North American soft pines from the beginning. The family we know as Balfouriana is an old lineage in western North America. The first identifiable fossils of something like a bristlecone pine come from strata in northern Nevada dated at about 40 million years ago. They have short needles, as do some slow-growing White Mountain trees. This means they appeared or arrived at a time marked first by a cooling and drying trend and subsequently by great mountain-building activity in the Rockies and then the Sierra, when continental relationships were beginning to resemble those of today. They lived through the gradual changes from worldwide warm climates to today's abrupt changes of climate regimes and patterns of climatic zoning. During this period of relatively rapid evolution for pines, they survived cooling temperatures of the second half of the Tertiary and also periodic drought.

About 2 million years ago, they began to weather what Mirov calls the grand glacial eras of the Pleistocene. In Mirov's time, this epoch was imagined to include four glacial expansions. Now several more have been identified. Bristlecones, below the farthest southward extent of these glaciations, were adapted to repeated alterations between glacial and very warm dry periods, which continued on a smaller scale during the Holocene. The bristlecone, probably very close to being an original inhabitant of the modern geological West, has lived and survived the large climatic fluctuations that preceded the changes modern humans have experienced, and which seem, by contrast, much subdued in scale.

Piñon pines probably began to evolve in what is now Mexico about 25 million years ago, from the same ancestors as bristlecones, and they proved the most resilient pines in this semi-arid regime. They are, as a result, the most widespread species of pine in the southwestern United States. The genetic makeup of whitebark—perhaps the most "primitive" of the five-needle southwestern pines—and of foxtail, limber, and bristlecone pines was not so sharply modified by adaptation to conditions, perhaps because, like aspen and Jeffrey pines, they were farther north, in a moister, cooler region and could escape drought by retreating periodically to the emerging mountains of the Great Basin as island populations. Sugar pine, western white, and other pines in the Great Basin made neither successful changes nor migrations. They disappeared from the Great Basin.

Migrations of bristlecone pines were part of a rhythm including much larger and widespread movements of coniferous forests. During the Quaternary glaciations beginning about 2 million years ago, pines marched—to use a paleobotanist's military metaphor—toward the equator, not in one continuous dispersion, but flowing back and forth, sometimes eddying in a region, their march south accelerated by glacial epochs and retarded by interglacial intervals when they retreated into the mountains. These glacial epochs expunged any sign of ancestral pines north of California, Colorado, and Nevada, because these areas are close to the southern edge of continental glacial advances.

This same era was, for the pines of the Great Basin, a time when adversity took another form as well. For more than 20 million years the Rockies had blocked moisture from entering the Basin from the east. About 2 million years ago, the three-hundred-mile-long north-south chain of the Sierra, so beneficial to the conifers on its west slope, began ascending to today's great wall, nearly three miles high in the sky. As it rose, it blocked the flow of moisture into the Great Basin from the west and transformed a temperate region into a cold desert bounded by a double rain shadow. The Sierra closed the Great Basin and impoverished even its own eastern slopes, locking the lands of its eastern shadow in a prison—or a sanctuary—where the remaining populations of soft pines, the limber, whitebark, foxtail, and Great Basin bristlecone continued to vibrate with sharp fluctuations of climate.

The bristlecone pine populations, as a set of characters in this story, seem driven by change and eminently adapted to an environment of harsh conditions. Their ability to continue a cycle of life under conditions which periodically abbreviate and lengthen that cycle, to adapt not primarily by genetic but by geographical migration, constitutes a form of freedom offset by a tremendous necessity. The story of the Great Basin's contingent history and irreversible changes seems met by a primitive, unrelenting, opportunistic yet flexible creature, now ensconced in mountain islands. Islands, because of their isolation, contain, shelter, create, and constitute interesting kinds of populations.

Island Biogeography

In the late 1960s many American biologists were thinking about island populations at the same time that some botanists were thinking of the islands of bristlecone forests. Biologists attempting to refigure theories of evolution discovered that they also faced critical and urgent contemporary problems of diminishing global biological diversity. It would seem at first glance that biogeography, the study of geographical distributions of organisms, would be a straightforward matter of mapping and cataloging. But modern commentators point out that this simple definition hides the complexity of the subject. If organisms such as the bristlecone are presently distributed in nonrandom patterns, then this requires an explanation of processes, requires something more than the broadbrush narrative above, requires a story which can reconstruct biotic history as a plot with causes and effects. Island biogeography wishes to derive present-day distributions in a way useful to those who wish to keep these populations viable. Patterns, in other words, cross processes in the thinking of a biogeographer, and their crossing is a prelude to management.

Biogeographers are interested in the nature of the patterns they construct and worry about their accuracy, whether patterns constitute a biological reality or a human representation, something objective or subjective, factual or perceptual. Biogeographers call the patterns they construct models and know that the narratives they infer reflect the questions they ask. Though the discipline grounds itself in careful mapping of past distributions, a largely descriptive task, the aim is to resolve patterns partially with historical explanations through ecological, evolutionary, and geological stories, but also to create models of the processes that produce patterns. Consequently, the maps of spatial distributions, arrayed as sequences, reflect on the methods of the discipline.

As the preceding chapter should make clear, patterns of plants in the present are easiest to map, and yet frequently such patterns fail to reveal an accurate picture of the past. Consider two issues. First, the present interglacial age in which we live constitutes an unusual climatic era and consequently an unusual bioclimatic regime which probably is typical for no more than 10 percent of the last two million years. Second, most recently, a difference between the present and the past is dramatized by what one paleoecologist calls "the puzzling absence of ponderosa pine from most of the interior West during the last glaciation." What is typical now has not been typical in the recent or more distant past.

Robert H. MacArthur and Edward O. Wilson defined the explicit link between biogeography's theory and practice in *The Theory of Island Biogeography* (1967). They wrote that "the study of insular biogeography has contributed a major part of evolutionary theory and much of its clearest documentation." They sought out insularity not only because they could study biogeographical processes unmodified by humans in such regimes, but conversely they considered the study essential because insularity's "principles apply, and will apply to an accelerating extent in the future to formerly continuous natural habitats now being broken up by the encroachment of civilization."

MacArthur and Wilson, for instance, were interested in the attributes that "preadapted" species to be "good colonizers": their ability to inhabit places which were superior points of departure, their possession of high dispersal power, their preferred habitats being superior as points of arrival. Island biogeography has always been concerned not just with patterns but with the limits those patterns reveal, of the past and for the future. There is something different in the Great Basin: the species-area relationships may be similar to those of oceanic islands, for example, but for geographical reasons explained by geological history, extinction without subsequent replacement has characterized the history of biogeography here, resulting in an "impoverished" taxa in a "severe" climate. Species in the Great Basin would be preadapted because they could survive and stick to the region.

Dendroclimatologists were interested in one aspect of the biogeography of bristlecones, perhaps a narrow one, when they asked about distribution of only a single species and framed the question in terms of the climate, not the populations of bristlecones. A wider story opens when one recognizes the brevity of the bristlecone's status as a set of island populations. During the past two million years, during as many as ten interglacial periods, it has periodically become a set of island populations. Before that, where was it? What was it?

Dana K. Bailey's Story

All histories are told in the present, though based on mementos of a past. The modern history of the bristlecone is based primarily on its *phytogeography*, which includes the presence of at least four identi-

Dana K. Bailey in the Panamint Mountains, California. (Edwin C. Rockwell photo)

fiable and distinguishable populations of trees growing in distinct geographical regions of southwestern North America. In terms of taxonomy, these populations constitute the three (or maybe four) divisions of the *Pinus* subsection *balfourianae*. In 1970 Dana K. Bailey (1916–   ) identified these as population I, the Rocky Mountain bristlecone, growing primarily in Colorado, New Mexico, and Arizona, population II, the Great Basin bristlecone, which grows in California, Nevada, and Utah, and populations III and IV, the foxtail pines of California, inhabiting two islands in the Klamath Mountains to the north and in the southern Sierra. Such a history has not one, but three or four modern characters, siblings more or less, alive in the present. Consequently it is a concrete extension of the vague history sketched out in such broad strokes above, of the origin and dispersion of western pines during the Mesozoic era from the general area now occupied by the Bering Sea.

Bailey was, for most of his career, a geophysicist whose professional expertise was in the propagation, dispersion, and absorption of radiation in the earth's atmosphere. He fortuitously studied dendrochronology in the 1930s with A. E. Douglass at Arizona. He never took a formal course in botany, and is, by this criterion alone, an amateur botanist. He pursued a hobby of tree-ring dating among the Colorado bristlecones in the 1960s near his home in Boulder, Colorado. Because he could find no old bristlecones in the Rockies, in 1968 he began to explore the groves of the Great Basin, visiting the White Mountains and the Snake Range. These trees included not only specimens older than any he had cored in Colorado, but also they were different.

Bailey began his story at a time about twenty-seven million years ago, in the Oligocene epoch, because in 1923 identifiable fossils of a paleo-species known as *Pinus crossii* Knowlton were uncovered in Creede, Colorado, and similar fossils were dated at twenty-seven million years old in 1967. These fossils, found within a mile of living populations of bristlecones in Colorado, even more remarkably seem, in all details possible to identify in a fossil, essentially identical to the Rocky Mountain bristlecone pines. The trees had grown in conditions similar to those the present Rocky Mountain populations inhabit. Fossils identified as the same species, and apparently of comparable age, had also been found in the northern Great Basin.

Since the uplift of the Rockies had advanced considerably by twenty-seven million years ago, Bailey inferred that ancestral bristlecones migrated south along the Rockies, which is a route cut off from any migration close to the Pacific. He inferred that the foxtails in California probably followed a separate Pacific migration, perhaps somewhat later than those in Colorado. Bailey was careful about his next inference. If understanding of the geological history of western North America in the late 1960s was correct—no small inference, since plate tectonics was a new and radical idea at the time—no feasible routes of migration existed between the Californian and Rocky Mountain populations.

So four populations of ancestral bristlecones must have migrated by at least two separate routes, and at some time(s) populations of California foxtails and Great Basin bristlecones must have diverged.

The route of the Great Basin bristlecone was least clearly defined. Bailey found the following plausible. When the Great Basin was open to temperate Pacific air before the Sierra's orogeny, it was also the home of a continuous if not dense population of mixed conifers. Populations of trees in California were probably continuous, at least on a periodic basis, with populations in Nevada. As the Sierra rose over a period of five million years, the trees of the Great Basin were cut off from the populations of foxtails.

Bailey decided that the Great Basin bristlecone was relatively recently separated from foxtails in the Sierra and could constitute a subspecies of that population. Bristlecones responded to the desiccating climate of the Great Basin through a relatively rapid process of adaptation, especially for such a hitherto conservative species, acquiring cones with more scales and longer bristles, but also some key differences in needles, internal chemistry, and overall shape or structure.

Bailey imagined that the Great Basin trees were finally isolated from those in the Sierra by the Owens Valley and had always been cut off from populations in the Rockies by the lowlands and canyons of the Colorado River. Individual groups of the Great Basin were almost certainly not cut off from each other, certainly not in the last two million years when they probably inhabited lowlands several times during the Pleistocene glaciations.

Most recently, these forests have experienced global cooling of a large order, averaging as much as five degrees during a maximum of glaciation 11,000 to 22,000 years ago, and also an era of global warming of five degrees, perhaps, in the mid-Holocene, 4,500 to 7,500 years ago. They are a continuous population which only appears fragmented.

Bailey's natural history follows the Great Basin bristlecone as a species constrained for several million years by geographical boundaries in every cardinal direction. As an island population, it is an aggregate of the many groves we see growing in separate mountain ranges. Those qualities which make it different from the other populations evolved in place as responses to climatic fluctuations. By distinguishing Great Basin bristlecones from the other populations, Bailey perceived unique characteristics as developed in this place as adaptations to aridity. The Great Basin bristlecone of Bailey's story may be the apt or even ultimate arid North American conifer, embodying strategies appropriate to survival or adaptation to the Great Basin, distilled through nine thousand feet into the mountains.

William Critchfield Critiques Bailey's Story

Dana Bailey's bristlecone phytogeography, a story of trees as figures moving through a landscape, seems to make sense. It includes a coherent plot of dispersion, forking paths of migrating trees, and leads to the present island populations.

His story was supported by the results of the first detailed investigations of the internal and chemical compositions of various populations. When chemists tested the turpentines drawn from trees, the differences in chemistry between populations seemed to dramatize a sharp distinction between eastern and western trees. However, later investigations of needle and wood resin have produced certain anomalies. A stand found on Sentinel Peak in the Panamint Mountains, on the edge of Death Valley, has a turpentine chemistry closely allied to the Rocky Mountain populations. There are at least four chemically identifiable groups of bristlecone pines, in Colorado-New Mexico, Arizona, Utah-Nevada, and in the highly variable California populations.

Another way to understand the difference in populations is to engage in gardening and attempt to interbreed or cross them. The northern and southern foxtail populations are almost fully crossable. Crosses between California and Colorado bristlecone pines have been largely unsuccessful. The White Mountain bristlecone and the Sierra foxtail are fully compatible and reproduce in both directions (Sierra pollen to White Mountain flowers and vice versa). William Critchfield, who bred these trees, says "the most striking instance of discordance between genetic and other evidence of relationships in the *Balfourianae* is the complete crossability of western bristlecone and southern foxtail pines." It is striking because distinguishing features of these two populations are like those of closely related but separate pine species.

Critchfield's experiments in gardening allowed him to critique the polyphyletic origin of Bailey's story, the idea of a double lineage for bristlecone and foxtail pines. Bailey's is an unlikely story, Critchfield wrote, because the kind of convergent evolution he posited "must account for all of the diverse ways in which the eastern and western bristlecone pines resemble each other and differ from foxtail pine." And the most recent analysis of tree chemistry further sheds doubt that the Great Basin bristlecone evolved from a foxtail-pine-like ancestor. Perhaps, Critchfield considered, the Great Basin bristlecone is a product of ancient hybridization from *aristata* and *balfouriana* ancestral lines. Or, perhaps most satisfying to those who wish the Great Basin bristlecone pine to be THE ancient bristlecone pine, Critchfield suggested that perhaps all species of the complex Balfourianae family come from a "single ancestral line most closely resembling western bristlecone pine." The Great Basin bristlecone of this story is the original and is least changed.

Problematic Tree Stories

Even when it spread across the valleys the Great Basin bristlecone was a subalpine species. And in those valleys, people hunted now-extinct large mammals of the late Pleistocene Great Basin. But humans have not lived in the worlds of the bristlecone's deeper past, though they came out of it. They cannot live under the conditions it endures or has endured. They cannot experience what the bristlecone does on a daily basis, or for its range of years. What we call adaptation when we speak of ourselves is a much cruder process and of shorter term.

A perfectly objective biography of bristlecones would be a story in which humans play a role only as historians, readers, discerners, not as actors, and humans would create a tree's story only in the sense that they recover, construct, or reconstruct it from fragments. How, then, to know if the history of this tree makes sense? We expect the teller to get the details right and demand that the story be based on verifiable information. Yet details alone do not make a story seem believable or compelling. And someone is always introducing a new detail. The stories speak as if the historians know, who have not been there. Compelling stories are often composed of differences which seem to contradict common sense, because a history is also edifying and interesting if it is not at all capable of being our own. If the story is told well, we are apt to forget how strange it is; but when we think about good history we see it is only worth reading because it is strange.

If the competing versions of the bristlecone stories do not seem strange, it is because we are accustomed to their themes. The longevity of certain individual trees led scientists to investigate closely the unique qualities of the bristlecone. Longevity and sensitivity have made these trees useful too, and so these twin and perhaps contradictory characteristics became essential aspects of its told history, to be explained. If it is an error to speak of trees as if they have strategies, I am not alone in this error but only repeat what I have heard or read. This story which creates a species with volition facing adversity is tinged with a theory of evolution not widely held by scientists in the late twentieth century.

We are accustomed to looking at a tree that seems to adapt its shape to the wind, its presence to precipitation, that seems to meet competition by choosing places where only it can grow, that takes advantage of unique geological conditions. Just as dendrological studies may reveal rainfall, air and soil temperatures, the length of growing seasons, the history of winds, so investigators seem to want to say the tree itself has "learned" to use these factors to its advantage, to survive. When I retell this story I shape the tree so that its purpose is to survive the winds of change. How can my assumptions not be projections when I try to represent this tree?

Nevertheless, I follow other authors who speak of its strategies of survival. More than a hint of the error I describe is found in the continued fascination of Bailey and many other investigators with the architecture of the bristlecone, its habits of growth and branching, its stature or posture. These are not, strictly speaking, criteria for identification.

Postures of Survival

The bristlecone is a shape shifter. Schulman acknowledged as much when he found himself "thinking of these oldest individuals as tending to belong to one of three rough types or forms." Schulman's "massive slab," Pine Alpha, is one great mass of wood, as was Prometheus. He spoke of trees like the Patriarch as "eagles' aeries," with numerous separate diverging snags. The "pickaback" type, as distinguished from the "eagle's aerie," consisted of a line of several separate and sequential stems, mounting from the same base. This type can be sampled almost right to the heart through the straight strip of bark, and the rings indicate a continuous sequence of growth.

Strip growth itself is a strategy of shape shifting and seemed to Harold Fritts a way to reach quasi-equilibrium with the environment. Though not uniquely available to the bristlecone, this particular habit of growth reaches an extreme in old bristlecones.

Stephen Arno spoke in 1966 of the "ungainly, weedy" form of the bristlecone pine, twisted and multistemmed. LaMarche noted the "great variety of sizes and forms" the Great Basin bristlecone took. In stands of high density they grew tall and straight, with bark all around, and contrasted sharply with the older trees, isolated or in more open stands: "They are typically squat and gnarled and have many dead branches and large areas of exposed deadwood."

Most biologists hold environment responsible for the stunted growth-forms of many species when they are near or at timberline. At cold timberline, a particular kind of damage to trees is possible. If new shoots do not mature fully, they remain succulent rather than "hardening off" and can experience frost damage in fall and desiccation in winter. Above treeline, they are "reduced to progressively shorter krummholz (shrubby) forms," until they are shaped like great cushions along the ground. European biologists call this the "Kampfzone" or zone of struggle. In an interesting transition to this zone, trees often take on the "flag and mat" form, where stems of six to twelve feet, flagged with foliage, protrude from the luxuriant cushion of lower foliage. The flag stretches perhaps above the winter snow pack, while the cushion lies protected under it.

Though the Great Basin bristlecone rarely takes this shape, it grows in a band of krummholz on the broad and uniform limestone summit slope of Mount Washington in the Snake Range. In the year Bailey published his story of the bristlecone populations, Valmore LaMarche and Harold Mooney went east from the White Mountains to study this shape the tree so rarely assumes.

They surveyed the living trees on the slope and divided them into four lateral bands or zones. In a zone from elevation 11,160 to 11,240 feet (3,402–3,426 m), trees grew about 600 centimeters tall, in a "forest" proper. In an area between 11,240 and 11,360 feet (3,426–3,463 m), trees reached 300 to 400 centimeters, and comprised the "tall dwarf" zone. Between 11,360 and 11,440 feet (3,463–3,487 m), in the "short dwarf" zone, trees grew 200–300 centimeters tall. Above 11,440 feet (3,487 m), in krummholz, no tree grew over 200 centimeters tall. Between the short dwarf and krummholz, LaMarche and Mooney found the flag and mat form.

A relict population of dead trees on the same slope revealed the same zonal pattern. When they sampled these remnants, LaMarche and Mooney determined that the dead stand existed between four and two thousand years ago, with each zonal form found in its resting place. The zonation of dead trees seemed to parallel the zones of living trees, except that the old zones were displaced upward, and tall dwarf trees grew nearly to the summit at 11,676 feet (3,559 m). A krummholz zone probably did not exist in the Snake Range two thousand years ago.

The obvious conclusion to their study is that there is no separate race of krummholz bristlecones. Krummholz in these stands appeared over a period too short to allow racial differentiation, and in a place where no "refugia" exist for a race of krummholz trees.

However, the obvious meaning may not be as interesting as the implied meaning. LaMarche and Mooney found a pronounced krummholz zone on Mount Washington, but not in the White Mountains. The bristlecone does not often grow as krummholz because it is resistant to the chief cause of this form, winter desiccation. And though winter conditions are directly responsible for desiccation, trees are vulnerable to damage as a result of a variety of conditions during the previous warm season. The difference on Mount Washington might be found in the fact that the White Mountains receive half the precipitation of the Snake Range. Trees subjected to summer drought may be triggered by the environment to produce leaves which are drought resistant and thus able to withstand winter desiccation. Drought may prepare the foliage for frost by altering its growing season.

The Great Basin bristlecone pine does not, literally, respond to environmental stress by assuming a certain posture, but certain possibilities make it particularly able to endure conditions near timberline as a result of its shapes. These patterns of growth may have received the most intense scrutiny given to the architecture of any species of tree. Forms of the trees bear witness to damaging events, particularly the severe influence of the rain shadow of the Sierra, which is strongest in the west and weakest in the eastern Great Basin. The advent of a rain shadow, a negative event of sorts which depressed a great deal of the diverse vegetation in the young ranges to the east, did not harm the bristlecone because of its unique placement and its set of possible shapes in the conditions of the Great Basin.

Some of the austerities of bristlecone life can be examined in a laboratory. The soil for instance. Bristlecones, because they grow on dolomite, seem tolerant of the characteristic low phosphorus levels in this mineral. Tolerance of mineral deficiency probably allows the trees to grow where sage does not. Conversely, phosphorus deficiency may limit their growth. In wet years, when they receive an excess of moisture, they produce relatively uniform large rings, but these are narrow enough to create dense wood, perhaps because nutrient deficiency sets the upper limit to ring width.

Researchers subjected young, twenty- to forty-year-old trees to lowering soil moisture levels. Photosynthesis and nighttime respira-

Datable needles on a male branch of a White Mountain bristlecone pine. The year 1960, indicated by the pen, was a year of low available moisture, as can be seen from the very short needles. Photograph made in June 1969 before the needles of that year had developed. (D. K. Bailey)

tion (the release of food within the tree) were plotted against soil moisture, indicating relatively constant metabolism down to the "wilting point" at a soil moisture level of about 7 percent.

To know the way temperature affected the metabolic rhythms of the bristlecone's annual photosynthetic year, several researchers measured the relationship among photosynthesis, respiration, and temperature. Metabolism rises rapidly as the temperature rises above freezing; past 15 degrees centigrade the increase in photosynthesis levels off, while respiration continues to increase up to 30 degrees centigrade. Trees maximize their net photosynthesis at about 15 degrees centigrade.

Outside the laboratory, the needles face a complex austerity. The typical fifteen- to thirty-year longevity of bristlecone needles (not the tree's extreme needle longevity, documented at forty-five years) provides stability for the trees during periods of stress; and stress is reflected by a needle's length, which grows shorter when it emerges during austere years. Bailey stripped the needles from one tree limb and sorted them by year. He found their length correlated to ring widths. Older needles are somewhat more efficient at photosynthesis, perhaps because younger ones are more tightly wrapped by the young fascicle. Older trees may nevertheless slightly decrease their efficiency of photosynthesis.

Harold Fritts correlated the so-called root/shoot ratio with the width of strip on strip-bark trees. The width of the strip of live cambium increased or decreased slowly with changing conditions and could be correlated to the changes in the tree's crown and roots.

Yet the average width of the annual rings in these trees remained remarkably constant over these periods of time, suggesting that rate of metabolism was independent of quantity of growth in old trees.

In extended (fifteen- to thirty-year) periods of low spring and summer temperatures at high elevations, as the trees slowly drop needles, the total photosynthetic area of a tree grows smaller, and this causes a marked reduction in ring width. Because needles are held so long by trees, their gross numbers change slowly, and a tree's recovery might take as long as the time it took to shed needles. Individual bristlecone pines react slowly; they weather sharp changes by metabolically averaging them out.

All of these responses to austere conditions are related to the shape or posture the trees take. To say it another way, the gestures trees make may reveal their ability to survive change. Bailey knew that he was telling the story of a tree he would distinguish by the name *longaeva*. He did not have the kind of data which allow more recent paleobotanists to see that these gestures evolved in a world of extinctions. They are compelling gestures of long-lived trees in a world where slow but catastrophic change led to extinction without subsequent replacement. To speak of these gestures is to speak of acts, and to portray trees as actors.

Though taxonomists are not primarily interested in the architecture of trees, Bailey, following other observers, noted a markedly different stature among trees of the family Balfourianae. In 1980 Mastrogiuseppe and Mastrogiuseppe compared the growth habits and branching of the Klamath, Great Basin, and Sierra populations.

Though the Sierra population closely resembles the Great Basin population in key aspects, the upright branching of the Sierra population gives it an appearance more like the Rocky Mountain population, whereas the pendulous branching of the Great Basin population seems more similar to the downswept branching of the Klamath population. Also, the foxtails in the Sierra and Klamath populations normally retain their "initial leader," the growing tip of their main stem. Bristlecone pines don't, and that is why they seem to send so many naked vertical snags skyward.

If these gestures of trees constituted a principal distinction for identification of trees, they would also confuse the story, as Bailey acknowledged. Since the 1870s commentators have been fascinated with the stature of individual trees, noting the "pendulous or spreading" branching habit of the often "short and twisted" Great Basin trees, as opposed to the more orderly "fastigiate" branching of limbs parallel to the main stem in Rocky Mountain populations. Foxtails in the Sierra stand erect on high ground, leaning but not sprawling. Likewise, the Great Basin trees twist but do not writhe. They give the impression of dignity under duress.

Kristina Connor and Ronald Lanner found in 1987 that a unique mode of growth and origin of vegetative organs creates the branching habit of the Great Basin bristlecone. Large numbers of so-called interfoliar branches contribute to their singular and stark architecture. Interfoliar branches depart from main stems at acute angles rather than in the generally perpendicular direction of the long-shoot lateral branches more prominent in most pines. The combination of many of the former and few of the latter gives the Great Basin bristlecone foliage its disorderly appearance. The effect of interfoliar branching is magnified by the added weight of a large mass of dense, long-retained needles. Bailey noted two forms of foliage on "better watered sites," both exhibiting a "pendulous habit": one type seems almost "weeping," and another is twisted into a "grotesque, tortured appearance."

Connor and Lanner argue that the growth habits of pines are not such a stereotyped affair as is often supposed, and it is their conclusion that this is a potentially important matter for evolutionary ecology. Perhaps an argument against stereotype leads to such figurative diction as "stark," "disordered," "weeping," and "tortured." Why should species of trees not have individual gestures, and why should they not be compared to human gestures? Well, of course these forms look like stances, not gestures, but this is because we do not see the postures change over time. Have they been pointing at something all these years?

Dana Bailey's Distinctions

Wandering around the Great Basin like Ferguson and Schulman, LaMarche, and others, Dana Bailey observed that bristlecone pines, all over the place, were not of the same species he had known in Colorado. His map of differing populations rests on the landscape of the West like three fingers, and even if it has its critics, it was sufficient for his argument in 1970.

In that year, he established the generally accepted contemporary taxonomy of *Pinus* subsection *balfourianae*. He reviewed the literature, the hundreds of samples in herbaria; he took actual samples from the four populations of the bristlecone-foxtail complex and distinguished three separate species, including a new species, *Pinus longaeva,* D. K. Bailey, the Great Basin species.

His proposition for a new species combined traditional methods of field study and laboratory work and included extremely close description of the trees' form, foliage, and cones compared to those of samples in a large set of herbaria. His description, written in the traditional Latin, begins with architecture: "*arbor pendulo-ramosa.*"

Because Bailey lived in Colorado, he recognized in the trees of the Great Basin external and internal differences from the population he knew first. Though he was fascinated with the tree's gestures, his fundamental distinction between populations came from a set of decisive differences in the structures of needles. The needles of the Rocky Mountain bristlecone (*Pinus aristata*) spread and splay as the fascicle binding them breaks down after a couple of years, giving the effect of a "soft brush." These needles are liberally dotted with a white, crusty resin exudation, a crazed surface that scatters light and makes them look, as Bailey put it, "dandruffy." The needles of the Great Basin population and California populations differ: the fascicles of Californian populations tend to remain closed for a much longer time; the needles of Great Basin trees are retained much longer. The needles of both these populations are longer lasting than those of the Rocky Mountain population. Closed fascicles give the visual effect of a "much coarser brush," even more pronounced in the California populations of foxtails whose needles are smoother, darker, and brighter than the Great Basin needles.

An internal examination of the needles explains their difference in appearance. The resin ducts in the Rocky Mountain populations are closer to the surface of the needles and often rupture, whereas the resin ducts of the California and Great Basin bristlecone populations are larger, more deeply buried in the needles, and sturdier. The rupture or leaking of ducts may be related partly to the chemistry of the trees' resins. Bailey writes that Rocky Mountain bristlecones have, from their resin, an "almost unpleasant . . . strong, spicy, pungent odor of turpentine." The California and Great Basin populations have a weaker but sweeter odor.

These differences in the resins may account not only for the appearance of needles, but also the colors of cones and weathered wood. In the Rocky Mountain populations the wood of old trees

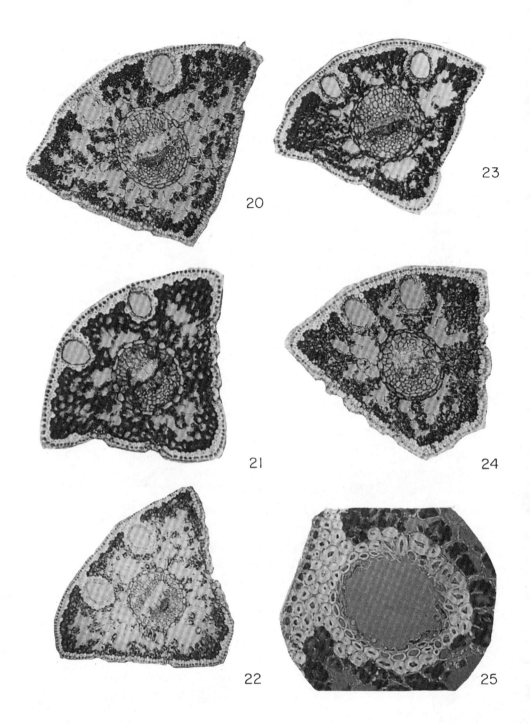

20

23

21

24

22

25

weathers to a buff or drab grayish brown. The western populations produce paler and often brilliant yellow or orange-brown surfaces of exposed wood.

The cones from the four populations do not show sharp differences, but gradations. The cones of Rocky Mountain bristlecones are most resinous and are the shortest. The bristles on the scales of the cones are much coarser in the Rocky Mountain populations and tend to be more delicate in the western trees—finer, shorter, and recurved when ripe among the Great Basin groves. The California populations have the fewest scales (averaging 82 per cone), the Great Basin the largest number (averaging 117); the Rocky Mountain number (averaging 108) is close to the Great Basin's. The Great Basin trees produce purple cones, but a significant number produce brilliant yellow-green cones instead. Bailey wrote that 1 percent are yellow-green, but Critchfield found a much higher proportion of this color in some places.

Bailey considered himself uniquely privileged to name a new species in 1970. As a worldwide genus, pines include only a few more than a hundred species. Why had nobody established his clear and important distinctions before 1970? Bailey's answer revealed his role as an amateur and his view of botany as a discipline. He believed that botanists of this century, assuming that issues of identification were settled long ago, "directed their interest and attention to less obvious elements." Further, problems of storage and transportation to herbaria often obscured distinctions necessary for close observation of needles and cones. But, most of all, the general perspective on the Great Basin came consistently from outside, from communities of botanists, from either the urban Pacific Coast or the urban "front range" of the Rocky Mountains. Neither population of researchers found it necessary to leave its own province for a wider perspective of all the populations of trees.

In naming a new species, the name-giver must, as a crowning and final act, choose a single sample from the population, the so-called holotype. Bailey's definitive sample of *Pinus longaeva,* including branch and mature cones, comes from a tree growing at about 10,400 feet in the quartzite boulders near Currey's WPN-114, in what was then Wheeler Peak Scenic Area and is now Great Basin National Park.

Bailey had produced a double argument, based on taxonomy and linked to phytogeography. His history is rooted in external

(opposite) **Magnified needle cross sections from Great Basin bristlecone pines: 20. from southern Utah; 21. from southern Nevada; 22 and 23. from eastern Nevada; 24. from White Mountains; 25. enlargement of duct of figure 22. (D. K. Bailey)**

The Money Tree as it appears in Dana K. Bailey's monograph. (D. K. Bailey)

details—cones and needles, pollen shape, seed wings, odor as it relates to gum turpentine, and color related to resin—but it is not entirely external or contingent. The close proximity and characteristic greater needle retention of the California and Great Basin populations suggested to him that the Great Basin species should be commonly called the "Great Basin" foxtail, and the *Pinus aristata* should be called the "Rocky Mountain" bristlecone. Interestingly, Bailey uses a photograph of an isolated single tree on Mount Washington to demonstrate the pendulous twisting form of the holotype. This image has come to be used nearly universally in the botanical literature. It is the tree Darwin Lambert and his friends called the Money Tree.

The Past and Presences

Choosing his sample so close to the oldest dead tree in the world, Bailey could hardly have ignored an irony in the name he chose, *longaeva,* nor could he have ignored the matter of the great age of some trees of this population. He was, in naming the species, not speaking of individuals. But when he recovered the Great Basin bristlecone as a presence, he also shaped its narrative, arguing in effect that we ought not to confuse one past with another, or confuse our own past with the past of some other, or the past of some other place. Bailey's account of the human confusion over species argues also that we should not mistake distinct and different presences, although at some point in the past, presences merge as a result of the inverted telescope and the de-forking of evolution.

His distinctions reveal precisely the adaptations in the Great Basin population which seem to make it better able to live longer. Everything of it seems slightly better adapted to conserve its life. The needles don't leak or decay, the cones are more fruitful, the parts last longer, and the response to duress is slower. Environment, as a determining factor, shapes or triggers responses which adapt the trees so well to extreme cold and dryness. Extremely careful research following Bailey's description has determined no indication of senescence—loss of reproductive power—as a result of aging in these trees.

The strategies revealed by taxonomic details speak of the resilience of individual trees faced with adversity. But is the Great Basin bristlecone population in danger from within, from inbreeding, or is it a fit and variable population? Normally this is asked in terms of *homozygosity,* which results from gradual loss of genetic variation. This is a distinct risk for island populations, leading quite possibly to an inability to adapt to changing conditions in the future. Conifers generally exhibit great genetic diversity within populations, and this is particularly true of the bristlecone, which is highly *heterozygous.*

Broad geographic range also might be considered a measure of success, in which case the Great Basin bristlecone pine would not be thought successful if judged by its present disposition. But Ronald Hiebert and J. L. Hamrick found greater genetic variability within isolated populations of the Great Basin than there is between separate populations, which reflects probably on their relatively recent communication during past ice ages, and predicts their success when the next one comes. So populations are genetically viable but geographically constrained at present, highly fragmented but not yet suffering from this fragmentation.

Seen through the wrong end of the telescope, the times of the bristlecone seem more uniform and less richly textured than they probably were. Time seems to move slowly back then, but as far as we know this is an illusion born of ignorance. Seen through the right end, every minute detail of a Great Basin bristlecone seems to embody precisely its history and place.

In human thinking, short spans of time cross long spans of time. Trees active during a brief summer season, for instance, live long. Is a causal relationship revealed where these two kinds of time cross? Trees do not think of themselves as long lived. They do not reflect upon their lives. We do. Let us return to the present, where we have been all along. The bristlecone stands before an observer like an object before the senses, an idea before the mind, and a presence to be reckoned with.

CHAPTER 8

Figures of a Tree

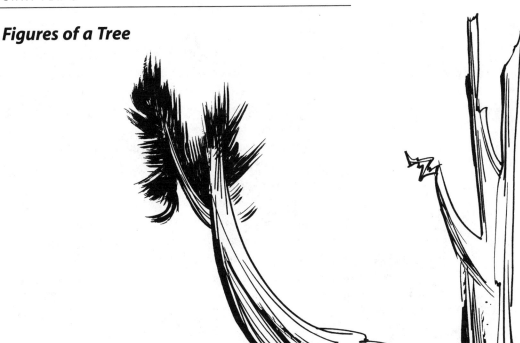

Dressed in thought and expressed in language, the bristlecone pine has come to mean many things beyond itself. Those who are not restrained by a specific discipline engage more freely in discourse about the trees, especially in unguarded and informal circumstances, where they reveal an intersection between Americans and an indigenous part of their landscape. When people speak of the tree, they reveal themselves and traces of their own history. Some of these traces are so familiar we scarcely notice them. But language surrounding the bristlecone also reveals the way knowledge becomes human, and the way revelations of bristlecone science have altered people's perceptions of their world.

When—consciously or not—people use words in what are called tropes, a seemingly simple process grows complex. Then one must read closely. Tropes are turns of language allowing deviations from the ordinary and principal signification of words and thus allowing transferences of meaning. To notice or mark a trope is to identify the linguistic form of a conceptual process that transfers meanings.

Some transferences are continuous. Metonymy substitutes an attributive or suggestive word for what is actually meant, as when one speaks of a tree as a snag. Synecdoche allows a part to stand for the whole, as the term foxtail does for the tree. In a larger sense, thinking of the bristlecone pine as embodying certain qualities of the Great Basin engages several forms of metonymy and synecdoche.

Metaphor—to speak, for instance, of a bristlecone pine as a gnome—always involves the comparison of like but discontinuous objects or ideas and engages ideas of similarity. When people personify a bristlecone pine, name it and speak of it as if it possessed human attributes, they engage in metaphor. An individual or a whole culture can engage in this activity. Antithesis on the other hand—to speak of a bristlecone pine by contrast to a sequoia, as great to small and as monument to dwarf—involves the juxtaposition of opposites and ideas of dissimilarity, or even contraries.

Sometimes tropes play with perspectives. Irony—to say that old trees are more dead than alive—and oxymoron—to designate trees, for example, as heroic pygmies—yoke opposite terms or meanings. Puns play on the meanings of words.

A second family of figures depends on the structure of a sentence. These are schemes that transform the order of words to disengage language from its ordinary meaning. Parallelism, antithesis, anastrophe (inversion of word order), parenthesis, apposition, ellipsis are such obvious strategies of language which create subtleties of meaning.

U.S. Forest Service brochure, pre-1970. (U.S. Forest Service)

U.S. Forest Service brochure, 1988. Note that humans have disappeared. (U.S. Forest Service)

Tropes and schemes: these figures of speech are postures, or positions of humans before trees, and these figures also construct word-trees, trees made of words. Quintilian (ca. A.D. 35—ca. 95), the first paid teacher in Rome, called them *figura,* meaning "any deviation, either in thought or expression, from the ordinary and simple method of speaking, a change analogous to the different positions our bodies assume when we sit down, lie down, or look back." Sometimes these figures pose, wear masks, and play tricks. They are often duplicitous. Every figure suggests its opposite: nobody knows why humans think in terms of opposites and dualities, yoking and distinguishing by pairs. But we do.

Language is a site of pairing because language reveals the interests of its users. Darwin Lambert established much of the figurative language concerning the bristlecone pine. As he says, "it is still a tree, anchored to the ground, but you have difficulty thinking of it as merely a tree." People choose trees to talk about and remark on these trees sometimes because they seem to embody images which express deep human desires. To paraphrase the French writer and teacher Roland Barthes, the site of such language is someone speaking within himself, amorously perhaps or otherwise, confronting the other (the loved object, perhaps), which does not seem to speak. This discourse is, according to Barthes, "of an extreme solitude," though spoken by thousands of people. Speaking in this way is not a matter of rhetoric alone, and not simply a posture or pose, but also gymnastic or choreographic, and is an image of the human body's gesture caught in action and not contemplated in repose—caught in scenes of language.

Because there are trees in these stories, I also think of the bristlecone groves as metonymies and metaphors for narrative texts, as Umberto Eco thinks of trees in *Six Walks in the Fictional Woods*. Eco explains that "a [narrative] wood is a garden of forking paths. Even when there are no well-trodden paths in a wood, everyone can trace his or her own path, deciding to go to the left or the right of a certain tree and making a choice at every tree encountered." Though it is not forbidden to use a text or a tree for daydreaming, Eco indicates that "daydreaming is not a public affair; it leads us to move within the narrative wood as if it were our own private garden."

Stories of the bristlecone have sometimes been a kind of public daydreaming. People have been told that certain trees, nearly five thousand years old, have stories to tell—and told that this is no dream. In adjusting their sense to the trees and what they have been told about them, people confront a dream and a reality, often in public. For that reason, I have chosen for this chapter not high literary figures but representative descriptions from widely distributed publications. Impressed by the science of the bristlecone, impressed with the age of individual trees, attempting to account for its value, real people speak in mixed and tangled figures, dramatizing a confusion, doubt, or agitation of mind appropriate to their experiences.

What follows, then, is a primer or lexicon, a selection of extracts containing gestures of language called out by the bristlecone pine. It does not pretend to be a complete handbook of the figures of the bristlecone, but only an anthology—which means, literally, a gathering of flowers. Confronted with the bristlecone pine, people assume postures, attitudes, gestures, flowers of the human mind when faced with the insoluble questions, and they leave a record. Following the paleobotanists, I collect these perspectives as an assemblage rather than attempting to synthesize them. They are like constellations of concepts, clusters of brilliant things, which, once taken in, are capable of possessing the mind. These entries are arranged by alphabet but also—thin and thick—they create their own contexts, like the growth rings of a live old tree, to be read for the patterns they may make.

The bristlecone pine can be anything the writer's language makes of it, but is not. With its five needles, bound together with a fascicle like the Pentateuch, it may seem a book to be read. It is a book because people take it for a book and read it in diverse ways. It may seem to speak, but does not. People read, speak, and write. In what follows, I offer extracts keyed to my bibliography—by author and date—and my own commentary.

A Handful of Bristlecone Pines

ADVERSITY

> To what may we ascribe the great longevity under adversity of trees such as those here reported?   —Edmund Schulman, 1954

> On the frontal ridge were two trees which Paul sometimes contemplated as he shoveled mud to stem a flow of irrigation water or as he worked a slab of rock with mallet and chisel. One of the trees on that high ridge was tall, straight, and conical; the other was curiously warped at midtrunk into a contorted bush. The crippled tree troubled him. It seemed cruelly deflected, thwarted in its movement toward the open sky. The commandments overweighted a man, bent him low, squeezed him into odd shapes like a gnarled, missprouted tree.
>
> —Levi Peterson, 1982

> Is it adversity to receive water, sunlight and soil nutrients regularly enough and in sufficient quantity to survive for thousands of years?   —Darwin Lambert, 1972

> These survivors of adversity become the Ancients.
>
> —U.S. Forest Service handout, 1996

> Adversity begets longevity.   —Stephen Trimble, 1989

Adversity is a term often used to describe conditions in the modern and ancient Great Basin. These environmental conditions are often described as harsh, as opposed to smooth or easy. Adversity also connotes human distress, trial, affliction, misfortune, calamity as a result of some contrary force. It has been associated by New World immigrants with spiritual and metaphysical fears.

Anne Bradstreet wrote in her *Meditations Divine and Moral* (1664), "There is no object that we see, no action that we do, no good that we enjoy, no evil that we feel or fear, but we may make some spiritual advantage of all; and he that makes such improvement is wise as well as pious." See lexicon entries for tenacity/struggle; longevity.

AGE / ETERNITY

> After studying a photograph of one of these trees, a friend of mine remarked enthusiastically, "Don't you wish we could all live to be that old?"
>
> To this his wife replied, "Who wants to be 4,000 years old, if she looks like that!" —Edmund Schulman, 1958

> However, the absence of any anatomical indications of vascular cambium aging suggests that among ancient bristlecone pine, eventual decline and death is due to external rather than internal causes. —Kristina Connor and Ronald Lanner, 1987

> Although these rugged trees have existed hundreds of years, it is only recently that their great age and natural beauty have awakened new interest in scientists and nature-lovers alike.
> —U.S.F.S. handout, 1970

"Age" and "elder" have no etymological connection. Age, as a representation of a period of existence, particularly as that period produces maturity, slides toward the idea of elder, indicating the earlier born, ancient individual, often suggesting prior standing or longer service.

Longevity is a necessary but not sufficient cause for wisdom. Not everyone grows wiser as he or she grows older, and wisdom is not necessarily passed from generation to generation. Nevertheless, the idea persists that certain trees know better because they have lived long. Longevity seems to apply particularly to individuals capable of communicating or being read. Creosote circles of the Mojave, though they may be more than eleven thousand years old, do not seem to be readable; they cannot be cross-dated; they are empty inside; consequently they do not seem to contain knowledge.

Alvin Noren's name for the largest bristlecone, Patriarch, denotes a virile individual. Schulman's name, Methuselah, specifically links longevity (969 years; Genesis 5:27) with patriarchy.

Age and eternity are sometimes continuous ideas. Those who speak of old bristlecones as figures of the eternal extrapolate four or five thousand years to the infinite. The eternal is also conceived as beyond human sentience, freed from human subjectivity. Milan Kundera wrote in 1995 of a "consolation in the nonsentience of nature. . . . The world of nonsentience is the world outside human life; it is eternity."

The bristlecone pine has been represented as timeful and beyond time, full of time and eternal; it has been conceived as finite and infinite, knowable and ultimately unknowable. See patriarch.

ANCIENT / MODERN

Those that grow the slowest, producing dense highly resinous wood that is resistant to rot and disease, are more likely to join the Fraternity of the 4,000 year old Ancients.

—U.S.F.S. handout, ca. 1980

The dense, resinous dead wood, exposed to ice driven by high winds, becomes beautifully sculpted and polished.

—U.S. National Park Service handout, 1995

In modern literature the Great Basin bristlecone is almost always referred to as the Ancient Bristlecone, and not simply because of some trees' numerical ages. One modern preoccupation with the ancient is enacted by celebrating life's continuity and another by preserving artifacts in hermetically sealed cases with meticulous care.

Ancient artifacts may be preserved not because they can be precisely dated, but because they offer a valuable path from the present that might fertilize or germinate some viable future. An aspiration to appropriate the ancient may be a gesture to create continuity between the past and the future. Those who wish to preserve the Ancient Bristlecone reveal an optimism that the United States, a two hundred-year-old country, has progenitors an order of magnitude older than itself that it can afford to support.

As a conception, the modern includes an idea that humans create the world in the act of perceiving it. For this reason the modern has been defined by cultural historians like Raymond Williams as including a sense of alienation, of loss and despair. Modernist poems like T. S. Eliot's "The Waste Land" have collected "fragments shored against my ruin." And to be modern is, for some, as it was for Matthew Arnold, to be between two worlds, one dead and the other powerless to be born. As an ideology, modernism includes a grim view of man, solitary by nature, fragmented, asocial, unable to enter into relationships.

Something that is modern might be set free from and broken off from values of the past. Modernism has been characterized by historical discontinuity and a liberation from inherited patterns, yet modernists have been greatly attracted to the old and primitive. Those who preserve ancient artifacts may seek an antidote for the modern, may seek power over the past, or may only collect decorative objects. Though ancient bristlecones may appear modern or antimodern, interest in them is certainly modern. See relic, solitude.

COMMUNITY / COMMUNICATION

> A beneficial fungus-rootlet relationship seems to be essential
> for successful establishment of trees at timberlines and on
> other severe sites.   —Stephen Arno, 1984

This microscopic relationship named *mycorrhizae* suggests microscopic biological relationships between species, carried on at the cellular level. Ronald Lanner wrote in 1988 of macrorelationships he calls "corvid seed-dispersal mutualisms." Fortuitously, he argues, "most populations of bristlecone pine are maintained by nutcrackers on sites to which the species is only partially adapted, but which it can tolerate," when "perpetuated by germination from seed caches."

A mutually advantageous relationship between two organisms is defined by ecologists as "facilitative" if the organisms can survive independently, or "obligative" if one species is incapable of surviving without the other. Within a human community, as Peter Høeg has written in *Borderliners,* there is "the inexplicable union in the consciousness of change and constancy." People create a common place and a common time as part of the process Høeg calls human fellowship, and conversely, when the individual is isolated for a long time, eternity seems to draw near.

Time and community cross when humans describe what they imagine to be their own obligative and facilitative relations with trees. John Muir, who sometimes likened Great Basin landscapes to "heaps of ashes dumped from the blazing sky," described the Sierra or western juniper (*Juniperus occidentalis*) in *The Mountains of Cali-*

fornia as "a singularly dull and taciturn tree, never speaking to one's heart."

Darwin Lambert warms toward bristlecone pines that "call for you to walk with them, touch them, communicate with them." He describes relations with trees as intimate, if one-sided. "We walked up to it and touched it, caressed the twisting, flowing grain of its naked wood . . . encircled its trunk with our four arms and our bodies—consciously to measure its surprising circumference, yet on a deeper level perhaps to embrace it as a fellow member of the lost community of life."—1972

Stephen Trimble in 1989 depicts bristlecones as meditative: "They do not share much. Bristlecones give almost as little of their personalities as lichens or starfish." They are, for him, "not cheery like piñons and junipers," but dignified, like old people, "not lofty like sequoias but godlike nonetheless." They are, in other words, closed books and seem to follow a romantic conception of duality between the open child and the closed adult.

Elna Bakker writes in *An Island Called California,* "Those with imagination can see a host of figures—tragic, joyous, pensive, pleading." People seek specific figures of trees that speak precisely to their own condition in time and space, because "there is a definite emotional impact upon meeting a 4,000 year old tree."—U.S.F.S. handout, n.d.

CONSCIOUSNESS

HE: The bristlecone pine has no consciousness.
SHE: You'd better not say that.

CROSS

In 1878 John Muir wrote in "Nevada's Timber Belt," "[Bristlecones] with two or three specialized branches pushed out at right angles to the trunk and densely clad with the tasseled sprays, take the form of beautiful ornamental crosses." Death in life and life in death alternate in doubles, triples, or quadruples—trees that are made up of several boles near the ground—whose whole structure makes "a perfect harp, ranged along the main wind-lines." The crossing images of harp strings in the wind suggest Heraclitean conflict of the bow and lyre in the nature of the tree, even for Muir, who eschewed conflict in nature.

When the bristlecone suggests the arboreal cross of Christian lore, it presents itself under two aspects. Some notice its architectural structure, the firm sculptured cross of dead and weathered wood, with all suggested by rigid shapes and textures, but others notice the sprays of live foliage which seem strangely superimposed on the structure and seem to represent some unnatural or even miraculous resurrection.

No doubt the icon called the botanical cross, tree cross, or verdant cross has some pagan origin "as the source of life in arid places." And it was "hijacked," Simon Schama writes in *Landscape and Memory,* by Christian iconography to suggest "the death that is no death." Green men, Bacchic vines, holy pagan trees, trees of life, figurative and actual, all converge in what he calls the "timber history of Christ." Trees sprout from the loins of Jesse, and the human voice sprouts from the limbs of a tree in a work by Chagall. At the center is a botanical miracle, the transformation of dead into living wood, the *lignum vitae,* the transformation of earth, air, water, and the sun's fire into life.

The awakening of a tree's life has always been the occasion for religious festival. Conversely, when humans perceive the tree's trunk echoing the twisted form of Christ on the cross, they represent their own agony. A complex of shape and meaning is rooted in this idea of the tree in winter, which superimposes two trees, of knowledge and of life. In southern Utah and the Owens Valley, people once used bristlecone pines as Christmas trees.

The prose describing a tree that crosses life and death can be structured by the rhetorical shape called *chiasmus,* such as the following I have written as examples: "Dying takes forever, and old ones are forever dying," or "Long suffering constitutes the beauty of suffering long."

"To have a body is, finally, to permit oneself to be described," writes Elaine Scarry in *The Body in Pain,* speaking of the representation of Christ, or more pertinently, speaking of the representation of human agony. Agony, for instance, seems eternally associated with the bristlecone. These trees seem to offer themselves to human ideas of agony.

It is said that the Jews had no word for cross and therefore referred to it as tree. Nevertheless, the very image of x, chi, chiasmus, a mirroring and doubling, superimposition and also inversion, suggests that human identity is iterative and paradoxical, but not what you would expect. To be crucified is to be nailed to a tree, insistently, like the thinking in this text. An *X* is the mark of the son of man, but also the mark made by the man who cannot write his name. It is a representation of the body, and a verbal abstraction of it. Insofar as one might be nailed to a cross or a tree, one's individual body would be superimposed upon the body of the world. One writes a sign: the cross.

Consequently I must continue to cross between perspectives, engaging in a continual recombination of ideas. The idea of recombination is sometimes spoken of using the biological, or genetic, concept of "chiasma" or crossing over. The term itself can only be defined by a story. In the process of chiasma, chromosomes of a homologous pair exchange equal segments with each other. First they synapse, or come together; then they break at corresponding points and exchange genetic material. This dance of information, enacted at times in the human body but not, apparently, in the body of a pine, results in a recombination of genes: structure remains the same, but the information is reshuffled in a way that humans think of as creative.

Such a metaphor for human thought seems especially strange, yet it is not. Human thought is pervaded with cross-references, cross-datings, crossroads, and crosscutting; it is engaged in focus on the crux of problems in an attempt to resolve some crisis. The bristlecone itself is frequently represented in terms which seem to pervade and yet cross many humanistic and scientific perspectives. The idea of eternal suffering and redemption, expressed in imagery closely associated with the cross, also has served scientists for experimental design. See snags.

DEATH / LIFE

Much of an older bristlecone pine is dead—beautifully and aesthetically dead, but dead all the same.   —Elna Bakker, 1971

Portions of the crown and cambium may die, new leaders may develop, and only a small strip of bark connecting the live top and roots may survive. This so-called 'strip-bark' tree apparently reaches a quasi equilibrium with its environment.

—Harold Fritts, 1969

Many trees are more dead than alive.

—Russ Johnson and Anne Johnson, 1978

Some writers have claimed that the 'lifeline' of a functioning
trunk results from an evolved response, on the part of the tree,
aimed at adjusting the amount of cambial tissue it can afford to
sustain. But this makes a virtue of necessity—to die slowly is not
an adaptation to one's environment. . . . Why does the Great
Basin bristlecone pine live so long? Perhaps the proper question
is, why does it take so long to die?   —Ronald Lanner, 1983

Representations of old bristlecone pines may be arrayed on a line
beginning with life and ending with death. Strip growth is associated with dieback. Lanner represents old dead bristlecones as snags
standing like "bleached tombstones." For him, a snag is a *memento
mori,* like the Sibyl of Cumae, who asked for eternal life but forgot
to ask for eternal youth, and so wished to die. A tree may even
represent death-in-life, a distinctly modernist idea, as opposed to
life-in-death, a more traditional Christian idea. See cross.

DESOLATION

Do not expect the bristlecone to rival the majesty of the Sequoias, however, for unlike the redwood forests' lush greens and
warm browns, the bristlecones' world is bleakly tan and gray
and white. It has no streams. —Genny Schumacher Smith, 1978

The vast open spaces and long range of colorful mountains are
very impressive and could be a scene on the surface of the
moon.   —U.S.F.S. handout, ca. 1970

The Schulman Grove and Patriarch Grove are the chief tourist
attractions in the White Mountains. The Patriarch Grove is more
admired by visitors, for two reasons. First, weathered trees are to be
found on relatively flat ground and are thus easy of access. Second,
the region surrounding the grove is open.

The alpine barrens, referred to as moonscape, frame bristlecones
with an openness appearing so bleak and desolate that it seems to
compliment their form, reinforcing a vision of trees as "scarred and
battered warriors," "starving for soil," and "clinging to life," in a
"forbidding world," tested by a "brutal climate." To be desolate is to
be abandoned, left alone in solitude. It is to be deserted in an arid,
barren, but spiritual landscape. See solitude, tenacity.

DREAM

I dreamed of a place where the trees would grow old, hidden in a branching canyon in the shadow of a steep mountain, where the sun reached only in some other season or time of day. It would soon be dark. Dry slopes led one way to stony ground and another way to the heavens. I looked for my shadow on each tree. They knew I had done what I had done. They moved now in the wind, toward my eyes.

I grasped a tight bunch of live needles. I would be blind for the rest of my days. Yet I was certain that a tree could choose me. I stood on unstable footing. I looked back down the canyon. I leaned against an old tree and rubbed my cheek against its band of sharp and odorless bark. Above me, ribbonlike cords rustled like my pain on pendulous limbs, dry for years and left, perhaps, by absent mothers.

FOXTAIL

> *a sort of tree*
> *its leaves are needles*
> *like a fox's brush*
> *(I call him fox because he looks that way)*
> *and call this other thing, a*
> *foxtail pine.*
>   —Gary Snyder, 1968

Fox means thick haired and bushy, but also implies wily, shy, crafty, or deceitful behavior. To be foxy is to be attractive and stylish, and in the 1960s it was to have hair. One can stain something, or fox it a reddish brown-yellow, the color of fox. There are grasses called foxtail, especially *Setaria,* that bear spikelets interdispersed with stiff bristles.

A tail is a fringe on the rear, hind, bottom, or last portion of a body. It is also the bottom of a page and can hide on the back of some surface, as in "heads or tails." To tail is to follow.

Tale, though indistinguishable from tail in spoken discourse, suggests guile and artifice, a literary composition or idle gossip, containing truth, legend, fiction, or falsehood. To speak of a fox tale would be redundant.

GHOSTS

Open a book about bristlecone pines, and the trees are discovered for you as presences. David Muench entitles photographic images assembled in *Timberline Ancients,* his collaboration with Darwin Lambert, "Bristlecone ghost," "Colossal bristlecone ghost," "Sculptured ghosts," and "Skeletal bristlecone ghost." He also calls one of his images a phantom. But Muench also speaks of timeless forms and names some forms with anthropogenic terms. Their "torsos" are "corkscrew," "twisted," and "serpentine." They possess massive sculptured arms.

By comparing bristlecone pines to ghosts and to humans, Muench discovers forms fantastic but real, figments of the human imagination, but perhaps also spirits. By comparing bristlecone forms to human forms, he makes them real like us, but also we become fantastic. They have been here so long, and our visits are so brief. They are embodied and we are disembodied. They are real and we are spectral. But then we remember they are only photographs.

Who is the ghost? Humans invent many kinds of ghosts, ghost stories, ghost dances, ghost towns, ghost riders, and ghost writers, perhaps of the purple sage.

GOTHIC

Sometimes the wood of a bristlecone pine evokes, even in a dendrochronologist, religious awe. Darwin Lambert described Wes Ferguson handling a sample of bristlecone wood, in a hotel room in New York City. "Mystery glowed from its smooth polish, its wonderfully fine grains," Lambert reported in 1972. Ferguson said, "You may find it hard to believe, as I do . . . that the tree which produced this wood died a thousand years before Christ—after a long lifetime."

Belief goes beyond chronology, to the measure of men. LaMarche, for instance, once wrote in a letter to Lambert: "The lifespan of a single ancient tree encompasses the whole period of the development of our urban, technological western culture. Can we build anything that we can be sure will survive for 5,000 years?"

A German tourist I met seemed to revel in the arid Southwest, typical for him of the landscape of the American West—typical, that is, of the landscape he had seen in art books and read about in westerns. It was August, 105 degrees in Bishop, California, which didn't bother him because he aspired to mountains marked by vertical effects of pointed arch and vault, sought forests of mysterious stained wood, trees with slender spires and intricate traceries. He imagined a gothic world: medieval, natural, primitive, wild, free, authentic, romantic, suggesting all the extravagances of an irregular fancy and perhaps something portentously gloomy. Perhaps he was engaged in a religious pilgrimage.

GROTESQUE

> The resin droplets often seen on the wounded limbs of a pine
> tree broken by the north wind are tear drops shed by Pitys when
> she thinks of her youth, of her lover Boreas, and, most likely, of
> Pan. . . . The origin of the legend of Pitys . . . is easy to under-
> stand; anyone can see that a pine tree weeps glistening tears.
>   —Nicholas Mirov, 1976

> You feel you are meeting a very important person, perhaps a
> figure from mythology, half this, half that, like the Grecian Pan
> or his nymph-friend Pitys who, tradition says, was crushed
> against a rock by the bitter North Wind, then transformed by
> the mother-Earth into a pine, or like a dragon-king of ancient
> China who battled droughts and distributed the rain.
>   —Darwin Lambert, 1972

> [T]hese grotesque little fighters to the arid-east have bested even
> the great sequoias, long looked up to as the mighty giants of
> age.   —David Muench, 1972

Darwin Lambert speaks of an era—1958–61—when he and his colleagues named bristlecone characters. He speaks in a recent letter of having friends among the trees during those years, especially the tree he named Socrates. What he wrote then, he sees in retrospect, "certainly indicates clearly the feeling of the ancient ones in personal-mythological terms was far advanced."

He and Dana K. Bailey corresponded in 1972 about appropriate imagery for describing the trees. Bailey complained of Muench's "grotesque little fighters," writing, "The imagery is wrong, suggesting much bouncy, nervous energy, when in point of fact what is remarkable about the ancient trees is the sense of serenity and peace in the face of great environmental hostility, and the scars of a very long life in the hostile environment, which they impart."

The bristlecone is commonly portrayed as grotesque, deformed, distorted, gnarled, weird. These comparisons establish it, strangely, as mediator between the human and not-human. The grotesque has traditionally included fantastic interweavings of human and animal forms, decorated with flowers and foliage. The grotesque has functioned as a middle ground. Sherwood Anderson wrote in *Winesburg, Ohio* of grotesques as "figures that went before the eyes of the writer." See tenacity/struggle; picturesque, personae.

LONGEVITY

The capacity of these trees to live so fantastically long may—when we come to understand it fully—perhaps serve as a guide-post on the road to understanding of longevity in general.
—Edmund Schulman, 1958

Schulman was professionally interested in the causes of great longevity in trees. Is there any reason to imagine that longevity in trees and longevity in general are related? Some would like to imagine that knowledge of a tree's longevity might serve to extend the lives of humans. There is no evidence that this is anything but a fantasy. See survival.

MARTYR

In "A Letter of Solidarity," Utah writer Terry Tempest Williams tells a story:

A friend the other day told me a story of walking up a particular ridge where a bristlecone pine stood, one of the oldest trees on Earth. He considered it his Elder and went to pay his respects as he had done year after year. When he finally found his way to the tree, it had been cut down. The body of the bristlecone pine lay on its side sawed into pieces. He stood before the stump for some time and then pulled out his pocketknife and made a small cut along the tip of his thumb. He let the blood drip onto the stump.

The Williams narrative, loosely based on the story of the tree called Prometheus, contains traces of its time and place. The idea of the tree as "Elder" takes on a particular theological coloring in Utah's culture, where young men join the lay priesthood of the

Church of Jesus Christ of Latter-day Saints (Mormons), become elders, and prepare to go on missions. The suggestion of symmetry between the whorls of the print of a thumb and whorls of the rings of the tree stump, and the transfusion of blood from one to the other, reminds us of a belated transfusion, an age-old martyrdom, or perhaps even the somewhat obscure Mormon idea of "blood atonement."

The idea of solidarity, of a community of interests, is displaced from the tree to the friend, who might be like Darwin Lambert, to the narrator, and then solidarity is offered to the reader in the form of a letter speaking for wilderness in Utah. Williams adapts the strategy of Lambert's "Martyr for a Species" of 1968 by continuing to use Prometheus as "a martyr to save the other ancients."

The search for the True Cross, the finding of splinters of the relic, the theft of relics and their use for religious rituals: all are suggested in stories of the tree named Prometheus. Some devotees of bristlecones visit the site of the now-dead tree and follow the distribution of the materials of which it was made. See cross; relic.

NOSTALGIA

The following dialogue is a composite from the writings of John Muir and from his biographer, Linnie Marsh Wolfe.

"There were giants in those days," a 68-year-old Emerson said to 33-year-old Muir, while they walked through a sequoia grove in 1871.

Muir replied, "You are yourself a Sequoia. . . . Stop and get acquainted with your big brethren."

Muir reported, "The old man sadly shook his head, and then, taking one more look upward at the grand domes of verdure, commented in his slow hesitant way: 'The wonder is that we can see these trees and not wonder more!'"

Men imagine that trees represent a time when men were gods. In this anecdote, sequoias feed a desire for return. In the late twentieth century, old bristlecones do not replace a nostalgia that the sequoias served in the nineteenth century, but offer instead a more tortured idea of an unknown past shaped by the observer's perspective of the present.

The desire to reinhabit a mythical past remains. Bristlecone pines sometimes appear in that light of that desire, to the sightseer and the scientist. Perhaps it is the same desire, differently expressed.

Some people desire to know this thing intimately, some would like to understand its past, while others would like to possess the past it embodies. These desires are multiple and would seem to be at odds with one another.

PATRIARCH

Would the seeds from an eroded old bristlecone pine tree germinate? —Edmund Schulman, 1958

Schulman consulted with botanist Frits W. Went. Went pro-
cessed seeds from an eroded old bristlecone and from "a slender but tall young tree." Both trees generated progeny, germinated equally sturdy seedlings.

We found no evidence of deleterious mutations accumulating
in the pollen and seeds of ancient bristlecone pine trees. . . .
Seed germinability was unrelated to tree age.
—Kristina Connor and Ronald Lanner, 1991

Schulman conceived trees in entirely male terms. He named one form of old tree the pickaback form and described an old specimen as a pickaback tree with several sequential stems in a "Junior-Dad-Granddad" sequence. One old tree's sequence included a "Great-granddad Pickaback." The stems are all of one tree which seems to appropriate the branching of the "sons" to lengthen the life of the "Dad," or "Granddad."

The Patriarch Tree, though only a few yards from a parking lot, is introduced by a trail sign. Recently, a wooden sign was replaced with an aluminum one. The last time I saw the wooden sign, someone had altered the gender of its monumental name by refigur-ing one letter with a penknife. See ancient; stunted/monumental.

PERSONAE

Each bristlecone pine, from the young sapling to ancient relic,
has an individual character. —U.S.F.S. handout, ca. 1980

Their weird, hobgoblin shapes with arms reaching and turning
at all angles, like the illustrations in the *Wizard of Oz,* give one
the feeling of being in a strange world. The trees are fantastic;
each one is a character to meet. —Adolph Murie, 1959

Then I saw—stooped as under a burden, with roots like claws
grasping the ground—a magnificent monster standing alone.
. . . Not far away were more colossi, some still larger and more
grotesque.   —Darwin Lambert, 1968

They had a haunting allure, a wizened character that gave great
meaning to each twist in its trunk, and each scar in its bark.
They had survived droughts and mudslides and terrifying win-
ters. . . . They bent with the wind, flourished in the warmth of
an early spring, yet knew the waste of impetuosity. They'd
learned to relish the Earth's meager offerings.   —Jim Sloan, 1993

Old trees are often described as individual personages. Any old
tree, no matter what its specific age, might be identified as "the
world's oldest living inhabitant." This individualization makes no
literal or scientific sense, but suggests that ideas slide between species
and individual, and between individual trees and mythic creatures.

Lambert, Adolph Murie, David Brower, and other advocates
of Great Basin National Park named certain trees: Socrates, The
Giant, Prometheus, Storm King, Buddha. Robert Waite, a later
park advocate, named a dead member of the fossil timberline of
Mount Washington "Moses" because of its "majestic form." See
grotesque.

PICTURESQUE

[O]n the roughest ledges of crumbling limestone are lowly old
giants, five or six feet in diameter, that have braved the storms
of more than a thousand years. But whether old or young, shel-
tered or exposed to the wildest gales, this tree is ever found to be
irrepressibly and extravagantly picturesque, offering a richer
and more varied series of forms to the artist than any other species I have seen.   —John Muir, 1878

At last the tree may attain a height of 40 or 50 feet, and if
crowded by others will retain for some time a handsome spire-
like form. But it cannot forever restrain the picturesque eccentric in its nature, and before long the symmetry is broken by the
shooting out and up of long snaggy arms.
                          —Donald Culross Peattie, 1953

They are among the world's most photogenic trees, half the
time resembling something else.   —Elna Bakker, 1971

The picturesque is a historically changing and distinctly cultural ideology or construction that frames the trees. Yet people prefer to believe that trees are inherently picturesque. See snags, cross.

POVERTY / UGLINESS

The Indians preferred tall, straight young trees for building timbers. . . . Driven, however, by an entirely different need, we began sampling such 'worthless' veterans.
—Edmund Schulman, 1958

Schulman wrote of "underprivileged" trees and "battered dwarfs." "Like Battered Derelicts on a Beach, Living Driftwood Clings to a Cliff," reads one of his *National Geographic* photo captions, which has informed many texts since the 1950s. Schulman's essay concludes, "[P]erhaps their misshapen and battered stems will give us answers of great beauty."

The bristlecone tree is a dwarf, an ogre, a misshapen giant, an abstract sculpture, an old man. . . . It is ugly, bizarre, absurd, or it is startlingly beautiful.   —Darwin Lambert, 1972

The bristlecone pine is not a tall and stately thing of beauty, nor do its leaves glisten and blow in the summer winds. The trees are short and squat, most of them reaching no more than twenty-five feet in height. And they don't have leaves—but instead short needles tufted to stubby branches giving them the appearance of fox tails.   —U.S.F.S. handout, ca. 1970

We have adopted the bristlecone pine as our emblem, primarily because the college has, we hope, some of the same characteristics as the bristlecone. . . . We don't like lean years, but if they come, we'll be like the bristlecone pine, we'll adjust and even try to take advantage of the situation.
—Royden C. Braithwaite, President, in a speech given at
Southern Utah State College, ca. 1970

They were stunted, and their thick trunks were twisted and pockmarked, ravaged by time and the harsh weather. In some eyes, they were pitiful, for they merely survived and never thrived. They had little stature. Most looked nearly dead, barely hanging on with a thin, troubled crown, or a dangling branch.
—Jim Sloan, 1993

Lambert and Sloan have both written of the death of Prometheus. In these narratives, Lambert's "gnomes" are ugly and beautiful at the same time, and Sloan's are capable of vibrating between these poles. Perhaps modern Americans oscillate between ideas of ugliness and beauty, between uselessness and use, poverty and wealth. Americans are ambivalent about their abundance. The bristlecone, perceived as a distorted, disturbed, twisted, and changed form, is impoverished and ugly: a victim. Perceived as an entity capable of simplifying its rudimentary life, it is sublime. See personae; stunted/monumental.

RELIC / COLLECTING

> As the great ages of these trees and the beauty of both the trees and their environment became known, visits to bristlecone-pine localities took on the nature of pilgrimages.
> —Charles W. Ferguson, 1968

Ferguson spoke of the samples of 1956 and 1957 as collections. He noted in 1968 that many visitors "collect ornamental wood," because they consider this activity "a moral right" and "beautiful sculpturing of the bristlecone wood makes it particularly desirable." This meant, as he wrote, "I must compete with the public for my basic research material; a small, often quite attractive piece of wood that may hold the solution to a dendrochronological problem may become someone's personal memento."

Some cultures distinguish themselves not by what they contribute, but by what they collect. The bristlecone, which speaks and is spoken of, which collects data and is collected, seems a particular case in point in the history of this preoccupation.

Perhaps individuals collect these things because they can feel something—the tree of life, or what it represents—dying in them day by day. Indoors, they may feel estranged from something outdoors for so long that it fades and seems silly in its distance, like a story forgotten or not properly heeded. So someone carries a piece of the forest home for interior decoration.

This is a problem because bristlecone pines are conceived by scientists as a set of relict populations, persistent remnants of an otherwise extinct flora, left unchanged by their isolation until recently. When people think of bristlecone pines as "relics," not "relicts," they take them for venerated objects, remains of martyrs, souvenirs or mementos, but they also collect fragments of the trees because they are valuable traces of the past.

SNAGS AND THE ELEMENTS

> When life finally ceases, the snags stand like elegant ghosts for a thousand years more. They continue to be polished by wind-driven ice and sand, the wood not decaying but rather eroding away. —U.S.F.S. handout, n.d.

> As centuries pass and the trees are battered by the elements, they become sculpted into astonishingly beautiful shapes and forms. —U.S.F.S. handout, n.d.

> The elements have molded the trees into unusual abstract sculptures. —U.S.F.S. handout, n.d.

A snag is something sharp, or something sharpened. As snags, the trees are passive. They are objects, not individuals, shaped by exposure to the elements. The elements are, in turn, a set of rudimentary principles. Earth, air, fire, and water. Element may denote a letter of the alphabet. Even in death, snags resist the elements.

A snag is a point. However, the point of a snag, or as someone might say, the pith of these snaggy descriptions, may be that the snag presents a hooked point and catches, holds, or snatches the attention. Snag is also a verb. A snag may act, by becoming a *memento mori*. See tenacity; ghosts; cross.

SOLITUDE / INSOMNIA

> Forty centuries of living in this high wind-swept and inhospitable land—and yet the bristlecone pine continues its vigil. —Russ Johnson and Anne Johnson, 1978

A vigil is sometimes conducted alone, in wakefulness. Those who are vigilant are sometimes appointed to watch in the place of others, for a change or event. Sometimes they take this task on their own initiative. Vigilance might seem an odd conception for a tree that is active for such a short season.

Like the vigilant, the insomniac is awake when others are asleep; the insomniac sees what others miss. Insomnia is a kind of vigilance. Vigilant trees do not lie down, rest, sleep, or go indoors.

In some stories, individuals need no friends. They are isolate.

What seems expressive, what seems to objectify the inner experience of these individuals is self-contained. Conceived as isolate, trees seem to enact a lonely dance of death. Their death is their life. People try to take photographs of single trees, uncomplicated by relations with any others. See community/solitude, communications.

SPEECH, WRITING, AND DIALOGUE

A. E. Douglass described what he called the signature rings of trees in "The Secret of the Southwest Solved by Talkative Tree Rings," in *National Geographic* in 1929. His language portrays trees writing their own identities and autobiographies. Because trees are not self-conscious speakers or writers, their writings must be accurate records.

Douglass's theory of language is traceable to Emerson's essay "Nature," which spoke confidently of interrogating "the great apparition" of Nature. Because Emerson believed that "words are signs of natural facts," he could trust that "whatever curiosity the order of things has awakened in our minds, the order of things can satisfy."

M. G. L. Baillie, of the Paleoecology Centre, Queen's University, Belfast, writes, "When the trees told Val LaMarche that there had been a major volcanically related environmental event in the 1620s B.C., some people accused them of lying—but they didn't lie." Trees don't lie, nor can you successfully lie to a tree, Baillie continues, as he criticizes his own figurative language: "There's nothing supernatural about this; it's just that trees are rooted in the real world."

Because people have cast them in the role of Socrates, bristlecone pines seem to ask questions and serve as lie detectors. People have dialogues with them, as they once had dialogues with philosophers in the marketplace.

Darwin Lambert framed *Timberline Ancients* with a pair of dialogues with the tree he named Socrates, who grows close to the dead Prometheus tree. Socrates has a "tall, dignified trunk" and "a dense, somewhat umbrella like crown." Like the historical Socrates, he is not a writer, but asks questions Lambert transcribes as: "What are you doing here, man?" "And what's so different, really, between surviving as an individual and surviving as a species or a culture?"

When the man moralizes "That you and we live together on a small planet floating in space and time too vast to be fathomed,"

Socrates replies, "Did you need to construct such truths so laboriously from artificially broken down fragments of fact? Why didn't you simply feel it?"

Socrates is a talkative if fictional tree, yet his last puzzling question leads out of thought, not into it. The fiction of talking trees also evades a set of major problems faced by contemporary theorists of language.

When Douglass, Baillie, and Lambert write as if trees could talk, or present trees as persons expressing their immediate, present, living identity in spoken speech, they seem to erase the real work of dendrochronology, the reading of records by people. When writers present trees as if they could write, they may be representing trees as bodies, whose meanings are deferred, absent, deadly, and determined from differences. Tree-rings are withdrawn from trees, abstracted, counted, cross-dated, read, interpreted, compared, checked, and re-read by a community of readers. Writers have no reason to put words on paper unless they imagine that the words will be read. See community/communication.

STUNTED / MONUMENTAL

> These stunted pines of upper tree-line grow only to heights of
> 20 to 40 feet while across the Sierra the giant sequoia grows 200
> to 270 feet in height.   —Russ Johnson and Anne Johnson, 1978

Something monumental is large and exceptional. The opposite of a monumental tree is a small and commonplace tree. To be stunted is to be stubborn and hindered, to be in some sense conflicted.

Bristlecones have been named as if they were monuments, but not as the sequoias have been, for generals or politicians. Bristlecones have been named for biblical, mythical, and intellectual characters. See personae.

STURDY / STUBBORN

> As the tree continues to grow, it endures all of the extreme con-
> ditions of its environment.   —Ronald Lanner, 1983

A dendrochronologist seeking a sensitive tree-ring series chooses a tree with a short bole and broad trunk. This tree is stubborn, hindered, but strong. It has suffered damage but recovered; it has endured. Such a tree is rarely overturned. Its continuous record can be read.

This tree, which seems to be an objective correlative to a certain kind of life, also challenges a way of thinking and writing that has led the investigator to it. It confirms and denies a method of study ingrained in the American tradition, one based on the reciprocity of the world and the perceiving mind, and one which prefers to believe with Thoreau that—perhaps sometime in the past, but not so frequently at present—the faith of a philosopher or scientist was identical with his system and his view of the universe.

Through his fifty-year career as a scholar of nature writing, Sherman Paul explored the idea "or way of thinking about the relatedness of man and the universe." He began in the early 1950s with Emerson's early belief in the "fundamental correspondence of man to the world," expressed as a doctrine of *correspondence,* that links words, things, spirit, and nature.

The young Emerson believed that "the mind must think by means of matter," and he wrote in "Nature" that every change in the world writes a record in the human mind. "Nature is a vehicle of thought," he wrote. This is revealed in human language, because:

1. Words are signs of natural facts.
2. Particular natural facts are symbols of particular spiritual facts.
3. Nature is the symbol of spirit.

How can something in Lanner's tree, that endures extreme conditions and continues to grow, correspond to something in the human spirit? According to Sherman Paul, Emerson believed that a man's *temperament,* his constitution or habit of mind, especially as determined by his physical constitution or natural disposition, allowed him to believe. Perhaps a modern person can believe, with Emerson, that the universe is friendly, beneficent, lawful, and related in every part. Without the will to believe, the doctrine of correspondence loses its efficacy.

According to Stephen Whicher, at the age of forty Emerson was not so confident as he had been as a young man and "contrived to rescue his old hope from his new skepticism, the resulting shock of opposites making 'Experience,' as he finally called it, probably his strongest essay." In the most skeptical section of "Experience," Emerson wrote: "Life is not intellectual or critical, but sturdy." Such a perspective is not characteristic of Emerson generally, for whom a tree is never simply a tree. But in this mood, life seems stubborn and perversely unyielding. That is the best he can say, and he counts the implications of sturdy life. "Nature does not like to be observed, and likes that we should be her fools and playmates," he continues. From this angle of vision, all attempts at deciphering are pointless: "Nature hates peeping and our mothers speak her very sense when they say, 'Children, eat your victuals, and say no more of it.'"

From such a perspective, every attempt to find out what the bristlecone might be telling would create an allegory of allegorizing, because the doctrine of correspondence breaks down. As Emerson wrote, in this mood life appears superficial: "We live among surfaces, and the true art of life is to skate well on them." Yet surfaces too are subject to the doctrine of correspondence. If the bristlecone were saying only that life is stunted, sturdy, and stubborn, if the bristlecone were saying only that life endures, some might find the story too horrible. Emerson did, and returned to a more complacent view. See community/communication.

SURVIVAL

> Here in the White Mountains, the ancient trees have survived more than 40 centuries, exceeding the age of the oldest giant sequoia by 1,500 years.   —U.S.F.S. handout, n.d.

A gypsy with dark and troubled eyes leads a small clan in Cormac McCarthy's *The Crossing*. He says, "[T]he great trouble with the world was that that which survived was held in hard evidence as to past events. A false authority clung to what persisted, as if those artifacts of the past which had endured had done so by some act of their own will. Yet the witness could not survive the witnessing."

A disproportionate number of the men who worked with bristlecone pines died young. Some hastened their own death. Joe Griggs was a heavy smoker. Valmore LaMarche was a serious drinker. Like others of their generation, they lived in a country that devised the strategy of protecting its way of life by deploying nuclear weapons for "mutually assured destruction."

TENACITY / STRUGGLE

> With most of its wood dead, growth barely continuing through a thin ribbon of bark, the aged tree's tenacity to maintain life is impressive.   —U.S.F.S. handout, n.d.

Their short stature and broken crowns give no hint of their age, but their massive trunks tell a tale of centuries of indomitable will and struggle, and their buttressed bases seem to grip the thin soil with wildcat claws.   —Donald Culross Peattie, 1953

It is not quite the same thing to say that a tree endures and forbears as it is to say it perseveres and persists. Those who describe trees as struggling and suggest they contend or grapple are speaking also of a certain modern human dilemma. Someplace behind the range of meanings here is Darwinian theory, and perhaps behind that the more ancient idea of a deposed king.

People are not like trees. Those who entered universities in the nuclear age were introduced as part of their general education to existentialism and to its premise that human reason cannot explain the enigma of the universe. Albert Camus was read frequently by this generation of students. One popular book by Camus, *The Myth of Sisyphus and Other Essays,* begins, "There is but one serious philosophical problem, and that is suicide."

TREE OF KNOWLEDGE / TREE OF LIFE

The bristlecone pine is a bible of earth and life beginning to be read—this realization came after my first visit with a tree-ring scientist.   —Darwin Lambert, 1972

Lambert's conception of scientific knowledge contrasts with the foot-slogging and eye-burning work dendrochronologists practiced in the 1960s. And it evades the prohibitions of the reading of knowledge, grounded by mystical traditions with reference to the unworthiness of the readers. Mythical figures who broke these prohibitions include Prometheus, Sisyphus, and perhaps Oedipus. Socrates paid dearly for his desire for knowledge. Camus comments, "Galileo, who held a scientific truth of great importance, abjured it with the greatest ease as soon as it endangered his life. In a certain sense, he did right."

Leo Schaya, an expert on the cosmic tree of life, writes in *The Universal Meaning of the Kabbalah,* "The *Zohar* teaches that the first Tables emanated from the Tree of Life, but that Israel, by worshipping the golden calf, 'was judged unworthy of benefitting from them.' Therefore Moses, following the divine command, gave the people other Tables, 'which came from the side of the Tree of Good and Evil.'" The Tree of Good and Evil is a second and perhaps secondary tree of knowledge. Its law, called the Ten Commandments, is made of positive precepts and negative commandments, of what is permitted and what is forbidden.

The tree of life persists for Judaism, which eschews icons yet includes powerful iconographic images of renewal and protection. The menorah, a tree of light often cast in brass, silver, or even gold, frequently takes on the shape of a many-branching tree or pillar of life. Sometimes the menorah tree is cast in letters that spell out "Shalom" in Hebrew. One sees mezuzahs too, guardians of the home, that encase a sacred scroll with sculptured vines. People rarely extract the scroll, hidden within, and read it. The pithy text of the scroll begins, "Hear, O Israel! The Lord is our God, The Lord alone" (Deuteronomy 6:4).

Modern images of the tree of life proliferate, like Chagall's stained glass image at the Art Institute of Chicago. Chagall's translucent window is called "Theater."

YOUTH

> With their bristled cones dripping pitch on a warm afternoon, they exude all the freshness of youth.
> —U.S.F.S. handout, ca. 1980

> Not all bristlecones attain great age. Trees anchored to more moist slopes grow fat and tall, produce less dense wood, and succumb at an earlier age. —U.S.F.S. handout, ca. 1980

> The Great Basin Desert's youth is startling. Think of it this way: a single ancient bristlecone pine, more than forty-five hundred years old, has lived through the entire span of what we might call the modern biological world of the Great Basin. It has lived twice as long as what we call the modern historical world. And it still lives. —Stephen Trimble, 1989

> See age.

CHAPTER 9

An Aesthetic of Bristlecones

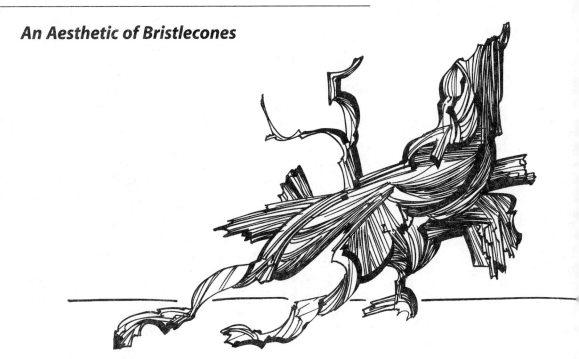

Dominance and Submission

On a typical summer morning, it is cool in the small, shady parking lot high on the flank of Wheeler Peak at an elevation of 9,886 feet (3,013 m). Here, at the end of the scenic drive at Great Basin National Park, people of all kinds step out of their cars to follow a well-maintained trail that climbs switchbacks for 600 vertical feet and then traverses a ridge through Engelmann spruce to the mouth of the canyon made by Wheeler Glacier.

The Wheeler Peak bristlecone grove is small, containing only about eight thousand trees. It is not typical, because it grows on quartzite, because the grove has a northeastern exposure, and because, as a park brochure says, "the dense resinous wood, exposed to winter ice driven by high winds, becomes beautifully sculpted." The commercially produced brochure called *Official Map and Guide* says "the wood actually erodes like stone," and an "unofficial" guide promises the "rich gleam" of exposed wood.

A young couple with two small blond children begin their walk. Several older men and women carry cameras and tripods, anticipating the place where limber pine and then bristlecone pine appear on the hillside. Near tree line, near the mouth of Wheeler Peak's glacial cirque, someone lingers on a short loop of trail and reads aloud the small interpretive signs. An old man fusses with a tripod on the rocky slope. A woman with long dark hair and long legs and a man of middle age with short muscular legs and gray hair leave the trail. They carry large daypacks across a jumble of quartzite blocks, stopping now and then to study a tree, and approach a steep but short moraine a few hundred yards to the east, where the oldest trees grow.

The trail in the Snake Range is even more evasive than the one in the Schulman Grove of the White Mountains. It never approaches the specific trees Darwin Lambert and his allies named so monumentally and contemplated as exceptional aesthetic objects.

The trees on the moraine have a powerful presence and awaken a complex of human responses. People begin to speak in the first person when faced with them. And to contemplate the eternal. Keith Trexler told the following story to Darwin Lambert. There was a man, Milan "Mike" Drakulich, who operated the D-X Ranch Inn on Sacramento Pass, a few miles from Wheeler Peak, and who also worked for the Forest Service. On August 6, 1964, on orders of District Ranger Donald Cox, Mike hiked up to the Prometheus Tree with the chain saw crew. This may have been the first time any of the crew had seen this tree, or had been on the Wheeler Peak moraine. Cox pointed to the tree and told Mike to saw it down, Lambert reports. "He walked over to the tree and touched it. 'I'm not cutting this tree,' he said." Cox could get Mike to prepare the chain saw and fuel it, but he could not make Mike use it. And the tree was cut by other men the next day. A part-time Forest Service laborer—a man who was no effete aesthete—touched the tree and then refused an order to cut it. This was no small act of mutiny. It was a powerful, if symbolic, gesture. Unlike Donald Currey, Mike Drakulich apparently was unable to do the act which Schulman had described, that required hardening the human heart. Why would a human have to harden his heart to cut a tree?

Mike Drakulich refused to cut the tree because it looked old, perhaps, though nobody knew at the time how old it would be. Surely he responded primarily because of what it seemed to be. His response was, in part, aesthetic.

"Aesthetics," Terry Eagleton writes in *The Ideology of the Aesthetic*, "is born as a discourse of the body." Because the discourse must include the body of the perceiver and the body perceived, there are at least two ways to consider Drakulich's aesthetic response to the tree. He reached out and touched the tree. So too I begin here with the salient concrete aspects of the old bristlecone pine, experienced by touch, smell, sound, and sight. The tree meant something to him. Any discussion of the concrete aspects of a tree must cross with the abstract idea of a pine. As free particulars, the trees seemed to stir some primitive materialism in Drakulich.

Eagleton calls this "the body's long inarticulate rebellion against the tyranny of the theoretical." Drakulich did not want the idea of the tree for science, but wanted the tree itself to stand. Lambert tells this story he has heard from Trexler as if it is a little secret, lost in the history of WPN-114. He tells this story to validate a personal response to the tree, and to disseminate that response, to permit thinking of the tree as more than an object for scientific analysis. When he refused to cut Prometheus, Drakulich engaged in a social act: aesthetic responses link people to each other by their shared responses; these responses can also destroy social cohesion.

Surfaces

The trees near timberline on Wheeler Peak seem shaped by the wind with such precision, portions of their trunks abraded by the snow-laden and ice-filled blasts that come out of Wheeler Peak's cirque, that their lower sections are often eroded like desert boulders near the ground where abrasives are carried by the wind. This results in bright buttresses of wood which glisten as if newly cut. The wood is so sharply etched that you do not casually rub your hand across the surface for fear of cutting your flesh.

There is a certain nearly universal human pleasure in newly cut wood, the way the grain seems nearly translucent where it is open to the senses. The surface, freshly exposed and warmed by the sun, invites touch, and the smell of resin from the warm surface flows from the tree like blood from a clean wound, exuding a smell some call spicy. The brightness of new-cut wood is not like the brightness of cut and sanded wood, nor like the brightness of a finished surface. It is radiant and yet unfinished, therefore fragile, in the way a new piece of pine would be if made into a human object or implement.

The surfaces of these storm-abraded bristlecones are not evenly exposed but cut into sharp but not splintery ridges because they are made of such close-grained wood. They appear to be cut precisely by a sharp tool, especially in the smoothness of their facets and edges.

The evaporative power of wind in the Great Basin ranges quenches rot, but not entirely. Many if not most of the old trees on Wheeler Peak are streaked by the slow weeping of their sap, and by dripping water over many centuries. Because the Snake Range, and especially the cirque of Wheeler Peak, receives over twice the pre-cipitation of the White Mountains, many trees do exhibit heart rot.

It is the exception, rather than the rule, that the eroded surfaces of bristlecones are bright. Bright wood is a rarity on the western and eastern sides of the Great Basin and is most common at timberline. People are drawn to timberline trees at Patriarch Grove, Mount Washington, or Wheeler Peak because they seem idealized. At the north rim of Cedar Breaks in southwestern Utah, as in most places the bristlecones grow, the abrasives of wood are limestone and dolomite particles combined with icy snow. Stone chips often dust the surfaces of the trees or embed themselves in the grain, the dead wood acquiring a streaked or mottled texture of gold and gray, seeming to be a mixture of fresh and ancient surfaces.

Wind blows out of the Wheeler Peak cirque and scours certain trees in exposed locations. More generally across the Great Basin, south winds are the most vigorous and precede each winter storm. Because of the direction of the prevailing winds, which are them-selves a condition of older growth, the bright or weathered faces of scoured wood seem to confront the sunlight, especially in the fall and spring when the sun is lower on the horizon, and they seem almost to offer themselves to it and catch its brightness.

The bright-edged buttresses of the old trees face up-canyon on Wheeler Peak, generally to the southwest. It is the same in the Patri-arch Grove near the California border, at Cedar Breaks, on Mount Charleston near the southern tip of Nevada, and near Mount Mo-riah. In many, if not in all old groves, walking from up-canyon, or from the south, with the wind at your back, you face exposed wood. You see and hear only hints of the moving foliage hidden behind the buttresses of naked wood.

To see these trees with the wind insistent on your back is to encounter them from the direction of forces that have shaped them. Aesthetic qualities of groves and individuals are created by the prevailing wind, which is also the direction from which light flows. On a bright morning when they seem created by light, this is not an illusion. On dry south-exposed slopes, where an observer encoun-ters wind and cold, they seem created by cold and exposure. Wind, cold, and light seem to conspire at timberline, creating a certain order among trees.

Although each tree seems remarkably individual in such places, the trees also seem strangely though not precisely congruent. Be-cause, as one approaches the old bristlecones, they seem individually to represent some complex relation between order and disorder, uniqueness and commonness. The way they grow seems harmonious and also tumultuous. Each is alike and all are different. Old and young, live and dead, they possess a common order of time and of space, which are the coordinates used to describe aesthetic objects.

Photographers with the sun on their backs find these sites seductive, and they select the dead wood as an object of focus. As so many amateur and professional photographers seek to capture the texture of sculptured wood in changing light, they scarcely notice, perhaps, the hidden foliage, and ignore the sound of the wind blowing through it.

Look at the tree from its lee side—as the long-legged woman does from where she has gone to hide from the cold wind. You can't see anything of the sharp lines. Instead, you are engulfed in a huge undifferentiated mass of impenetrable foliage. Even if the sun is behind you, there is little difference in the light values between the lit (forward) and shadowed (receding) foliage. She knows that the human eye and brain require sharp value changes within a mass to perceive or "read" a form. Leonardo da Vinci, for instance, produced what we call realistic painting by creating the illusion of three dimensions, or volume. He did this by emphasizing wide value-steps between light and shade. Traditional painters of landscape rely a great deal on value contrasts to make their pictures readable.

Looking into thick bristlecone foliage may be a frustrating and unpleasant experience for an artist, precisely because it won't allow looking in, nor will it allow that satisfying experience of seeing, recognizing, or imposing form. The foliage resists all her attempts to make sense of it. Its dark form is obdurate. She asks how its form or gesture could possibly have anything to do with the trunk and branches. The foliage reminds her ceaselessly that she does not know enough yet to see and understand. She almost wishes that this evidence of life were not there, because it is easier to imagine a dead tree's past foliage than to reconcile herself with a live tree's extravagance.

A Touch of Life

The foliage of old Great Basin bristlecones seems at a distance, to one who does not have to draw it, dignified but electrical. The limbs do not leap about in the wind, nor do they make a high-pitched whine. Moving air brings out low notes, and none of the whistling heard in forests of long-needled pines. The limbs deploy themselves in a diverging pattern, and the heavy foliage sways in stately rhythms when blown.

A tight cluster of needles, when grasped, feels dense and heavy, almost as if it is shaking your hand. A tuft of needles does not flow through the hand in so disorderly a way as a bottle brush or crush so delicately as a fox's brush. It feels more substantial, a little like deer hair, springy and not quite slippery. The rounded shapes of individual five-needle bundles feel like tubes split longitudinally. It is difficult to run your hand up a sprig of foliage. The directions of the needles say "the other way," and as you follow their direction, you can feel the incremental changes of each year's growth, thicker and thinner, longer and shorter.

It is a sturdy foliage, and the cones too are sturdy. The bristles on the old ones are too fragile to penetrate the skin of your hand, and the young cones, when they release their seeds, are so full of sap that they defy handling. Shake a newly opened cone in the fall, and the seeds drift to the ground, so small that they are difficult to pick up without destroying their delicate mayfly-like wings.

As for the bark, it is a homely line of life, and like skin it changes with use. Nobody knows how to touch it. Handling the trees, you are constantly reminded of contrasts between their concrete aspects: the substantial, resilient, and sturdy; the ethereal, fragile, and delicate; rough and smooth; accessible feelings and hidden ones.

Smell

The primeval smell of any pine comes from "essential oils," as they are called by Nicholas Mirov, which emanate from the pores of the needles, providing that "delicate and ephemeral piney fragrance." For someone smelling the tree at some distance, that smell combines with the smell of resin from the bark, which also consists of volatile and nonvolatile oils. Closer inspection reveals that the smells of bark and needles are not the same. The quantities and varieties of these oils and resins have been carefully cataloged and measured. But knowing what they are is not the same as smelling them.

Substance

The man with short legs has been reminded of the degree to which a bristlecone of five thousand years is substantial and ethereal. He has imagined surfaces and hidden foliage when witnessing their absence, looking down at the remains of the Prometheus Tree which now lie scattered on the pale, striated, rectilinear quartzite boulders amid drifts of needles, mostly from Engelmann spruce. There, encircling the stump, a few fragments of the tree lie in disarray, and one massive remnant fades into the grays of the forest floor. Though hardly in a thick forest, this site seems strangely dark, as if some luster of life has been lost and in this place is irretrievable.

He has been reminded that living bristlecone pines speak to all the senses. They are striking material objects, and that is what allows them to be made into aesthetic representations. The wind, the sharp blue of the sky, the sharp temperature changes between sun and shade up high, are compatible with their qualities, so opposite from anesthesia. There is nothing subjective about these conditions or the trees shaped by them. There is something subjective in the way people represent them.

At the time Muir was speaking of the bristlecones in the clichéd language of the "blighted and twisted tree" so frequently expressed in paintings known as picturesque, the idea of the aesthetic had become quite narrow. The idea of beauty as the visual only—of the aesthetic as distinguished from the useful, of art as distinguished from society—allowed many to sneer at aesthetics and use "aesthetic" as a common derogatory term. But few who work in the bristlecone forests, whether Forest Service sawyers or university-trained dendrochronologists, dare to sneer at the aesthetic qualities of these trees.

Shapes

A standing live tree presents itself as a shape, as a falling tree does, and a tree like the bristlecone which falls so slowly, sometimes long after it has ceased to live, presents itself to aesthetic judgment as a set of shapes or forms, whole and fragmented, representing perhaps the stages in its life, even when downed by wind and erosion and broken into pieces or remnants.

A tree cut down by people becomes something very ordinary, part of business as usual. Something has gone out of it in terms of its shape, its relation to its environment, and its concrete appeal to the senses. The loss of color, the loss of smell, the dissolving of form seem somehow related to the human act of cutting it away from its roots, for we always remember what we were taught, that half a tree is underground, and hidden. When humans cut down or cut up a tree, its fragments do not feel or look like the pieces left from elemental deconstructions.

An artist notices what a naturally fallen tree looks like. Its roots suddenly become upward-reaching branches formed in powerful, tusklike curves and very expressive. What had once been branches break on impact, or are later crushed under the trunk's weight, remaining as shattered stumps like half-amputated legs. It is as if, she thinks, by falling the tree is resurrected and begins a whole new life as something else, which she will draw. The whole thing starts all over.

Perhaps this is why people, for time out of mind, have been collecting weathered wood, worn shells, smoothed stones. Not just for interior decoration, but for their comforting feel or form, which comes from slow change. Sometimes people say that such objects are "nature's art," or "nature's sculpture," in the way they speak of trees as being picturesque. This always involves looking at natural objects as if they obeyed (or disobeyed) the aesthetic principles of objects made by people.

Because they are remnants, because worked by the elements of sun, wind, water, rock, and cold, old bristlecone pines and their fragments seem something that suffered and endured with dignity and grace. Prometheus was named before it was cut; other trees and fragments are similarly perceived. For this kind of perception depends upon the beholder. A piece of wood representing some abstraction—representing some personage or living being who witnesses and suffers for witnessing its truth—is valued for its ability to reproduce a religious theme.

When people speak of fragments from older bristlecone pines as relics or tokens, they are saying these are "remains" but are saying something more, that remaining is in some sense sublime. Sublime objects are inescapably linked with the idea of deity, and they are, for that reason, icons. When people see them, they think of more than one thing at a time.

So the seeming longevity of the trees under adversity which so interests the dendro-scientists also lends itself to an abstraction for those who go to bristlecone forests for aesthetic pleasure. Their long lives seem a wonder and their shapes recall their endurance. People collect the pieces of those trees for the purposes of interior decorating, without doubt, the way some criminals illegally collect archaeological pieces, pots and potsherds. Perhaps they are naïve, or driven by nostalgia, or crass consumerism. The attraction to this old wood, and even the desire to collect a precious piece, is not simply consumerism, though surely bristlecone snags have become little more than souvenirs for many.

For many collectors they are relics in the full religious sense, like pieces of the Cross, or the bones of saints. Ferguson's piece of wood, offered "to be felt and smelled," contained some mystery of touch, smell, and texture in "its wonderfully fine grains." It contained something more.

There are also people to debunk this religious awe. Michael Kelsey reports that one rancher near Great Basin National Park told him, "If you gave a man a chain saw and let him start cutting, and kept him supplied with gasoline, he could never in his lifetime cut down all the bristlecone pines in the Snake Range." But in the 1990s there is a sense that cutting a bristlecone is sinful. And such a religious sense has led some writers to speak of martyrdom in terms of the fate of the trees in human hands. Ideology has been part of people's aesthetic response to bristlecones too.

Most aesthetic discussions of these trees turn on the significance of the wood, what the tree represents. Whether the wood is a resource or a treasure, a great store of mementos or a marketable commodity, it has acquired importance beyond curiosity, leading to a discourse going far beyond the trees.

People in the Woods

Watching others and watching one's self respond to the bristlecone pines is a complex affair. It is impossible not to be disaffected and complicitous at the same time. Given a chance to wander among the old trees, people will choose or at least turn their attention to particular trees offered by a particular place, trees whose aesthetic forms seem to "make sense" or strike the imagination. It is true with all of us. Some will, perhaps, stretch toward forms which seem strange or alien, while others will seek the exact tree that speaks to their condition, the former seeking to understand what is at first incomprehensible or maybe even to accept uncertainty, while the latter seek, perhaps, some comfort.

In the places where most people go to choose a tree that speaks to their condition, the trees have already been chosen and have already been marked for their utility. Not grossly, as in a forest flagged for cutting, but marked nevertheless. Usually these marks are not so obvious as in the grove on Wheeler Peak moraine where one tree near the Prometheus has been cut across its face with a broad **v**. Why? one wonders. The tree gives no answer. Looking closely at the trees in an old grove, you can see small holes left by the increment borer, and aluminum tags the size of small Band-Aids are pinned to many trees and even fragments in the Schulman Grove, the Patriarch Grove, and elsewhere, as labels identifying them. Some people, in the recent past, have already chosen, have mapped the groves and marked them. Yet people repeat this process.

Gestures of the Groves

She believes that to get a sense of "reading" a healthily foliaged, high-altitude tree one has to stand back quite a distance, perhaps as far as a hundred or several hundred yards, to see its gesture, its overall motive, its expressiveness—which is how the prevailing wind wrote on the landscape, perhaps aided by the earth's spin and the moon's pull.

The trees grow and become more complicated at the same time, presenting a problem to the artist. Because old bristlecones do not retain their initial "leader," they branch by dying. They suggest an aesthetic of disinclination, reluctance, indisposition, an aesthetic of negation, or of forking, seeing things more than one way. Through branching, they grow complex, and through weathering they are simplified. They grow more concrete, but also lose detail; they go through levels of abstraction, seem to become more abstract. As a result of their growing and weathering, living and dying, this tension between complexity and abstraction can be disturbing.

Each grove is different, of course. The partially uprooted old trees on the easily eroded pink limestone of the Wasatch Formation at Cedar Breaks have been called the "Twisted Forest"; there the oldest trees may have experienced as much as forty inches of soil loss and stand in seemingly awkward postures. The artist imagines that some Cedar Breaks trees seem to stand on tiptoe, or are doing some weird, jerky kind of dance upon elongated spider legs. Others seem as if they ought to fall down this very minute because on one side erosion has left the roots entirely free of the soil, so that there must be thousands of pounds of tree weight held up on the other side by the frailest thread of root. Still others seem to squat atop a squirming mass of snakelike roots. In contrast, the old trees on Wheeler Peak seem embedded in the rocks on which they grow, the bases of some of the oldest encased in several feet of erosion-resistant Prospect Mountain quartzite. Some in the White Mountains seem to clutch the rocks on which they grow with a sense of firm rootedness.

Bristlecone and Sky. Watercolor on paper, 30″ x 22″

Sketches for these paintings were drawn in the White Mountains of California, at Mt. Charleston, Mt. Washington, Wheeler Peak, and Mt. Moriah in Nevada, and at Powell Point, the Markagunt Plateau, and the Wah Wah Mountains in Utah. *Artwork by Valerie Cohen.*

Red Daybreak. Watercolor on paper, 22″ x 30″

Mother Courage. Watercolor on paper, 22″ x 30″

Desert Range. Watercolor on paper, 22″ x 30″

In the Wild Animal Park. Watercolor on paper, 22″ x 30″

Bristlecone with Curly Root. Watercolor on paper, 22″ x 30″

Two Thousand Years Later. Watercolor on paper, 22″ x 30″

Bristlecone on the Edge. Watercolor on paper, 30″ x 22″

Drawing a Tree

Each grove has its own gestures, and walking through a grove of old trees seems like walking in a contemporary sculpture garden, looking at a set of arrayed abstractions, or maybe a sequence of them. This sequentiality may be related to geography. Near Cedar Breaks the trees are sometimes arranged in rows as a result of erosional patterns, and on Mount Moriah they seem arranged in ridgetop strips, or gathered in protected hollows. Everywhere, the wind seems to play a role in their distribution. But sequentiality is also created by the perceiver's choices.

People have for at least several centuries been interested in tree forms that suggest struggle. Muir, for instance, commented on the "rocky angularity" of the Sierra juniper (*Juniperus occidentalis*) growing under stressful conditions: "Its fine color and odd picturesqueness always catch an artist's eye, but to me the Juniper seems a singularly dull and taciturn tree, never speaking to one's heart." He found it "silent, cold, and rigid."

Muir's aesthetic taste is of another century. A modern viewer like Darwin Lambert likes to think that bristlecones are "ultramodern at the same time as they are ancient," and he literally embraces such trees. Both speak as if they perceived a timeless tree, but both perspectives are shaped by their historical context and reveal their own present.

The artist asks herself, "Why do I like to draw the dead and very aged forms?" She looks through her sketchbook, seeing that she likes them—and now she is speaking of her drawings—because they are so simple. These forms attest to the fact that all drawings are based on only four types of lines—the horizontal, vertical, diagonal, and curve—and these lines are all you need to convey an emotion. Hook them together right, says her teacher Milford Zornes, and you get something that looks like Arabic writing; you get moving lines. Zornes says: Horizontal is your foundation. Vertical is your support, which conveys power. The diagonal supports, but not so well. Diagonals are subordinate to horizontals and verticals and "can do mischief if you don't keep them under control." Curves are connectors.

"They are voluptuous," she realizes, "but for me curves are a real problem with bristlecones. If you get close enough to see the tree, you see only curves and forget that if you stood back far enough, you'd see the tree's true geometric form, which is a vertical cone . . . I get too wrapped up in curves," she says, "and that makes bad paintings.

"Another reason I particularly like drawing old bristlecones and western junipers. Their hard value-contrasts—between lit wood and dark high-altitude sky, between lit wood and shadows, between lit wood and foliage—seem to make things very easy. But the value-contrast can be a crutch that woos me away from making a truer statement about the tree. I have tried to narrow this value range in order to explore color instead, warm against cool, intense against muted. Which makes everything harder.

"When I draw these trees, I know that nobody will guess if I get it wrong. Because each tree is different, they seem to give you license to make them twist and turn, go any way you want. This feels like freedom, if you contrast it to the precise proportions you have to master in the drawing of a human face. However, there are very definite rules circumscribing the drawing of bristlecones. They are vertical forms. Their branches depart the trunk at identifiable angles. Their branches taper in ways that can be replicated. Their roots grip the ground in exact ways that call for decisive lines. Fuzzy lines won't work. You have to understand their rules and characteristic gestures. You have to operate within them."

A Modernist Form

Like others of his generation, Lambert learned the aesthetic of trees through modern art. Anyone who has been to school knows that Picasso's cubism, for instance, takes the abstract elements of an experience, fragmenting them into what he called "destructions," and rearranges them in a new order he called a "sum of destructions." It is not much of an exaggeration to describe the life of an old bristlecone as a sum of destructions, and perhaps it is no coincidence that the popularity of bristlecones as images has arrived in an era when people place inexpensive prints of cubist paintings on their walls.

That is to oversimplify, perhaps. One need not consider the many formulaic definitions of cubism to remember that their range reveals a consistent artistic intention to disturb and challenge the viewer's preconceptions. Cubists did not merely distort objects and space to produce flat decorative effects; they also departed from a single point of view and from symmetry in the aesthetic object, and often attempted to establish a set of transformations from the concrete to the abstract or a series of ever more disturbing images which depart from "reality." The very departure or disturbance led to those adverse reactions to cubism by certain political movements which saw it as decadent, subversive, or incomprehensible.

The bristlecone has no such intention, and people who view it as a modernistic sculpture are doing something similar to what was done by those who sought the picturesque a century and a half ago. They are choosing a tree that fits an aesthetic preoccupation created not by nature but by the culture of modern art. Yet aesthetic responses to bristlecones may be subversive, because trees are capable of changing the perceiver's sense of his or her own body.

Consider what happens when a painting is about its perceiver. Milan Kundera has abstracted an incident concerning Max Brod in 1911, from the diary of Franz Kafka:

> In his 1911 diary [Kafka] tells this story: one day the two of them went to see a Cubist painter, Willi Nowak, who had just finished a series of lithograph portraits of Brod; in the Picasso pattern as we know it, the first drawing was realistic whereas the others, says Kafka, moved further and further off from their subject and wound up extremely abstract. Brod was uncomfortable; he didn't like any of the drawings except for the first one, which, by contrast, pleased him greatly because, Kafka notes with tender irony, "beyond its looking like him, it had noble and serene lines around the mouth and eyes."

Like people looking at a series of abstract lithographs, perhaps of themselves, some may feel compelled to choose a specific individual bristlecone tree. And an artist may discover in her sketchbooks representations of these trees which reveal her view of herself. She knows that people are always choosing themselves. She says, "My truest picture—my most expressive design, most pleasing division of space, most accurate shape—is usually the on-site pencil sketch. Never again will I see that accurate first impression. Even if I go back to look at it again and again, every visit is less true. Every successive painting made from that sketch is a step away from what I thought the tree really looked like, though often—but not always— a step toward a better painting. And what might the bristlecone say, if I could show it the portrait I had drawn?"

It is hard for the man to make sense of this. How can a self-portrait also be an accurate rendition of a tree? What connection between self and truth is in that first sketch that she is willing to leave behind for a better painting? In a series of trees, some may also prefer the first one, the realistic one, which is often noble and serene, and turn away from those which follow images moving further off the subject perhaps, which may even seem freakish. Moving further off the subject toward what? Do we have to choose and say which one we like? So too with her paintings. The drawings lead to a series of abstractions. Though she does not know where a series will lead, she must follow it, but not too far.

Even the cubists "dwelt bravely on this outermost frontier of representation and refused to go over the top into pure forms," writes Roger Shattuck. In this "withdrawal from the abyss," Picasso, for instance, was one who "was too young and vigorous to relinquish his belief in the sensible world." "There *is* an abyss," she says. "It seems to me that there is an impossible break or gulf between going pretty far into the abstract and going all the way over to the non-representational. I sometimes believed that it was my own cowardice or limited intellect that kept me on this side. It makes me feel a little better to remember my teacher's axiom, that all paintings are abstract, made from pigment arranged in a pleasing way on paper."

There is a certain exercise for those who view abstractions, suggested by an art critic in 1912: pick out a detail that contains the key to the whole, stare at it for a long time, and the model will appear.

Representative Snapshots

From the timberline and the edge of artistic representation one can drive down to Great Basin National Park's visitors' center, to be reminded that, in the last three decades, bristlecones have blossomed in color and into a mass market. Captured by more than a handful of photographers, typically as twisted golden snags in front of a sky darkened by the ubiquitous polarizing filter, these representations are mechanically reproduced as trees in books, calendars, notecards, and postcards, by companies such as Galen Rowell's Mountain Light, Beautyway of Arizona, and Nature's Design of California. Most of these reproductions from color transparencies are sold as decorative items. In this sense, the images are part of a late twentieth-century mass market, without human relationships. As Raymond Williams explains in *Keywords,* "the relative decline of *customer* . . . is significant here, in that *customer* had always implied some degree of regular and continuing relationship to a supplier, whereas *consumer* indicates the more abstract figure in a more abstract market."

Many of the photographs of bristlecones are little more than snapshots. Their compositions are so unvarying that they may reveal more about public perceptions than about the artist's aesthetic. Publications promoting tourism include human figures. Occasionally they juxtapose a child or a beautiful young woman next to the tree. Sometimes the Forest Service publications show scientists at work on trees, with borers. Yet many of the recent photographs seem to depict the same isolated snag over and over again, an image without distinction for a market without individuals.

Photographs taken by W. Robert Moore in 1957 for Schulman's *National Geographic* article are interesting because their subject and composition are not representative of more recent images. They constitute the earliest widespread public representations of a bristlecone forest. Moore's photographs of trees have people in them, looking, working, walking, kneeling, and sometimes touching. People frequently are the center of his compositions: he crops off the top of the Patriarch Tree in order to center our attention on a group of people picnicking. In other photos the angles made by human bodies as they stand on steep slopes are juxtaposed against the angles made by leaning dead trees. As a technical aside, one photograph with Moore in it is captioned: "The forest is so resinous that its exudations gummed the camera lenses of W. Robert Moore (right), veteran chief of the National Geographic Society's Foreign Editorial Staff."

Moore's photographs are crowded with resinous trees, and this effect is emphasized in pictures shot looking downhill through forests, where trees on a hillside seem crowded, almost like crowds of people, which gives the impression that human scale is commensurate with the scale of the trees. Moore's trees are not isolated from one another. He allows bristlecones to burst out of the photographic frame and extend beyond its boundaries. Jumbles of trees near and far, from foreground to middle distance, create levels of space, all filled with limbs at many angles.

David Muench's images constitute a contrast to Moore's. His interpretations of bristlecones in the 1970s are still frequently republished. Muench argues in his tour de force collection in *Timberline Ancients* that the aesthetic intentions of the photographer consist of an attempt to capture the "clarity and excitement of detail" and "delight in the bristlecones' tremendous form and textures." The tree constitutes a sculpture for him, which the photographer attempts to "see" in two dimensions. One caption reads: "The bristlecone pine might be looked upon not as the subject for art but as art in itself." Muench argues explicitly, "Cameras should only be an extension of your eye."

Because his photographs are composed, exposed, developed, and reproduced, his representations of trees become, in the making, always more and less than extensions of his eye. In this sense, his photographs, like those of Moore, are abstractions, where something is gained by emphasis or selection, and something is lost too. Muench conceived, for instance, the trees of "Twisted Forest" near Cedar Breaks as "a Japanese garden in grotesque," but most frequently he conceives of them as individuals. Muench has been closely allied to such organizations as the National Parks and Conservation Association. By omitting images of humans, his photographs implicitly argue an ethic suggested by preservationist organizations in the late 1950s: "Take only photographs, leave only footprints."

His photographs typically isolate an individual tree by selecting and carefully centering the tree on the page, as if to offset or make up for the asymmetry of its limbs. Perhaps his trees are so exclusively isolated because they are found in timberline locations, which makes it irresistible to abstract the vertical tree in a bleak horizontal environment. But the effect is that of portraiture. To isolate a single tree for representation is to choose it and to discover it for the person who sees it through its portrait.

Often Muench and other photographers accentuate the isolation of trees by foregrounding or backgrounding them. Many of his images are close-ups of the details of the cones and bark and, most of all, the weathered exposed wood. Muench's images include dramatic effects, the artist says, the whole tree often framed with chemical turquoise or flat blue skies, or with gory and sanguine sunsets.

Those images, like Stephen Trimble's photograph on the cover of Lanner's *Trees of the Great Basin,* depict nobility. Trees appear exalted and elevated when their portraits are taken from ground level. The viewer of such a photograph looks uphill at the tree, which is framed against sky, clouds, or a rocky outcrop. Such a perspective magnifies the scale of the trees and their importance in the landscape. Also, in such photographs the colors of the weathered wood are often enhanced by careful exposure or developing strategy to produce an unbearable warmth and richness. The effect is probably meant to be religious. It is as if the perceiver stands at the feet of a gleaming god. Unfortunately, this compositional strategy is shared by commercial photographers who create similar iconic effects in images of gleaming Cuisinarts and imposing vacuum cleaners.

The artist grows impatient in the visitors' center. She asks her husband, "How can any discussion of these photographs proceed unless you identify every American's basic, culturally learned premise that the camera equals reality? People have to realize that they see selectively and have been taught to do so, or they can never look at a piece of art.

"When modern representations of bristlecone pines seem to be of no composition at all, or seem deliberately uncomposed," she says, "still, the trees are being 'discovered' for the viewer, through a surreptitious 'reading in' of ideas. Honesty in art demands admitting that the artist's work is to read out and compose. Dishonesty consists of reading in and pretending not to. Abstraction is honest because it subtracts and says so. This is why I hate the bulls-eye composition."

When the photographer says that the tree itself is already a work of art and the photograph only records the tree's own work of creating itself as an aesthetic object, a careful observer finds strategies of depiction and representation. Most photographs of bristlecone pines are not transparent but opaque. It is not possible to see through them. Of this one can be certain: the trees do not represent themselves as photographs. People represent them, and represent their place and time in doing so.

Composition creates a viewer's experience of a tree. If trees in a picture look like they are about to fall over, and as composed they seem to lead the viewer's attention out of the picture, they create what some people find unpleasant lines. Indeed, some of Muench's images represent the tree as something so linear in its structure that it leans and grows awkward, unstable, and unbalanced. The depictions he produces which are most stable are also the most stunted forms, their textures chaotic, even turbulent. Some captions emphasize this aspect of the trees, labeling them as ghosts, phantoms, corkscrews, twisted torsos. Perhaps this is a deliberate strategy to capture the absurd twist or curve, the peculiar trait, accident, or vagary in the quirky lives of trees on windblown slopes. For he also indicates that he carried a heavy camera and large tripod to photograph these trees, "stable equipment" necessary "if for nothing else than something for me to hold on to myself."

An obvious distinction separates the close-up photograph meant to provide some intimacy with the subject from the open or long-range shot. Photographs of the strip bark and weathered wood emphasize arcing lines of grain, bulges and discontinuities, stains of dust, sap, and water. Because compositional patterns of weathered wood repeat other patterns of whole trees living and dead, they suggest a symmetry between the parts and the whole, and perhaps something more, that the tree, even as it approaches its own death, is congruent with its own form. In this strategy of representation, Muench seems to discover for his viewer something very different, that the bristlecones—rather than being timeful—present a symmetrical design, a set of what he calls "timeless forms."

Beyond Representation

Most popular photographic representations pretend not to admit of judgments such as those made by nineteenth-century critics, which distinguish in a literal way between "monstrous," "less erroneous," and "true" pictures. Paradoxically, by the late twentieth century the very concept of "objective" representational art—even if still widely admired by the general public—had been pretty much demolished by the scholars, critics, and historians of representation in art. Indeed, the popular images of bristlecones are largely fantasies and freaks. When the artist speaks of "true" paintings, she is not talking about a literal but a figurative truth.

"Every representation," writes W. J. T. Mitchell, "exacts some cost, in the form of lost immediacy, presence, or truth, in the gap between intention and realization, original and copy." Since it is not possible to distinguish a disinterested image of a bristlecone pine, representations inhabit and exploit the gaps they open. Sometimes this discontinuity between art and life, Mitchell says, "is as ample as the gap between life and death." The images of bristlecones are not only about what they are, but about how people express them, and there is plenty of evidence that people respond to the figures of bristlecones as if they were figures embodying the gap between life and death.

The certainty and precision of modern photographic technology allow great resolution of detail. Yet just as biogeographers find no certain symmetry or order in the history of the bristlecone, as they obtain more precisely resolved pictures of its distribution and the conditions under which it has lived, so too the closer photographers get, the less certain their images seem. Like the dendroclimatologist who attempts to see *through* trees and glimpse something beyond the individuals, the photographer often reveals not simply the tree, the text in it, or what the tree reveals, but also the photographer, his skill, and what he seeks. Every photograph limits its own readings, even as every artist steps away from the first sketch, in search of something else.

Defamiliarization

Nobody can speak of every photographer or photograph of bristle-cone pines. The photographs described here often make the trees seem familiar, pretending verisimilitude to make trees part of our family. Such art seems to identify nature with culture. But many artists, by baring their devices and dramatizing that their images are not transparent but opaque, call attention to the grounds of their work. There is a value to those works of art which defamiliarize the trees and create in the perceiver a confusion, or muddle. This confusion allows, as Eagleton writes, "the dense particulars of perception" to "be made luminous to thought."

As a source of knowledge, bristlecones make journeys in the minds of people, and one of those journeys is aesthetic. Like the other journeys, this one has forking paths. Artists themselves work in the realm of the intuitive, not the deductive, but the process of their work includes something very much like "reading" forms or shapes and "writing" compositions. The process is intimately connected to their medium.

The fragrance of pines, Mirov wrote twenty years ago, is not so exuberant as that of flowers, because it is a primitive smell. "The difference between the fragrance of flowers and that of pines is about the same as the difference between a water color painting and a wood engraving; in one the desired effect is achieved by using a palette of many colors; in the other the effect is evoked by using only black and white." By its austerity, the black-and-white medium demands disciplined composition, at the same time as it releases the image and allows it to be evocative.

Because the artist is a watercolorist, she knows that this process is more complex. She does not begin with paint. She often draws where it is too steep to put up an easel and in groves too remote to be reached with anything but a sketchbook. She makes paintings in a studio, where it does not rain or snow, and no wind blows the paper from the easel. The process, for her, includes many drawings in the field and a series of paintings, usually beginning with watercolors in black and white. When she paints bristlecones, she is conscious of creating abstractions of her drawings, which are of trees which have already been abstracted by the elements. "To tell the truth," she admits, "I am not conscious of the long process that removes the extraneous then, but only later when someone points it out. I always believe I'm making it 'look like it looks,' and yet if I try to make it 'look like it looks,' when I paint, I make a bad painting."

Though particularly interested in painting trees which exhibit "longevity under adversity," she does not restrict her work to bristlecone pines. What does it matter that many of her paintings are of trees of other species? Every tree is not a bristlecone, but bristlecones share certain characteristic forms with other trees under certain conditions, sometimes suggesting the limits of these forms. They seem to be sculptured, they often exhibit strip growth, they take on Schulman's types, they fork or diverge, exhibiting the "dis-" form—evidence of discontinuities and disturbances.

She likes to be where the bristlecones grow, in unpeopled landscapes, though she also paints cars, jungles, rivers, bridges, factories, and crowds of people. Though she has tried to teach herself that all subject matter is more or less equal, she likes the bristlecones and junipers best because, as she says, they are in the nicest places to spend a day, and because they are "loveliest of all."

She draws and paints and repaints, altering all the compositional elements she controls. Her aim is not to represent the tree, but to get the painting right, and yet there is no separating the two. A painting is always some combination of the contingent and the certain, the accidental and the inevitable. The medium is neither perfectly forgiving nor entirely unforgiving, and the medium's own laws sometimes produce accidental effects that are better than effects the artist could have intended. Just as there is no such thing as a bristlecone science, but dendrochronology, ecology, paleoclimatology, disciplines which study the tree using a particular method, so too there is no such thing as a bristlecone artist.

There are, however, people who have learned to work with the trees, artists, scientists, managers, and others. Their working with the trees consists, at the very least, in knowing the tools they use, knowing the subject, knowing the object of interest, and desiring not to tell any lies.

CHAPTER 10

The Trees in Town

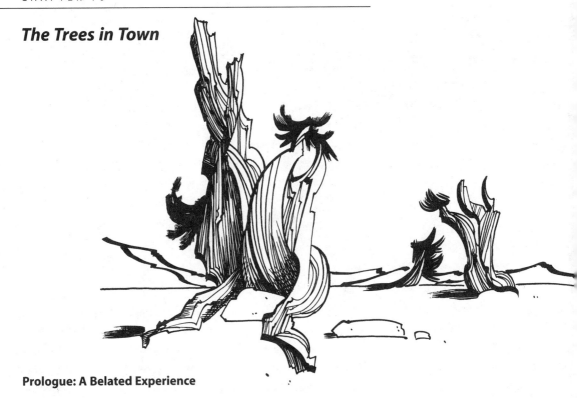

Prologue: A Belated Experience

A full-page color advertisement for Nikon Corporation in *Outside* magazine's 1995 Christmas shopping issue featured a photograph entitled *Bristlecone Pine* by Galen Rowell. Like most of his bristlecone photos, this one—of a Rocky Mountain bristlecone—highlights a spiky fragment. The photo dramatizes a special trick of light: an aura right behind the tip of the dead snag shields the sun from his lens, while the weathered wood facing the viewer is nevertheless warmly but unevenly lit, as if with a klieg light. The bright, detailed grain and streaks of the snag, which should be in shadow, contrast strangely with a dark blue sky containing a few shreds of windblown cloud. The image is overlaid by a crisp white text about the speed of light and its impact.

"I hit Mt. Evans too late to catch the natural light that would make those ancient pines come alive," Rowell comments in his small printed endorsement of Nikon equipment. His pine, bathed in light coming from many directions, seems to defy common sense because it is produced by technology and is, as all photos are, a virtual reality. He relied, as he says, upon the meters and flash attachments Nikon produces to "match the impact of natural light," expose the foreground perfectly, achieve a "creative exposure," and recreate a daylight which had passed. Rowell's point is sufficiently complex to bear stating: a photographic system allowed him to create the illusion of an experience he has missed and promises that the consumer can replicate this belated experience.

"In principle," as Walter Benjamin pointed out some sixty years ago, "a work of art has always been reproducible." His essay "The Work of Art in the Age of Mechanical Reproduction" is fittingly translated and reprinted in a book entitled *Illuminations*. He did not mean what the Nikon advertisement means. In our age, reproduction has been enacted in ways Benjamin could hardly have anticipated. Yet what he noticed still applies, that reproduction strangely replaces and destroys the original. "Even the most perfect reproduction of a work of art is lacking in one element," he wrote, "its presence in time and space, its unique existence at the place where it happens to be." For "uniqueness of a work of art," he thought, was "inseparable from its being imbedded in the fabric of tradition." But, says my friend Richard White, it cannot stay there: the world changes around it.

In a culture whose fabric of tradition cannot contain the avalanche of images it produces, the captions below magazine illustrations reveal the way reproduction disconnects a work of art from its tradition. They do this, Benjamin noticed, by *prescribing* a way of observing and dictating the meaning for an experience. Such prescriptions are necessary in a changing world, and they are coercive.

In an avalanche of ever more technically perfect images, the giving famishes the craving, not for the experience, but for the image of it. Rowell's photo is not a pure aesthetic object: it is part of an advertisement. It says: Imagine buying the equipment that will allow you to go to the same place and take the same photograph. Susan Sontag explained in 1977 how the logic of the tourist's photograph contradicts itself: "A way of certifying experience, taking photographs is also a way of refusing it—by limiting experience to a search for the photogenic, by converting experience into an image, a souvenir." In this way, the experience is commodified, or as I prefer to say, owned.

Benjamin believed that "one of the foremost tasks of art has always been the creation of demand which could be fully satisfied only later" by new forms and techniques. Now, even with the possibility of instant satisfaction that comes from collecting and accumulating photographs, some people who visit the bristlecones do not take pictures but buy postcards instead. Sometimes, according to Sontag, "tourists feel compelled to put a camera between themselves and whatever is remarkable," taking photographs which replicate the images of postcards. In this way, the photograph in our own age has become a tool owned by travel industries; by visiting the bristlecones, a tourist can acquire or replicate photographs like the ones that led him to these trees.

At present, the postcard is sent from the place of its origin, a video is bought at a visitors' center in a national park, and a photograph is exposed where light falls upon the earth. Trees do not express themselves with foliage or architecture, do not express themselves as picturesque images. Insofar as they can be said to have intentions, they intend—like humans—to live, breathe, grow, and propagate themselves. People go to the places where the images they have seen were captured and attempt to recapture the way images made them feel about these intentions. Sometimes tourists authorize their experiences with a camera and in so doing capture the same images, as a part of their lives, even if they repeat the experience to which they have been exposed. In this sense they are sensitively dependent on the conditions which initially caught their attention and brought them to the trees. This mass experience of replicated images propagates an avalanche or chain reaction upon which the modern tourist industry depends. At a certain critical moment, Ely, Nevada, hoped to capitalize on this chain reaction by appropriating the image of the bristlecone, and in so doing began to refigure its history and perhaps its future.

A Tourist Economy

> Every tree sends its fibres forth in search of the Wild.
> The cities import it at any price.   —Thoreau, "Walking"

Ely, the county seat of White Pine County, is an unplanned experiment created by conditions not present in late twentieth-century Nevada. It was once a planned experiment. Now, according to the chamber of commerce, northeast Nevada "offers a progressive, full service community combined with the serene, uncomplicated quality of life of the rural West." This is the kind of story one expects from such a source, but it should not be ignored for that reason. Within such stories, people tell and retell their histories, trying to get them right. But the stories diverge. Though a town's history may not be whatever its people want it to be, they reveal what they desire by the way they tell their history, to themselves and to others.

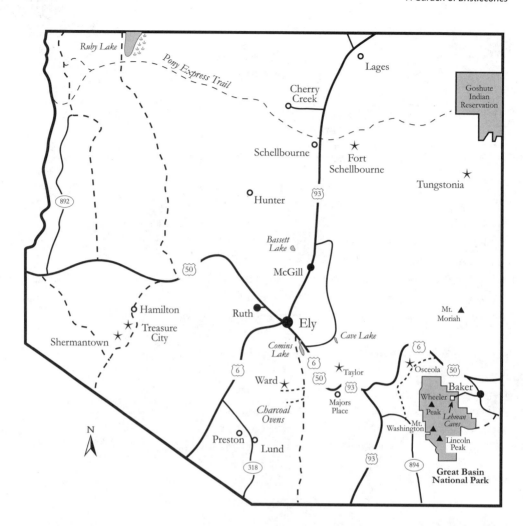

White Pine County, Nevada. (Adapted from map by White Pine Chamber of Commerce)

With an average annual precipitation of 9.27 inches, and a ninety-day growing season, White Pine County had a population of about 9,500 in 1993. Now it is larger. White Pine County is named not for the white pine, but for the limber pine. Its county seat, Ely, sitting at nearly 7,000 feet in elevation and surrounded by mountains, contains more than half the county's population and has been a regional center of business and commerce for more than a century.

Attracting visitors has been a difficult task recently. David Toll, who has produced and updated *The Compleat Nevada Traveler* for more than forty years, explained in 1993 that the present map of Ely reveals the city's recent past, and that one must read backward to understand the city's structure. The central "watershed event" in the history of modern Ely has been the departure of Kennecott

Copper in the late 1970s, and "nothing has quite taken up the economic slack." Kennecott stopped mining ore in nearby Ruth in 1978 and stopped smelting ore in nearby McGill in 1983. This explains why Ely, which lies between Ruth and McGill, seemed in 1993 somehow suspended in time and space.

At one time the Nevada Northern Railway linked these towns with each other and with the rest of the world. In 1906 it became the chief line of commerce for the region, connecting mining and milling to the Southern Pacific in the north, near Wells. When Kennecott Copper left Ely, it donated the so-called ghost train to the city. The train was restored and ran as a tourist attraction first in May 1987, as part of the celebration of Ely's centennial. The ghost train seems one image of Ely's hinged and connected functions. In the past the train connected extraction and manufacture and linked separate but interdependent communities. Now it links a possible past of mining to a possible present of tourism.

That is only half the story. When it was restored, the train's urban and technological appeal was first paired to a wilder attraction, Great Basin National Park, dedicated during Ely's centennial year, on August 15, 1987. Historical and natural preservation pulled the city in new directions, but as Toll wrote in 1993, there is "still a gap to fill before Ely completely recovers its stride." People in northeastern Nevada found him a bit too pessimistic about mining and too optimistic about tourism. The copper mine has been bought and sold several times since Kennecott left. It is presently owned by Broken Hill Proprietary, an Australian corporation. In July 1995 the pits in Ruth reopened, and milling resumed there in December. The mine employed 430 people. Surprisingly, the railroad was refurbished in the early 1990s so that it could transport concentrate from the mill to Arizona for smelting. Now it is both a tourist attraction and a mode of industrial transport.

Jack Fleming, who writes history for the *Ely Daily Times* newspaper, comments, "In a nutshell, that means again more people, more production and more payroll. Sort of full circle!" Sort of a quasi-cycle. Five thousand people applied for the four hundred new jobs that would last about fifteen years. These applicants were not the people who lost their jobs a little over fifteen years ago. And the "project," as the corporation calls it, will mine and concentrate the remaining 252 million tons of ore for only fifteen years. People speak of this era as "licking the bowl."

Romancing Nevada's Past, another tourist guide, also appeared in

1994. It was written by a younger man, Shawn Hall, then assistant director of the Northeastern Nevada Museum in Elko, who believed that "White Pine has rebounded from adversity," with the advent of microscopic gold mining run by a different set of corporations. Microscopic gold has had a minor effect on Ely, while it has recently allowed a major boom in Elko, a couple of hundred miles to the north. Most people, including the manager of the White Pine Chamber of Commerce, figure that renewed mining activity has simply deferred a crisis. Ely is at a historical crossroads, according to such a view, and must use the next fifteen years to diversify its economy and way of life.

Ely is also at a spatial crossroads, between east–west running U.S. Highway 50 and north–south running U.S. Highway 93. Perhaps that is why, as a Nevada Commission on Tourism brochure states, it is a hub and "has grown to be the largest city in Eastern Nevada." At present there are many motels in Ely, most of them pretty run down, with parking lots filled by pickup trucks. They have been used over the years by transient workers. If you ask advice at the office of the Humboldt National Forest, however, you are likely to be directed to the Bristlecone Motel, which, from the street, looks like the most inviting motel in Ely.

Toll believes "Ely's greatest attraction for visitors may not be in town at all, but in the magnificent surroundings." Some people residing in Ely are not satisfied with such a view. The White Pine Museum—"Preserving Eastern Nevada's Heritage"—was opened in 1959 to display the human history of the region. In 1975 the city built the Bristlecone Convention Center and Visitor's Bureau, run by the White Pine County Fair and Recreation Board, which "Extends an Open Invitation for You to 'EXPERIENCE THE UNEXPECTED.'" The foyer of the convention center boasts a world's-oldest-living-tree display. Every August since 1982 the city has invited tourists to a local crafts festival called Bristlecone Arts in the Park.

For tourists driving into town from the west, Ely is the last town and the terminus for their trip across the state. Highway 50, on which they arrive, was called the "Loneliest Road in America" in 1986 by a *Life* magazine writer who found no services, no attractions, and that drivers needed survival skills to make the journey. A couple of young graduates from the University of California, working for the Nevada Commission on Tourism, saw an opportunity and inverted *Life*'s idea to promote the route, pointing out that the highway traverses "Pony Express territory" and roughly parallels the ephemeral route used by riders in 1860 and 1861, before they were replaced by the telegraph.

A visitor may have his *Highway 50 Survival Brochure* validated with an "I Survived" stamp in Fernly, Fallon, Austin, and Eureka, and finally in Ely, at the museum or the chamber of commerce. Soon he will receive a certificate and a bumper sticker. He can buy a T-shirt. The commission also suggests a "93 Caravan," traveling U.S. Highway 93 through Nevada's "small friendly towns," from Jackpot in the north to Boulder City in the south. Highway 93 is also a possible, but not likely, route for transport of high-level nuclear waste to the proposed waste repository at Yucca Mountain.

Some people in Ely want visitors to do more than drive through town, and a particular segment is justly proud of a great many recreational possibilities in White Pine County, as one can discover in the foyer of the convention center.

Adults also come to Nevada to gamble, as the Commission on Tourism's brochures and maps continually remind, with the graphic of a woman's well-manicured, bright red thumbnail turning up an ace of hearts at the bottom right-hand corner, revealing the slogan "Discover Both Sides of Nevada."

Both Sides

The graphic is a signature of sorts. Both sides of Nevada: a postcard or a playing card has two sides. With a playing card, the message is hidden by the back, and so too, perhaps the image on the postcard hides the authentic message on the back. But the issue may well be the reverse, as when someone writes in Ely on a bristlecone post-card, "Wish you were here." What is hidden and what is displayed? In the simplest reading, as the official state map for 1995–96 states, the two sides are Lady Luck and Mother Nature. One image of Nevada is well known and the other hidden. The Nevada Commission on Tourism encodes and decodes a great many more readings in the image it creates with this signature. After all, the mining history of Nevada has spent more than a century writing "Wish you were here" on the Lady Luck side of the card that said Mother Nature.

Nevada's hole card is an ace of hearts because it is a single win-ning card, but also because the commission wishes to portray Ne-vada as the Heart of the West. The card is also a version of a map of the state's body. Northern and central Nevada are, according to the

Nevada Commission on Tourism *Nevada Visitors Guide,* the heart
of the state, and the triangular southern tip, Las Vegas, nearly five
hundred miles south of Ely, is a little lower—so to speak—where
a visitor can feel the state's fast-paced pulse. The Nevada Commission on Tourism suggests that traveling from west to east, from the
paired cities of Reno and Carson City, the metropolis and seat of
government, one travels back in history, perhaps away from the
brain and other parts and toward something more essential. This
fiction locks Ely in the past.

A kind of cultural shadow falls across northeastern Nevada, cast
by the western urban centers where people read Ely's condition
according to their own and try to write it too. The southern urban
delights of Las Vegas are paraded as a contrast to Ely. According to
this vision, gaming, the future, fantasy, experience, and culture
flourish in the big cities, while the northeast reveals a more austere
life, gambling of a different sort, inherited from the historic past of
mining and ranching. The northeastern reality reveals—according
to those who live there—something more substantial, and not necessarily a reality that retains an innocence of nature. People perceive
their cultures as cultures.

In the section of the Commission on Tourism's 1995 *Nevada Visitors
Guide* devoted to Ely, one page is striking. A small blond girl in a
bright magenta fleece jacket and Levis nestles comfortably among
green piney boughs, leans against a large weathered unmistakable
tree trunk, reading a book. "If only trees could talk," the text
begins, "these would sure have some tales to tell. After all, they're
the oldest living things on earth! They're Bristlecone Pines, just
one of the wild wonders of Eastern Nevada's Great Basin National
Park." The elder tree, used to establish a crucial selling point, becomes a kindly grandparent to a new generation and is effective
because it is affecting.

This is, literally, an image of family values. Taken on Wheeler
Peak by Linda Dufurrena—a rancher and professional photographer whose work is often devoted to portraying modern Great
Basin ranching in a favorable light—its provenance reveals a great
deal. The photographer had in mind a picture including an entire
class from the Baker School encircling one of the old trees living on
the nearby mountain in Great Basin National Park. Stormy weather
interfered, and so she posed her granddaughter Magan under an
old tree in September 1990. She sold the image through R. & R.

If only trees could talk.

Discover
Both Sides Of
NEVADA.

These would sure have some tales to tell. After all, they're the oldest living things on earth! They're Bristlecone Pines, just one of the wild wonders of Eastern Nevada's Great Basin National Park.

Come discover this magical place for yourself. But keep your ears open, you never know what you might hear!

Call 1-800-NEVADA-8.

Nevada Commission On Tourism, P.O. Box 30032, Reno, NV 89520

Magan Dufurrena as she appears in the 1995 Nevada Visitors Guide. (Linda Dufurrena photo, courtesy Nevada Commission on Tourism)

Advertising to the commission, which framed it with text. The image of Magan Dufurrena in her tree is a striking image of one way Northeastern Nevada might regain its vitality, by capitalizing on accumulated resources of the past.

A Visit to the Pits

Toll's guide of 1993 indicates that the economic downturn "has precluded widespread restoration," and so Ely has the familiar look of "early 20th century small town architecture . . . Norman Rockwell would have liked." Toll's guide does not talk about the weeds growing through cracks in the sidewalk on Main Street. The *1995 White Pine County Visitor's Guidebook,* in actuality a free handout printed by the *Ely Daily Times*, used Ely's stagnation to make a virtue of necessity: "White Pine has preserved its western history for the visitor to enjoy." One always gets a queasy feeling from such statements, as if a guilty secret is being divulged. Something valuable and irreplaceable is being sold to those who, unable to appreciate it, will acquire only transitory pleasure, unaware that it is being sold by those who have suffered and have nothing else to sell.

Ely has been the commercial center of White Pine County for over a century because of the modern uses of copper. When Kennecott left Ely, it left the railroad, the McGill smelter with its 750-foot-high smokestack and several thousand acres of tailings, the pits at Ruth, and people with modern needs. These reveal the way Kennecott had developed three separate enclaves where segregated populations lived and worked near the pits, near the tailings and smokestack, and in the commercial center.

To understand this tripartite cultural geography, a visitor might begin by going west, and backward in time, eight miles up the canyon from Ely. Near Ruth, ore was mined and became the natural resource upon which Ely's cultural geography was built. Ruth is, most obviously, an open pit, as Ely's visitor's guide jokes: "The view is the pits, fortunately." Named for the daughter of a local mine owner, it peaked, or to speak more precisely, reached bottom before the crash of 1929, as a town of more than two thousand. Kennecott, owner of "The Richest Hole on Earth" near Salt Lake City, began buying up mining claims around Ruth in 1915, assumed complete control of Ruth's Liberty Pit in 1958, and moved the whole town of Ruth to uncover a new hole under the original townsite.

At the place where you can look into Ruth's presently inactive Liberty Pit, the whole landscape in the foreground and middle-ground is disturbed in an almost incomprehensible way. A large display has been constructed near a picnic table for Magma Nevada Mining Company by People for the West. Magma owned the mines until January of 1996. The three-part display identifies mining machines, explains mining history, details mining technology, and outlines the significance of this landscape.

The Liberty Pit is one of five major developed copper deposits in the Robinson mining district which have produced more than 4 billion pounds of copper from 350 million tons of ore. As the display's text indicates, under the heading A MEASURE OF YOUR SHARE OF THE DISTURBANCE, "If you or your family has two automobiles and a house, then you are responsible for about 600 pounds of copper consumption, requiring mining of about 30 tons of ore, or about 100 total tons of disturbance."

A Return to Town

The diverse possibilities of traditional ways of life in Ely have been obscured by disturbances of the recent past and by a sharp conflict between those who value the past and those who call what comes next "progress." The processes of species shifting, market making, land taking, boundary setting, state forming, and self-shaping seem sometimes less like a readable history than a set of cards shuffled in some game of chance. Gradually, people have stopped talking about the prior rights of historic ways of life and have started to wonder whether ways of life can be combined: tourism with ranching, elk and antelope with cattle, mining and trees.

Mining is the joker. In the 1976 edition of his guide, Toll placed Ely in the region called "Mining Country," as opposed to the "Big Bonanza Country" of Virginia City on the western edge of Nevada, where he edited briefly the *Gold Hill News*. He described Ely as a "bustling town" of more than seven thousand. Kennecott, employer of fifteen hundred people, produced more than half the jobs in White Pine County. "The Kennecott influence is felt everywhere," he wrote in 1976. Because Kennecott's headquarters were in Utah, Ely was "more of a satrapy of Salt Lake City than of Carson or Reno or Las Vegas." Television, newspapers, and wholesale supplies came from Salt Lake City. The managerial class came from there and from points east. Economic conditions in Ely were determined by this influence from the east, but social conditions were not, according to Toll. Drinking and gambling at the Hotel Nevada were—aside from some brothels on the west side of town—the "undisputed center of after-dark activity." Such a view, a tourist's view, fails to see inside the domestic life of the county seat.

Reading Backward

Although writing in the present, Toll was writing of the past in 1976 because he was so near a central discontinuity in the life of Ely. Because this discontinuity is so recent, though not the only one in Ely's history, it seems to mark a divide between a city built by copper's turbulent history and a city that tried to build something else, but was still struggling to free itself from the benevolent tyranny of a single corporation.

A flying leap into Ely's past reveals a set of ambiguities and discontinuities. If you looked up Ely in Leigh's *Nevada Place Names: Their Origin and Significance* in 1964, you learned it was named for John Ely of Pioche, who supplied $5,000 as a loan to A. J. Underhill to lay out the townsite in 1889. This happened after the town inherited the county seat of White Pine County from Hamilton in 1887. Hamilton was a silver camp and boomtown, a commercial center like Ely that linked Treasure City, a mining encampment above, to Shermantown, where available water permitted milling below. Hamilton never recovered from a devastating fire in 1873 and was dealt its final blow when its courthouse burned in 1885. Because Hamilton is a ghost town, or, as the Nevada map calls it, a "site," its history can and has been written. Because Ely has not finished its history, even its past continues to change.

Ely had been established as a gold mining camp in 1868 but got its identity and stability from copper. A newer historical source, Helen Carlson's *Nevada Place Names: A Geographical Dictionary* (1974), links Ely's name to copper, making the strong case that Ely acquired its name in 1878 in honor of Smith Ely, president of the Selby Copper Mines and Smelting Company, and that the loan of $5,000 was not for a townsite but a courthouse. The source of Ely's name is not a trivial matter, because Ely may be the same town in a different place with a new name. Towns migrated in Nevada and were sometimes inhabited by the same people, who shifted their identities. Flourishing towns and ghost towns are connected materially and socially. It is often hard to keep track of their names or identities. For instance, a photograph of Ely in 1888 shows a few buildings in a gently sloping sage-covered valley. The lumber for these early buildings came from structures salvaged in Ward, Taylor, and other nearby mining towns that had expired.

The first newspaper in Ely, the *White Pine News,* began in 1868 at Treasure City, moving downhill to Hamilton in 1870. It stayed there for a decade, then migrated to the boomtown of Cherry Creek for a few years, on to Taylor in its boom years of 1885–88, and arrived in Ely shortly after it became the county seat. Moving a letterpress in eastern Nevada in the nineteenth century was no minor affair. Though the name of the news remained constant, owners changed and reversed its political orientations. Nevertheless, the *White Pine News* constitutes the most continuous historical record of White Pine County.

A Trip to McGill

Thirteen miles northwest of Ely, ore from Ruth was smelted at McGill because ample water could be captured there. It was a city built and controlled entirely by Kennecott. Like Ruth, McGill peaked in the late 1920s as a company town of about three thousand. McGill had been a cattle ranch, bought with money made in the Big Bonanza. As Toll described the scene at McGill in 1976, the place had a "gothic atmosphere," the enormous smelter brooding over an eerie gloom, "intensified by a haze of dust raised by the wind from the smelter's waste heaps and by smoke heaving out of two tall chimneys."

Those who lived in McGill did not think of it as a wasteland. To understand how it came to be depicted only as an environmental disaster, one must uncover the history Toll's description erases. Before the Great Depression, more people lived in Ruth and McGill than now live in Ely, but consider who they were and how they lived. The benevolent company carefully populated McGill with poorly paid Greek, Slavic, and Japanese laborers in separate enclaves commonly called "Greek Town," "Austrian Town," and "Jap Town." The company sent Serbian immigrants to work in Ruth and placed Croatians in McGill. These socially segregated populations were housed and maintained by the paternalistic corporation as "foreigners" in separate low but stratified social and economic conditions, with identities valued below those of "white" immigrants from England, Ireland, Scotland, Germany, France, Sweden, Denmark, and Norway. Even as individual members of these populations improved their economic status and engaged in broader social intercourse, they found the geographic barriers impermeable until after World War II. Ruth and McGill are now virtually empty. Where have the people gone? The Japanese did not return after their internment during the war. A few of the others live in Ely. Some remember White Pine at annual picnics in Reno.

So mining in Ruth and smelting in McGill were carried on by groups who could not live in "white" town. In half a century, more than a billion dollars' worth of copper came out of the pits at Ruth, flowed down through Ely, on to the smelter at McGill, and then north to the Southern Pacific, but in an unpredictable and sometimes turbulent pattern.

Kennecott is now described in Ely's newspaper as "the last copper lord to reign in White Pine" because it closed the mines in 1978 and sold out, leaving more than fifteen hundred workers without a living and the town in dire straits. Depending on your perspective, the smelter closed primarily because of globally low copper prices, cheaper ore and smelting elsewhere, or because the smelter could not comply with strict new standards set by the Environmental Protection Agency without expensive repairs.

Next as proprietor came Alta Gold, soon followed by Magma Nevada Mining Company, which promised to reopen the mines and did so before selling to Broken Hill Proprietary. Meanwhile, in the 1980s and early 1990s, as Ely was in danger of becoming a ghost town, the *Ely Daily Times* tried to see this turbulent history as cyclical, though perhaps irreversibly and seriously disturbed by federal intervention. The conditions of McGill's boom times will never return. The new copper lord will not be a benevolent corporation, as Kennecott was in the past. And having been whipsawed by the volatility of the mining industry in the twentieth century, the city of Ely hoped to diversify its economic base, partly with tourism. Not because tourism is inherently better than extracting and smelting ore, but because a tourist industry might fill a gap between the past and the future.

An Exhibit

At the Bristlecone Convention Center, copper seems remarkably absent. A large snag of weathered wood about eight feet long leans in the corner of the foyer with a plaque in front of it which reads, "This Bristlecone Pine Tree is one of the world's oldest living things. It was brought from the top of Ward Mountain by Stu Hevenstrite of the Ely Rotary Club for the Bristlecone Convention Center. Permit issued by the Bureau of Land Management, courtesy of Mr. Robert Schultz, June 1976."

This strange plaque, including information about a federal permit, its letters engraved on some plasticized material, is perhaps explained by reference to the larger display. Between the two entry doors to the main hall, named redundantly the Bristlecone Room, stands a somewhat hastily built showcase about eight feet wide and six feet tall, made of a dark walnut laminate often used to "spruce

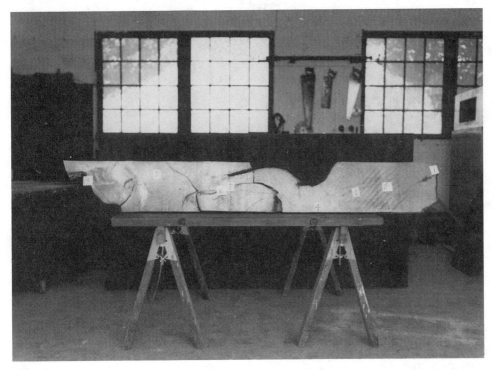

Prometheus slab in Nevada Northern Railway's Ely workshop. (U.S. Forest Service)

up" old interior walls in this region. The showcase is headed by a sign saying BRISTLECONE PINE WORLD'S OLDEST LIVING THING spelled out in brasslike stamped metal letters of the sort used for addresses and names on the fronts of houses. Ely is a city made by copper, but not much made of it. It is also a city of imported wood. The exhibit consists primarily of a one-inch-thick transverse slice of bright, close-grained pine, a foot wide by about seven feet long.

This great slab completely dominates the exhibit, mounted diagonally across a green enamel background, surrounded by a few eight-by-ten-inch glossy photographs of live trees, cones, and people walking in the woods. It is smoothly varnished, and its series of rings appears continuous. The slab is from the tree called Prometheus or WPN-114, though nothing in the display case says so. A small engraved copper plate mounted below the slab indicates that it is presented by Humboldt National Forest, United States Forest Service, and the Nevada Mines Division of Kennecott Copper Corporation, "prepared as a community service by Kaiser Advertising." Kathy Kaiser designed the exhibit to be placed in a cabinet donated by Howard Winn, general manager of Kennecott's local operations.

The display itself includes some text, the main portion ending "Journey back into history by reading the dates down from the bark

Prometheus slab in the exhibit at the Bristlecone Convention Center, Ely. (U.S. Forest Service)

(1964)." This is the historical journey at present, as indicated by small labels mounted on the slab of Prometheus:

A.D. 1964	Bark
A.D. 1945	Atomic Age
A.D. 1776	Independence
A.D. 1620	Pilgrims Land
A.D. 1492	Columbus
A.D. 1096	1st Crusades
A.D. 510	Mohammed Born
A.D. 476	Rome Falls
1 B.C.	Christ Born
753 B.C.	Rome Founded
1184 B.C.	Battle of Troy
1450 B.C.	Moses Exodus
1950 B.C.	Hammurabi Rules
3000 B.C.	Pyramid Built.

Such a standard tree-date exhibit was made a cliché by a round of sequoia wood in Sequoia National Park at mid-century. A similar tree-date exhibit appears as a two-page drawing in Russ and Anne Johnson's pamphlet *The Ancient Bristlecone Pine Forest*, printed by Chalfant Press of Bishop, California, near the western edge of the Great Basin. The Johnson chronology, first published in 1970, is able to bring history up to its date, and can be compared to the "eastern" bristlecone chronology at Ely:

A.D. 1969   The first man walks on the moon
A.D. 1100   The Religious Crusades to Jerusalem in search of the
            Holy Grail

THE BIRTH OF CHRIST
(The Beginning of Christianity)

332 B.C.   Alexander the Great conquers Egypt
1300 B.C.   The 18th Egyptian Dynasty
2635 B.C.   Babylon flourished as a nation.

The history of Ely's exhibit is in itself interesting. A gift to the
community by a stable federal agency and by a corporation which
has recently abandoned the region, it has been moved, and its
chronology has been altered.

The display was placed in the lobby of the Hotel Nevada in July
1965. It remained for some time in a corner between slot machines
and an entrance to a restaurant, where it deteriorated. The original
labels that marked historical events fell off, and the finish on the slab
grew opaque. The district ranger was appalled that the exhibit was
ignored and not maintained. Finally, in 1983, it was refurbished to
its present state and moved to the Bristlecone Convention Center.

The original text for the exhibit was written in 1965. It stated
inaccurately: "The slab displayed here was taken from one of the
oldest bristlecone pine trees found in the Wheeler stand—but not
the oldest, in order to preserve what may be history's oldest living
thing." More pertinent, however, is the listing of "thirteen important events that occurred during the lifetime of the tree." These
were numbered and correlated to white triangles pasted to the slab
in the following order:

13   A.D. 1957   birth of the space age
12   A.D. 1945   Atomic Age ushered in
11   A.D. 1905   first airplane built
10   A.D. 1620   arrival of the Pilgrims at Plymouth Rock
9   A.D. 1000   arrival of Leif Eriksson in the New World
8   A.D. 510   birth of Mohammed
7   1 B.C.   birth of Christ
6   438 B.C.   Parthenon built in Athens
5   753 B.C.   founding of Rome
4   1184 B.C.   fall of Troy
3   1450 B.C.   exodus of Moses out of Egypt

This photo of a bristlecone pine appeared in the original Prometheus exhibit. The forest service hoped that this tree would be "history's oldest living thing." It was not. The tree is still alive on the slope of the Wheeler Peak moraine. (U.S. Forest Service)

| 2 | 2050 B.C. | rule of Hammurabi |
| 1 | 3000 B.C. | start of the great pyramids in Egypt. |

As is clear by the shifting dates for events and the shifting selection of "important" events, the historical journey was slightly different at the Hotel Nevada. A culture or city may forget or remember selectively, may write and rewrite changing sets of past events—and perhaps changing theories of history—upon the rings of the bristlecone. For instance, an undated note made when the exhibit was being refurbished, found in Forest Service files, indicates that one of the people working on the exhibit considered but rejected "Nevada Statehood" as an important date.

People have always written their names on the outside of living trees. Aspens magnify initials, valentines, love notes, and sometimes pornographic images carved into their bark over the years, as the trees grow and heal their wounds. Inscribing trees, people inscribe themselves and sign their presences, sometimes by disfiguring the trees, or even disfiguring themselves by recording their history and desire. So too some bristlecones have been tagged and even mutilated.

The bristlecone display brings the process of inscription to town and indoors in a way that seems stunning and silly. In a hall built for the bicentennial of the American Revolution, inscribed on the grain of the now-dead but once oldest known bristlecone pine, someone decided to delete the Parthenon, Leif Eriksson, the airplane and the space age, but added the fall of Rome, the First Crusade, Columbus, and remembered to include A.D. 1776. History remembered in the mid-1970s became less technological than a decade earlier, more Christian and less Greek. But these distinctions are created by inscribing or erasing single events, which makes it hard to read this history. None of these sets of events include the world wars or events that can be correlated directly to the cultural history of populations in Jap Town or Austrian Town. Greek Town has its events, of a distant and perhaps irrelevant past. But maybe I underestimate the power of popular culture to disseminate a universal view of history.

These linear versions of world history, though not certain about space travel, are more certain of atomic energy, the birth of certain religious figures, and the foundings of city states. The patterns they illustrate are not anchored at their beginnings or their ends, but at their centers, at the birth of Christ. They are all Christian histories. Other events seem—as written on this slab of bristlecone—more *contingent*: their dates, though probably not accurately affixed to the exact rings of the tree, include a chronology memorized by school children; their importance seems less logically necessary than subject to interpretation.

It is always possible that the events inscribed upon the bristlecone were chosen for aesthetic reasons, because their dates could be displayed in an evenly spaced series across the grain of the tree. Certainly the exhibitors have made history appear nearly uniform and quite linear, not twisted, uneven, or multiple. Also, both the text and the foreground for this exhibit have changed. These parts of the exhibit may be simply decorative or may occupy niches in the syntax of the display. After all, the slab is contained in a box or case and is the only essential item, whose superimposed images and texts can be adjusted, shifted, or even replaced. Donald Currey retained a second complete cross section of Prometheus which, according to Robert Starr Waite, then a geographer at Weber State College in Utah, could be exhibited at another place, presumably with another interpretive text and set of important events. Indeed, it is possible to conceive of a very large number of very thin slabs of Prometheus, on each of which might be inscribed a slightly or greatly different version of human history.

Ely's Past and Future

The bristlecone display at the Convention Center suggests that someone in Ely would like to connect the city's own story to something larger than itself and read its history into something more stable and lasting, which might serve as a foundation for its present and its future. The display at the Liberty Pit claims that the ore mined there is 111 million years old. Though the ore has not been used up, it will be.

And in such a short time. Strictly speaking, none of the key events in the life of Ely have been inscribed on the rings of the slab in the exhibit. If they had been, they would have been marked in a region comprising less than 2 percent of the slab's surface, crammed into a very brief portion of the Prometheus chronology. And then, what to mark? In the original exhibit, the birth of the space age stood alone, and in effect erased atomic bomb tests, talks of nuclear disarmament, and Schulman's discovery of the oldest tree, ignoring what people want to leave behind and inscribing what they want in the future, perhaps. Because the history of Ely has been shaped by changes in conditions of the sort not revealed by the rings of any bristlecone, the meaning of these changes would not correlate well with the shapes of the rings either.

Russell R. Elliott, the preeminent historian of the state of Nevada, grew up in McGill but spent his adult life as a professor in Reno. He wrote in 1990, "It is not pleasant watching one's hometown decay slowly into a ghost town." What he meant is almost certainly not the same as what those who grew up in Jap Town, Greek Town, or Austrian Town might express by the very same sentence. Because history is mobile and unstable in White Pine County, the texts by which it is read are also subject to multiple readings. Elliott concluded that "it seems safe to say that the White Pine copper industry is a thing of the past."

It is hard for a town to imagine that its history comprises only its past, what it reads in the newspaper, or what is written—sometimes by itself—in guides for tourists, or that it is not heir to a continuous or lasting tradition. In a region where courthouses containing all civic records burn down on a regular basis, newspapers become the primary and only continuous sources for history. Yet it is hard to base a present or future on sheer nostalgia. And it has been hard for Ely to accept the idea that one source for enabling its own future prosperity may come from the belated discovery of trees which were overlooked and found worthless for a century, and which as a consequence still surround and precede its presence.

Elliott decided that tourism would be "a central part of the economic future of White Pine County." The materials one can receive from the Nevada Commission on Tourism, and from Ely itself, suggest that Ely's future is partly predicated on tourism and the kinds of journeys tourists take. Many of these tours lead to a kind of dead-ended terminus, like McGill on Ely's historic railroad, and then return home. Other journeys, like the west-to-east transit of the tourist commission's version of Highway 50, lead nowhere on an isolated ribbon of highway to broken connections.

Tracing the provenance of the bristlecone display is of interest in this regard. Owned by the Forest Service, it has moved out of a private business and into a Convention Center. The convention center itself is meant to inscribe Ely's new beginning toward a viable future—and perhaps meant to erase some of the past—in hopes that the city's future will not be determined by the forces or conditions of its origin. It is not exactly a community center. The White Pine County Fair and Recreation Board charges nothing for its use if more than half the conventioneers are from out of the county. Although it is in town, the display is for out-of-towners, and the short history of its travels suggests some caution in the ways one might speak of "owning" or "marketing" the "world's oldest living thing."

Ely might wish now to own the trees and the mountains which they inhabit, but these resources are entirely in federal lands. Ely might wish to own the name or image of the bristlecone, as copywritten for postcards, tourist brochures, or calendars. Ely would like to own the bragging rights to the original or oldest tree, if not to own the national park in which the forests of bristlecone pines are displayed. Ely would like to own the images of the trees on the

walls of the chamber of commerce's office. Darwin Lambert remembers a photograph of the Money Tree, as he called it, taken by
Erwin Fehr, the same tree that Bailey also photographed for his
taxonomy. This tree is still represented in the chamber's offices,
portrayed in a small oil painting. Ely owns none of these images,
and the oldest tree is dead, yet the city may—indeed it must—use
memories of the past to preserve its own life.

CHAPTER 11

The Trees Just Out of Town

Conditions in and around Ely

It is probable that many old groves have been preserved, and that Ely has been kept from turning into a ghost town, partly because the U.S. Forest Service allowed Currey to section his tree. The stories that followed made the bristlecone well known and established its value. These forests would never again be perceived or managed as worthless. The ensuing debate, publicity, and critique of the Forest Service's policies also gave park advocates a foothold. Even the idea of a national park brought increased tourism and some measure of economic support for a floundering city.

Cross-date the development of bristlecone science, the crisis in Ely's health, the evolution of Forest Service policies, and the advent of Great Basin National Park. The idea of an old tree and the idea of a modern community in the Great Basin intersect strangely. The intersection reveals relations among individual acts and social stability, and between nature and culture. When Schulman made the bristlecone pines of the western Great Basin famous, people in Ely felt no urgent need to refigure the town's own future. When Darwin Lambert and his colleagues formed a national park committee in the mid-1950s, a national park seemed to most people in Ely like a luxury or amenity. When the National Park Service released the result of field investigations in the Wheeler Peak area in 1959, the report generated no controversy. Ely's crisis came two decades later; then it struggled to control its fate, perhaps by seizing a new idea of an old tree and an old idea of a new national park.

During the decade between the closing of the mines and the advent of Great Basin National Park, chaos reigned in Ely, and a great fluctuation of civic hope and despair. This was the era when local residents began to notice the high incidence of disease and death by cancer among rural and urban populations, and especially among children, who contracted leukemia with horrifying frequency. Most believed that these diseases were a legacy of the nuclear bombs exploded in southern Nevada over several decades, and yet a cause-and-effect relationship between those tests and the deaths was virtually impossible to prove by statistical means.

Opportunities and nightmares both seemed to present themselves to people in northeastern Nevada. Late in 1979, for instance, the U.S. Air Force offered to introduce the MX missile system, a network of ghost trains carrying—or pretending to carry, in a sort of shell game—nuclear missiles on tracks that would crisscross basins in an area the size of Pennsylvania. According to military planners, this huge military reserve—actually a target for Soviet nuclear missiles—would straddle the border of Utah and Nevada.

A concurrent proposal for a huge power plant in Spring Valley promised to burn Utah coal, employ citizens in White Pine County, pollute the air of the adjacent Snake Range, and take all the water of the basin used by cattle ranchers. As always, Ely anticipated the possible reopening of the mines. In the meantime it lobbied successfully for a large state penitentiary. As a mining town, Ely had been coherent. But when faced with power plants and a prison, new deployments of nuclear weapons and the legacy of nuclear testing, the community split and branched like an old tree, deeply divided over many of these and other issues of land use, resource conservation, and health.

A Modest Proposal

"A National park centering on Wheeler Peak is such a natural idea that it generated spontaneously in different people," writes Darwin Lambert. Lambert himself, born in Kamas, Utah, grew up in the failed agricultural settlement of Metropolis, Nevada, a native of the Great Basin. He managed the White Pine Chamber of Commerce (1949–56), edited Ely weekly and daily newspapers (1956–61), and was elected to the Nevada State Assembly in 1954. By 1955 he had begun working for a park with friends in the White Pine Chamber of Commerce and Mines, as it was then called. Members of the chamber saw the park as part of a plan for economic diversification and quite explicitly as a way to break Kennecott Copper's overwhelming dominance of Ely. John Kinnear, the local manager of Kennecott in 1959, encouraged this idea because he knew that Kennecott would be shutting down sometime soon and the county would need another good source of income. Lambert says he desired to "represent the Great Basin," as he puts it, in the national park system. His wife, Eileen Lambert, also joined the campaign, and both wrote articles proposing a wilderness park.

Lambert acquired colleagues and help, locally and nationally. In the early days he found an ally in Weldon Heald, the Sierra Club writer, who lived in Arizona, and he later received support from David Brower of the Sierra Club, who, even in the late 1950s was particularly desirous of removing bristlecone forests—if not all forests—from Forest Service jurisdiction. Lambert and his allies obtained support and written testimony from scientists like Adolph Murie and later from other academics. Early supporters of the park came from Ely, but not from communities like Baker, closer to Wheeler Peak.

Over the years, the most influential supporters came from west and east, especially from academic ranks at the University of Nevada in Reno, from California, from the Wasatch Front where urban Utahns live, from the National Park Service, and from the National Parks and Conservation Association, on whose board Lambert eventually served. The arguments made nationally were of a traditional sort, in magazines like *Audubon, National Parks, National Wildlife, Reader's Digest,* and the *Sierra Club Bulletin.* During the 1960 presidential elections Lambert used his newspaper the *Ely Daily Times* to put in a good word to national politicians. Richard Nixon, the Republican nominee, had married a woman who was born in Ely.

"Nevada is the only western state that does not have a national park," wrote M. Burrell Bybee, chairman of the White Pine chamber's Great Basin National Park Committee. This kind of appeal to local or state pride ran into conflict with those local residents who did not wish to transfer Forest Service lands to the Park Service for fear of losing privileges they valued, such as grazing, wood cutting, hunting, mining, and even the harvesting of pine nuts. Indeed, many Nevadans did not think a national park in Nevada was a natural idea at all. At least the Forest Service was supposed to consider local needs first, they thought. When, in 1966, Secretary of the Interior Stewart Udall pointed out the significant payroll, the millions spent on development, and the substantial economic advantages of a park, Ely people often responded that a park would curtail hunting.

The furor over hunting was symbolic: national parks didn't fit with the idea of life or their place that many locals had. Mike Drakulich, for instance, clearly valued the old bristlecones and acted on his values. But he thought the idea of a national park in Nevada was as absurd as the idea of importing elephants and said the chamber's pleas sounded like shouting "We must have elephants in Nevada!" Others, like Joe Griggs of Baker, didn't want to see half a million casual sightseers every year disrupting the quiet communion of local communities in their chosen places.

Nevada's politicians fought among themselves over who should receive custody of federal lands, who owned the resources, and what life they were part of. Nevada senators Alan Bible and Howard W. Cannon represented, as western senators often do, the larger and more urban constituency; they supported the park and introduced bills to a sympathetic Udall as early as 1961. Congressman Walter S. Baring, representing the Nevada of ranching and mining, drew support from labor unions when he thwarted the park bills in the U.S. House of Representatives.

A new campaign was started in the 1970s. By this time, as Wes Ferguson had explained in 1968, bristlecones were objects of growing and passionate public interest. Schulman's discoveries may have been less powerful as arguments for reserving bristlecone groves than the controversy surrounding the cutting of WPN-114, because the latter event was used by writers like Lambert and Rowell to attack on the Forest Service and to plead for preservation. Individual bristlecone pines were idealized and turned into aesthetic icons in Lambert and Muench's coffee table book *Timberline Ancients.*

Inside the Forest Service

The response of the Forest Service to the park proposals and the evolution of policies toward bristlecones in northeastern Nevada can be broken into two eras, the years before Currey cut his tree and the years following, when the WPN-114 problem dominated the discussion. In the summer of 1963, for instance, Donald Cox proposed to his supervisor, W. L. Hansen, that the Forest Service could publicize the virtues of managing its Wheeler Peak Scenic Area under multiple use by showing how it was "fully developing the recreational resource." Part of this development included a road-building project to provide access to the high country near Wheeler Peak moraine, a project which park advocates would later attack. In November of 1964, Cox suggested to his supervisor that the Forest Service put out a news story on WPN-114, using pictures of the slab to publicize the Wheeler Peak Scenic Area. In July 1965 Cox did publicize the display at the Hotel Nevada. Local Forest Service personnel did not anticipate any adverse reaction to their policies. Floyd Iverson, regional forester, hoped the scenic area might be managed as a national recreation area, like the Sawtooth Mountains in Idaho.

But by spring of 1966, Iverson was watching his hopes shattered by the scandal over Currey's tree. He was lecturing his subordinates in Elko and Ely about public relations. Iverson had studied forestry at the University of California. As regional forester between 1957 and 1970 he sought, according to Thomas Alexander in his 1987 history of the Forest Service in the Intermountain Region, "to advance the cause of stewardship" by paying greater attention to environmental concerns and "by emphasizing interdisciplinary rather than more narrowly professional values."

"Small incidents sometimes precipitate major incidents," Iverson reminded his colleagues. He had been besieged by a "deluge of statements" about the sectioning of WPN-114 from conservationists, preservationists, and prominent scientists. Consequently, he asked District Ranger Cox and his new supervisor to critique the process from the beginning as to the "basis for cutting down the tree." He wanted them to assess the degree to which multiple-use policies were followed. But he went further, asking why sections of the tree were not distributed equitably to scientific institutions, questioning the desirability of exhibiting a section at the Hotel Nevada. He asked about the appropriateness of "making use of this material for paperweights or mementos and distributing them to anyone." His concluding question speaks for itself: "How astute were we in having Kennecott Corporation as our primary cooperator in making the display in Ely—a corporation which represents an industry that has, over the years, done much to prevent the passage of enabling legislation for a Park?" He expected this critique to be carried out in two weeks.

As his memoranda in the region's archives demonstrate, Iverson was trying to reshape Forest Service thinking in the Elko-Ely region. Forest Service people were used to saying, as Don Wilcox, Ely district ranger in the 1970s, did, that the Park Service managed people but the Forest Service managed resources. But Iverson saw how the forest-tree of multiple use was disseminated as material and as information to the public. There was no separating people problems from resource problems.

Donald Cox, in turn, solicited Currey's explanations for cutting the tree and passed them on to Iverson, along with his answers to the other questions. After reviewing the responses, Iverson answered his own questions two months later. In his arguments, he did not distinguish matters of policy from matters of publicity. Though he found Currey's statements about the events convincing, he pointed out that Schulman had already cut one old tree. Iverson could not justify the Forest Service's "taking down another ancient tree—especially from a controversial area." He was concerned that nobody at the University of Nevada had been consulted about Currey's project: "It usually pays off to be tied in closely with the leading educational institution in a state such as Nevada." He didn't think the Hotel Nevada was a dignified setting for the exhibit, or a congressman's desk a place for mementos from old trees. He believed the Forest Service should avoid the appearance of any alliance with Kennecott. He hoped that this process of critique would be helpful in " 'steering' a course in the future."

The future pointed to taking advice. On September 15, 1966, the Forest Service announced that it had contracted with the Laboratory of Tree-Ring Research for a two-year "in-depth" study of bristlecone pine in east-central Nevada. As his report of 1970 indicated, Wes Ferguson carried out an extensive and wide-ranging survey of the eastern edge of bristlecone forests in the Great Basin, from the Ruby Mountains to Mount Charleston in the Spring Mountains, but he failed to turn up an older tree. Two other researchers from the University of Arizona embarked on an independent investigation of the ecological relationships of the bristlecone forests in the region. The motive for commissioning expensive surveys by a separate institution has been variously interpreted. The critics of the Forest Service considered this a futile attempt to locate an older tree and thus vindicate the agency. But inside the Forest Service, Ferguson's survey was perceived as a significant change in direction toward resource preservation and interpretation. Ferguson sought places where long chronologies could be developed by scientists.

In the process of completing his work, Ferguson teamed up with Joe Griggs. Griggs (1938–1988) grew up in Claremont, California, and came to settle in Baker in the early 1960s, after attending Pomona College and the University of California at Davis. He worked as a builder, mechanic, electrician, ranch hand, packer, and guide. At various times in his career he worked for the Park Service and the Forest Service. He liked the Forest Service better because it was a hands-on kind of agency and didn't treat resources as if they were part of an artificial museum. His brother-in-law Dean Baker was a cattleman. Griggs was also a political activist. He helped organize opposition to the MX missile system and served on the board of Citizen Alert, a group which concerned itself with issues of nuclear dangers, water politics, militarization, Native American rights, and rural autonomy in the Great Basin.

Ferguson and Griggs laid out an "age interpretation site" for the first representative stand of bristlecones the visitor would encounter when walking toward Wheeler Peak moraine from the end of the road built into the Wheeler Peak Scenic Area. Ferguson dated the trees. Griggs built the interpretive loop and helped design nine interpretive signs for the Forest Service. These were meant to tell a story. Except for the first sign, they are still used by Great Basin National Park. The park's short "self-guided" nature path is actually an early exercise in Forest Service interpretive development. The Bristlecone Loop departs from the trail that the Forest Service named for Fred Solace, memorializing the ranger who had died of a heart attack while carrying out a slab of Currey's tree. When the Park Service took over in 1987, it did not retain Solace's name. Many Forest Service people have never forgiven the park for this symbolic erasure.

A Concrete Plan

While the Forest Service was creating an interpretive program for the trees in the Wheeler Peak Scenic Area, park proponents renewed their campaign. They had in hand an elaborate and concrete proposal, Robert Starr Waite's 1974 doctoral dissertation in geography at UCLA, an encyclopedic, multilayered cultural and natural history of the region, including a detailed management plan. Though his dissertation was entitled "The Proposed Great Basin National Park," it expressed a highly personal plan. He reprinted this loosely constructed document of two volumes, comprising nearly a thousand pages of typescript, and distributed it widely—in Utah and to U.S. congressmen. Donald Currey would later praise Waite's singular role in the creation of the park as "a quest destined to become legendary."

Waite devoted a substantial portion of his proposal to the management of bristlecones, making standard arguments about their scientific and aesthetic value, and he included many photos of old trees. He noted that bristlecone pines were concentrated in four areas of the Snake Range. He did not propose the Mount Moriah stand, north of Sacramento Pass, for part of his park. However, he claimed that two groves on the Wheeler Peak moraine and on Mount Washington represented some of "the finest bristlecone pine displays in the western United States." His view had a precedent. Joe Griggs considered one grove on Mount Washington to be "like an art gallery."

The operative term for Waite was "display." He outlined a plan for a short spur trail to the Wheeler Peak Stand, as he called it, containing the famous stump of WPN-114. In 1974 he still believed, against all evidence, that a tree older than WPN-114 grew in the grove on Wheeler Peak, and he included a photograph, courtesy of Donald Cox, of a tree once believed to be older. The Forest Service, he reported somewhat fancifully, was "currently planning to establish an outdoor display at the site" of WPN-114, which he hoped would be prepared by "polishing the stump and treating it with a preservative, with the dates of the aforementioned historical events depicted on its surface." He also suggested that the stump and the hypothetical older tree would be enclosed "by a solid steel fence" to prevent vandalism. He knew that Donald Currey had retained a second cross section from his tree which might be exhibited in the future, along with additional cross sections which Waite believed should be taken from the trunk for display in museums and scientific institutions.

He described the Mount Washington stand as the "largest and most diverse" forest in the range. It included not only LaMarche and Mooney's "fossil timberline," but a twenty-acre tract of fire-killed forest and a youthful community of trees. The fossil trees, Waite wrote, were exceptionally picturesque, weathered and bleached white by the sun, with "a stark ghostly appearance." Indeed, he admired this area, as others have, because it contained all the aesthetic forms of bristlecone growth. Waite detailed its forms, quoting Muir and others. He planned a "Mt. Washington Bristlecone Pine Exhibit" and a "Self-Guided Nature Trail" for the area, which would denote the physical characteristics of the tree and its habitat. His proposal—or prophecy—is still cited by the park's general management plan, but none of his plans for recreational development for the bristlecones have been implemented, and there are no indications that they will be developed in the future by the means Waite advocated. The Waite plan—a park constructed for "brief 'outdoor classroom' expeditions"—was precisely an idea people like Joe Griggs abhorred but helped to create.

At an interagency meeting in 1973, including the Forest Service, the Bureau of Land Management, and the Park Service, a representative of the White Mountain District introduced an interpretive plan for the bristlecone reserves in the White Mountains. The rangers there expected to carry out 95 percent of the bristlecone pine interpretation in the Great Basin. The interpretive site already developed by Griggs and Ferguson was a model deemed sufficient for the eastern Great Basin. And the group was careful to stress that "the major story would involve the Bristlecone Pine and its relationship to other plant communities and environments of the Great Basin." The group aimed to create high-quality signs dealing with basic concepts, along trails requiring that visitors spend about one hour of time. They hoped to "interpret communities or stands, not individual trees."

The *National* Park

The Great Basin was getting national exposure. John McPhee's *Basin and Range,* printed serially in the *New Yorker* in 1980 and as a book the following year, brought the idea of the geological Great Basin to public attention. McPhee's informant in Nevada, the geologist Ken Deffeyes, pursued silver, and the nature of his noble pursuit became, in McPhee's hands, a little metaphor for the rediscovery of the Great Basin. What Deffeyes sought was something in demand that could not be replaced but that people wanted. Because no major silver mine had been discovered since 1915, the solution was "secondary recovery," the scavenging of lesser or out-of-the-way mines, whose unextracted silver rested in the piles of rubble left as waste by previous generations. And Deffeyes' ideas about silver, McPhee commented, might send the Deffeyes children to college.

In the early 1980s the Park Service began to reevaluate its options for a park in Nevada, throwing a wide net over Nevada's basins and ranges and engaging in its own secondary recovery. The Park Service considered the Snake Range and Spring Valley, the Grant Range and Railroad Valley, the Monitor Range and Big Smokey Valley, and the White Mountains and Fish Lake Valley. Park planners dismissed the Ruby Mountains because, though "magnificent," they were not "characteristic" of Great Basin geography. This kind of second thought was followed by public polls in rural and urban Nevada.

No time could have been worse for a new national park in terms of the local and national political climates. Ely was in depression following the closure of the mines. Many residents of White Pine County and especially of Baker were deeply distrustful of the government that had bombed them with nuclear fallout since the 1950s and now offered to wipe out their way of life with an MX missile system. They thought of the park as another way to "take our land away from us." Though the White Pine Chamber of Commerce favored both the MX scheme and the national park, rural residents of the Great Basin, as Lambert remembers, were "bothered by the national park idea as much as the MX." People in Ely, Baker, and the entire region were never debating the merits of a park, but rather were arguing about the shape of the future and their stake in the resources surrounding them. Sharp divisions in the community saddened almost everyone.

A new Park Service study came out when James Watt was secretary of the interior, and President Reagan opposed any additions to the national parks in 1981. As late as 1985, Donald Hodel, Reagan's second secretary of the interior, said his department could not afford a new national park. Congressman Harry Reid of southern Nevada responded that Hodel was expressing a familiar arrogant view that "Nevada is nothing more than a federal colony" to be used for bombing ranges and nuclear dumps, but not "good enough for a national park."

The Great Basin National Park of 1986 is a belated park on a number of grounds. At 77,082 acres—120 square miles—it is about three-quarters of the size intended by Lambert and his allies and half the size of Waite's 147,000-acre park "with the boundaries being drawn to conform with the greatest scenic, scientific, and recreational values." It does not include a basin and includes only part of an island range. But it is "not fatally small," as Lambert puts it, and is a great deal larger than the 44,000 acres Hodel once offered.

In the constraints put upon its management, it is a peculiar park. Senators Paul Laxalt of Nevada and Orrin Hatch of Utah established a singular "multiple-use aspect" of the park—singular in modern parks of the lower forty-eight states. The senators wished to protect the ranching operation of one specific family. At present, three permittees graze animals on four allotments in the park. Each permittee has rights fixed in perpetuity, set at the precise number of animals that were grazed under Forest Service regulation. But these ranchers, who knew from the beginning that the handwriting was on the wall and expected to get "regulated out," have found it too difficult to graze animals in a national park. They are apparently willing to sell their options, and The Nature Conservancy plans to buy them and contribute them to the park.

Water rights at the park are carefully protected for downstream users, and the park ends where the range becomes basin. The park is an island within the National Forest and retains only the federal water rights originally established in Humboldt National Forest and Lehman Caves National Monument. Great Basin National Park is also a mountain island, shaped, as wilderness advocates like to say, like a "starfish" or "wilderness on the rocks," it contains only representative mountain landscapes. But it contains all of Waite's substantial groves of bristlecones, highlighted on the current *Official Map and Guide* in yellow. Two of these are significant for the history of bristlecone science, the Wheeler Peak stand Currey studied and from which Bailey took his holotype, and the one LaMarche and Mooney studied on Mount Washington, where Bailey's photo was taken.

Though a few bristlecone pines are protected in several other national parks, the current management plan points out that "none contain trees that are as old or as stressed as those in Great Basin National Park." The park has proposed specific management strategies, which consist largely of controlling human traffic: "Because of the extremely long life span of the bristlecone pines and the extremely slow rates of growth and recovery after damage, all impacts on bristlecones must be appraised from a longer term outlook."

It is hard to imagine a management strategy that stretches for thousands of years. Grazing of domestic livestock has not been permitted in the areas where old bristlecones grow, though this is a minor issue because there is little forage to attract cows or sheep. Primarily, the park plans to limit vandalism by visitors, addressing inadvertent physical damage from autos by closing a jeep road into the Mount Washington stand at the park boundary and by preventing soil compaction from off-trail hikers on the trail near the Wheeler Peak stand.

The Bristlecone Forest as a Management Category

Go where you will in the high mountains of Nevada and you will find bristlecones. There is an abundance of them. The reasons advanced for preserving old-growth forests in the twentieth century do not seem to apply to these groves. These are not the last bristlecones. They are not endangered by lumber companies. They do not create a major watershed for human habitation and agriculture.

Recreational possibilities in the groves are limited but conceivable. Arguments advanced in 1963, for instance, for the protection of "the last redwoods" in a national park because they were a "vanishing scenic resource" would not precisely apply to the bristlecones. The language of redwood preservation—"the last of an ancient race," "land of majestic forms," "a land of serenity and grace," "of wet and wildness"—could be used by writers like Darwin Lambert only in a limited way for bristlecone pines. The idea of protecting such a "useless" species did not appear until the late 1950s and did not seem compelling until the 1960s. Strategies for protecting such forests were consequently unclear. The plans for reserving and managing them evolved piecemeal from their uses, as they were discovered.

Yet many bristlecone forests fit the definition of wilderness in the Wilderness Act of 1964 quite precisely: "where man himself is a visitor who does not remain." They are affected primarily by the forces of nature; they are often in places of solitude; they occur where preservation is a possibility; and they are of great scientific, educational, and historic value.

In "The Value of Wilderness," Roderick Nash summarizes the conventional arguments established in the 1960s. Wilderness, "a reservoir of natural ecological processes," sustains "biological diversity" and is also an ideological resource, or, as Nash says, a "formative influence on American national character," a "nourisher of American Arts and Letters," a church, and a "guardian of mental health." Wilderness, he argues, sustains human diversity by encouraging individuality; establishing wilderness is an exercise in defending individual minority rights. Declared wildernesses become educational resources for developing a popular "sense of environmental responsibility."

Wilderness, however, is managed. Manage, from *manus,* means to take in hand, handle, train, direct, wield, rule, or administer. It is hard to imagine a management plan other than "preservation" for trees thousands of years old. The idea of wilderness as the place where "the hand of man has not set foot," as David Brower once put it, seemed neatly applicable to bristlecones, and yet it is not. In a dynamic natural system that changes as slowly as a bristlecone forest, the rate of change sought by managers must approach zero. Managers cannot accomplish this goal by doing nothing.

Bristlecone reserves become a special case of wilderness management practices because the trees approach the status of art in a museum, with curators who are given a spiritual charge to preserve the archives or collection. According to the contemporary Forest Service directions, standards, and guidelines, management strategy calls for shielding forests from "unnatural events" and must consist primarily of guarding forests from outside disturbances, human and other.

Obvious methods of protection include fences, trail signs, preventive laws, and prohibitions. Fire suppression has been an absolute commandment in the bristlecone forests of the White Mountains, and no camping is permitted. These groves are managed almost as if they were in a gated and fenced park. Early in the 1970s, reserve managers decided to concentrate interpretive activities in small areas where public access had been established. Less obvious methods of protection include guile on the part of managers who hide the oldest trees or dissemble about their whereabouts. Foxy management has established a place in the groves.

Designated Reserves

Consider a few of the many places where bristlecones are now protected or preserved. All of these reveal choices about a human future and about past choices, driven by issues of access. All reveal the

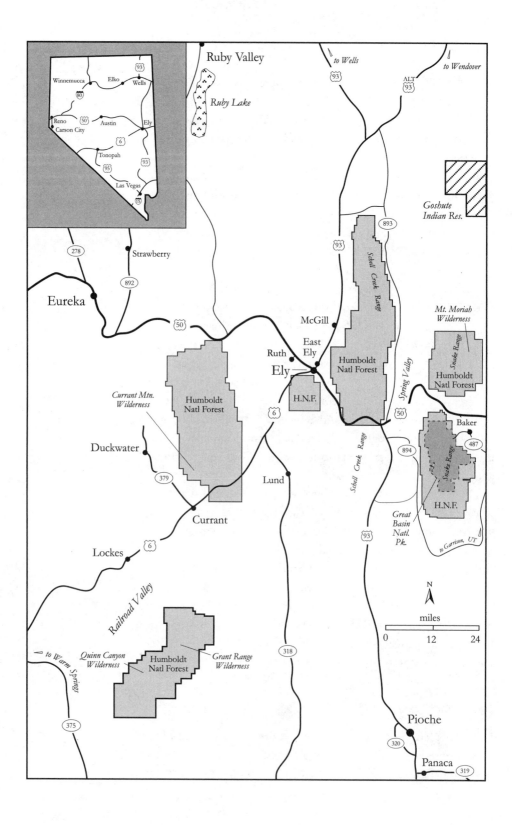

Ruby Valley

to Wells

to Wendover

Winnemucca • Elko • Wells
80
Reno • Austin • Ely
Carson City 50
6
Tonopah
95 93
Las Vegas

Ruby Lake

93

ALT
93

Goshute
Indian Res.

278

Strawberry

893

93

Eureka

892

50

McGill

Schell Creek Range

*Mt. Moriah
Wilderness*

East
Ely
Ruth
Ely

Humboldt
Natl Forest

Snake Range

Humboldt
Natl Forest

Spring Valley

50

Humboldt
Natl Forest

H.N.F.

*Currant Mtn.
Wilderness*

6

894

Baker
487

Duckwater

Schell Creek Range

Snake Range

H.N.F.

379

Lund

*Great
Basin
Natl.
Pk.*

Currant

93

to Garrison, UT

Lockes 6

N

Railroad Valley

miles

0   12   24

to Warm Springs

*Quinn Canyon
Wilderness*

Humboldt
Natl Forest

*Grant Range
Wilderness*

318

375

Pioche

320

Panaca

319

contradiction of human attention, which favors and destroys what it touches. I consider here only a few regions where bristlecones flourish. There are many others, some heavily used, like the Spring Mountains near Las Vegas, and some remote, like the Currant Mountain Wilderness, located forty miles southwest of Ely. Most of the high ranges in Nevada could be reserved. Many have been.

All bristlecone reserves were carved out of regions which had been managed by the U.S. Forest Service under the doctrine of multiple use. In the White Mountains, the research facilities built by the U.S. Navy were transferred in 1950 to the University of California. The first area of forest specifically singled out as a reserve was the Patriarch Grove, because it was strikingly scenic and because it contained the tree Alvin Noren had measured and proposed as the largest bristlecone. In 1958, as a result of Schulman's discoveries, 27,160 acres, including the Schulman and Patriarch Groves, were established by discretion of the chief of the Forest Service primarily for scientific research, but also for recreation. This area has grown in size and has been carefully monitored and developed as it has come under increasing pressure from tourism.

Great Basin National Park literally wrenched control of the southern Snake Range from the Forest Service. Recreation, at present, takes the forms established by the Forest Service, but it is now the chief purpose of the park where bristlecones are only one feature. Management plans for parks are always, like Waite's proposal, a prophecy, closely bound with issues of access and anticipated levels of visitation. In Great Basin National Park, bristlecones are managed to allow visitors to view the trees but also to keep viewers from the more sensitive groves. The designation of a park attracts visitors, as does the designation of special reserves and even of wilderness areas.

Management is dictated, to a great extent, by matters of access and proximity. Great Basin National Park is widely touted by the state of Nevada at the same time the newspaper in Ely hopes to bring in crowds by promising that the park is "far enough off the major tourist byways that there's still plenty of solitude for those seeking it."

Parks and declared wildernesses become the subjects of guidebooks, like John Hart's *Hiking the Great Basin* (1991) and Michael Kelsey's *Hiking and Climbing in the Great Basin National Park* (1988). Development does not always follow an elaborate physical plan, as in Waite's somewhat entrepreneurial proposal, but can

(opposite) **This map of the south portion of Humboldt National Forest indicates the discontinuity of the forest reserves— islands spread across the Great Basin. Note that these areas often contain smaller islands of wilderness within their borders. (adapted from the DeLorme *Nevada Atlas & Gazetteer* and U.S. Forest Service maps)**

result from widely disseminated knowledge as well. Places may have local significance. Local residents tend not to consider their landmarks as "features" or "attractions," and when they do, they may be revealing their own alienation from their locale. But the same places have different significances and uses for people who come specifically to "see the sights."

Mount Moriah Wilderness Area is a wilderness close to a park, and, one might imagine, receives a correspondingly greater recreational use. Perhaps not yet. But it will.

In stark contrast to the more accessible bristlecone groves, the Grant Range Wilderness, where Muir visited the bristlecones, includes 50,000 acres around Troy Peak and remains a remote and isolated management area. In some ways, areas like this are well protected by their inaccessibility and by the fact that no features are advertised. Neglect and ignorance—isn't this where the story of bristlecones began?—can protect a region or a species, but not for long. Nothing in this world can be hidden forever.

Research Natural Areas

In 1990 Nicholas S. Van Pelt of The Nature Conservancy and Thomas Swetnam of the Tree-Ring Lab demonstrated that sources of wood used in dendrochronology constituted valuable resources and were, in this aspect, "poorly understood forms of biodiversity." They pointed out that "chronology building represents a substantial societal investment" and that designation as federal Research Natural Areas could protect this investment.

Early in the 1990s the U.S. Forest Service began to expand a national network of what it called Research Natural Areas (RNAs). RNAs are lands protected for the purposes of maintaining biological diversity, unique or special species, or natural communities. By Forest Service standards, they "must be large enough to provide essentially unmodified conditions within their interiors." They are set aside as areas containing baseline conditions—the Forest Service uses the term "pristine" for these—of natural ecosystems. Because the Forest Service restricts these undisturbed systems or areas for conducting only nonmanipulative research and for the monitoring of relatively undisturbed natural processes, the RNAs serve as control areas for places where more manipulative research and management techniques are applied.

The Nature Conservancy has encouraged the process of creating

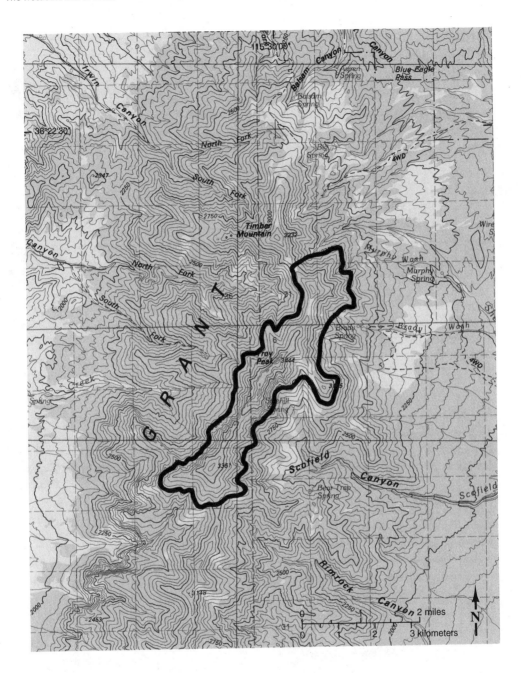

Proposed Troy Peak Research Natural Area. (from Quinn Canyon Range, Nevada [1:100 000-scale metric topographic map], U.S. Geological Survey, 1988)

Research National Areas and has often been engaged in identifying particular areas for consideration. Staff members of The Nature Conservancy have produced studies of these lands for the Forest Service, writing evaluations and proposals—by contract, cost sharing, or other means—and providing justifications for inclusion of such lands in the network. The Nature Conservancy has also com-

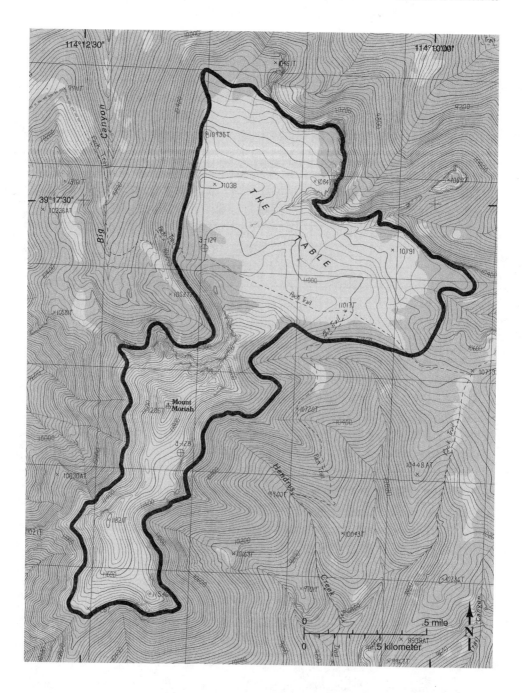

pleted the paperwork necessary for establishing candidate RNAs, supported their designation in the forest planning process, and helped to develop management strategies.

Two such areas, studied by staff of The Nature Conservancy and under consideration by the national Forest Service, are in the Grant

Range Wilderness and the Mount Moriah Wilderness. Both of these contain stands of bristlecones, but the bristlecone is not the sole reason for making these areas RNAs.

A biodiversity reserve is most effectively established within a wilderness area because this method of zoning allows managers to embed an island within an island. The high mountain ranges of the Great Basin—which are largely undisturbed, often treated by biogeographers as islands, and particularly interesting to conservation biologists—provide nearly ideal examples of regions where an RNA can be successfully created and maintained. This particular strategy of designation and management of RNAs allows the Forest Service and other agencies (the Bureau of Land Management in the Wah Wah Mountains of southern Utah, for instance) to update or revise wilderness management from within and manage from a more sophisticated biotic perspective than the Wilderness Act seems to incarnate.

Consequently, the Grant Range and Mount Moriah Wilderness are excellent RNA candidates. Established as wilderness areas in 1989, they are already managed to "protect bristlecone pine from unnatural events," to protect living trees and remnants from destruction or removal, and to carefully regulate wood cutting or disturbance.

The proposed Troy Peak Research National Area, an island of approximately 2,500 acres above 9,600 feet in elevation, encompasses most of the bristlecone pines on the peak, includes a habitat of desert bighorn sheep, and contains a couple of rare species of plants. Designation as an RNA appears to offer no conflicts with recreational use or wilderness designation. Livestock grazing is already minimal in the region because the Forest Service has been concerned for the welfare of a band of sixty to one hundred desert bighorn sheep resident in the range. The Humboldt National Forest had proposed an RNA on Mount Washington, in what is now the national park, and the Troy Peak RNA provides a similar ecological setting. It also includes some sensitive plant species (*Primula nevadensis* and *Silene nachlingerae*).

Like the Troy, the proposed Mount Moriah RNA of 1,800 acres includes subalpine forest, subalpine steppe, and alpine regions. Like Troy Peak, it includes habitats for bighorn sheep and *Silene nachlingerae*. Both regions include spectacular geomorphic features and major Great Basin mountain summits. On Mount Moriah, the RNA would include the unique region called The Table, an im-

(opposite) **Proposed Mount Moriah Research Natural Area. (from Mt. Moriah Quadrangle, Nevada, White Pine County, 7.5 minute series [topographic, 1:24 000 scale], Provisional Edition, U.S. Geological Survey, 1986)**

mense white plateau dotted with bristlecones, looking like a gigantic Zen garden high in the sky. What is the fate of these regions for the future? Perhaps, as protected islands, they should be considered forests in exile, awaiting the next ice age.

The modern history of the bristlecones is short and astonishing. How long it took for anyone to discover a use for them, how short a time it took for them to be studied, and how quickly their value was seen and protected. How many places they grow and how wonderfully. Yet now, after so much knowledge has been abstracted from these trees, their value still continues to change. Nobody knows what they mean for the future.

CHAPTER 12

Walks in Woods

After such knowledge, what forgiveness? Think now
History has many cunning passages, contrived corridors
And issues, deceives with whispering ambitions,
Guides us by vanities. Think now
She gives when our attention is distracted
And what she gives, gives with such supple confusions
That the giving famishes the craving.
                              —T. S. Eliot, "Gerontion"

Exposure

When I walk in this forest of the Great Basin, sometimes a great
sadness comes over me. Going to the bristlecone forests is not very
much like going home. I remind myself that this kind of forest
grows here, in a landscape of great beauty and of great terror. The
forests seem to offer an openness, not the protective openness of the
ponderosa forests of the Kaibab Plateau, nor the luxurious en-
closure of forests of the west slopes of the Sierra, but something else.

It does not take too long to learn where the old trees will be
growing, and I can find them now, in most ranges of this region.
What I feel in these forests, and especially on the ridges where the
old trees grow, is something personal and yet not personal at all. I
want to use the word consolation, yet know it is not the right word.
It is not that I accept these forests as a consolation, but that I find
they are where I belong some of the time. These forests do not
console. What I experience in them is not happiness, but it might
be joy.

In *National Geographic,* Edmund Schulman and friends sit on a
blanket as a foreground for the Patriarch Tree—"its age is a mere
1500 years"—as they "break their tree study with a picnic." The
friends seem to be a family. A father pours a cool drink out of a

metal jug for a young boy while the boy's mother watches. The picnic is contained in a cardboard carton marked "Burgie."

I have gazed at this photograph wondering what is wrong with it. Certainly it is posed. (As a child, I myself posed for such photographs which later appeared in *National Geographic*. I know how these images are constructed.) Schulman sits, somewhat awkwardly, on the right side of the blanket. I place my right hand over his image and see the family group, totally absorbed in its own drama, oblivious to its surroundings. I place my left hand over the family group and Schulman is alone, staring into space. There are two images here. They are not easily combined.

What is a picnic? I wonder about the Patriarch Grove as a site for a picnic. It does not seem an appropriate setting for a pleasant or amusingly carefree experience of eating in the open. The Patriarch Grove is certainly in the open. It is as exposed a place as can be imagined, and when I am there I feel exposed as I have felt part way up the face of El Capitan, surrounded on all sides by thousands of feet of vertical naked granite. This place, among the trees right below timberline, seems to me a place where one is not amusingly carefree, but rather a place that calls for thinking as carefully as one can.

Walking Around in a Daze

Time grows sacred high in these forests. A walk around an old tree might follow certain conventions, like a ritual, because one way to think is to walk around. A walk under the aspect of sacred time has often been depicted as a circular ritual, presided over by some god who stands left foot at the beginning of history and right foot at the end, making a gesture of Revelation, saying: "I am Alpha and Omega."

What is revealed? Consider a version of this walk invented three centuries ago by the Anglican cleric Thomas Burnet and discussed at length by Stephen Jay Gould in *Time's Arrow, Time's Cycle*. This is a walk of faith, where God's words and work, established in concord, lead to harmony. On this walk, the earth's history seems to move clockwise, in seven steps. It begins in chaos, the earth without form and void. Following the resolution of chaos into a series of smooth concentric layers, the earth assumes the perfection of paradise. The third step is the flood, a punishment for our sins. The waters retreat, leaving the cracked crust of the earth we live upon, "a broken and confused heap of bodies." In times to come, the earth shall be consumed with fire, made smooth again as descending soot and ashes establish concentric perfection. Finally the earth shall become a star. I think of Burnet's walk as an interesting narrative, but I do not believe it.

What can a modern person make of Burnet's theological-geological walk? It is an abstraction, unconnected to my experience. My generation has its own abstractions. I read a book where a mathematician speaks of genetic changes as one-dimensional and multi-dimensional random walks in random environments. David Ruelle writes in *Chance and Chaos,* "Random walks in a random environment are known to proceed very slowly, because to go from one mountain to another it is first necessary to climb down, and this is a very unlikely process." Ruelle writes that the random walk tends to be trapped on the tops of small mountains. The mountains he describes are models, like Burnet's earth, and the walks he takes are evolutionary-mathematical journeys. Nobody walks literally upon such mountains.

During the three-hundred-year transformation between Burnet's and Ruelle's thinking, the bristlecone itself stands unmoved and yet embodies time and change of an era an order of magnitude greater than this human history of mental travel. The bristlecone pine presents itself according to competing human theories of time. An observer faces at least one dilemma, torn between linear contingent history and a cyclical complete history. How to solve the Gordian knot of time? Reconstruct it, as Ferguson did? Cut it, as Currey did? Untie it, as Fritts attempted? Time is invisible, and yet it is embodied. People read it in trees. Can they read, resolve, untie time? My friend Michael Branch tells me that Emerson wrote, "That science is bankrupt which attempts to cut the knot which always spirit must untie."

As it seems to embody the line of time, a weathered snag might be an arrow or vector, or a quiver of them, pointing up or down, in or out, west to east, north to south. A tree seems to reach, from the ground upward into the sky. Many die in this act, but not entirely. Traveling through their own latitudes, bristlecone pines have been a unique phenomenon, born out of imperfect life and truly tentative. The oddness of each tree's form represents perhaps what Darwin found in life, a quirkiness characterized by abrupt twists or curves, peculiar traits, accidents, and vagaries.

This linear and contingent tree seems to suggest a world of irreversible change and in its form to represent some genealogical plot, be it progress or digress. Its complexity, according to the archetypal branching of any tree, becomes so stark and irregular, asymmetrical and sharp, that it suggests more than just a tree, as Darwin Lambert has observed.

Trees are so closely related to human ideas of time that humans, trees, and time cannot be untangled. Each tree embodies some idea of time. Each old tree is different from the next one. What holds them in common is, strangely, the differences people perceive in them. None seem to agree in position, value, structure, or function. Why are there different trees in similar positions? or similar trees in different positions?

Because each tree seems unique, each seems to reside outside human conceptions of time. If each tree behaved according to prominent human conceptions of time, then each tree would hide and display some perfect form, shaped according to some law of its immanent regularity, but difficult to perceive, just beyond the reach of understanding. Changeless and eternal, its life somehow concealing a symmetrical cycle, each unique tree—from this perspective— would reveal or reflect some set of recurring conditions or laws.

Each tree's history, as read by people who think obsessively of bristlecones, is told in terms of human time. This tree, in the present. Look at it. It expresses its life. Shall I treat the present tree as an object maintained by physical processes, revealing the work of physical conditions, or as a living being striving for a definite purpose? Or shall I depict it as a piece of architecture, as nature's sculpture?

Does change come to the tree from inside or outside? According to the perspective of time's arrow, a tree's life is a set of irreversible changes, like a chess game. Trees are faced with cooler climates, more complex life, catastrophe perhaps, or maybe the opposite. According to the perspective of time's cycle, the tree's changes have no direction except to elaborate some stately cycle, and a tree's form is a rational incarnation of rate and state. Every tree transacts some cyclical business with its environment. Yet if a tree's life is an actual cycle, its very regularity suggests a paradox and a psychological abyss. "If moments have no distinction, then they have no interest," writes Stephen Jay Gould. If everything in the form and meaning of a tree repeats, then no event has distinction. We enter the world of Herman Melville's "truest of all books," Ecclesiastes, in whose cycle, made of "the fine hammered steel of woe," "All is vanity."

As Ecclesiastes suggests, it depends on how old you are. A young man might be an empiricist, insisting that experience precedes expression, believing that any true theory of trees must rest on observation, be framed by a large body of evidence, which leads by induction to theory. The young man might be a creator of theories, but only after many renewed attempts at expression. Walk again and again in the forest, he might say, until you get it right. But an older man might be a theorist, believing that there is no such thing as pure induction, that all theories come from theory, that we are all victims of these ways of thinking, and every tree represents what we bring to our perception of it. It is a simplistic idea that any theory was born of, or triumphed entirely by, field work. It seems, finally, that one must be young and old to see the tree from its linear and cyclical aspects.

Do physical objects have purposes shaped in human terms? Final causes? Are they put here for us? Scientists are not supposed to believe this, but do they act as if they believe this? What does it mean when one spends a human life making a forest into a tool for reading time and change, or spends a life painting endlessly the forms of these trees, if not that they were put here for us and we were put here to utilize them? Beavers do not ask why they chew on trees, but surely humans do ask, even if they never know fully what they try to digest, or why.

All of this is a great deal to think while taking a walk in a bristlecone forest, but it is all there, potentially, for those who wish to approach.

Fidelity

People snatch up truths, as they do in Sherwood Anderson's *Winesburg, Ohio*. An old man might have a theory about snatching: "that the moment one of the people took one of the truths to himself, called it his truth, and tried to live his life by it, he became a grotesque and the truth he embraced became a falsehood."

There is the philosopher's tree, for instance, representing truth achieved through intellect, a tree of identity and difference. For this tree, the question of "the other" is a complex of questions, of the relations between the one and the many, the reduction of the many to the one. There is the artist's tree, of wholeness, harmony, and radiance, sought through strategies of silence, exile, and cunning. There is the sociologist's tree of the diaspora, sowed or scattered outside traditional homelands. There is the businessman's tree of commodity. The meanings of these trees are determined by the orientations of the minds grasping them. Several meanings might be grasped by a patient person who chooses carefully, who tries not to snatch, who places the meanings before the mind as an array without hierarchy. But nobody knows everything, and nobody can place ideas before the mind without making choices.

How then can one achieve fidelity to these trees? Some people attempt to know or love them all by loving one tree, in the belief that choosing to know can be choosing to love. These people some-times focus on an individual, seeking the one extravagant gesture containing them all. And others achieve fidelity by focusing on no one tree, but encounter one after another. Consider the following exercise, where I attempt to embody the bristlecone pines in lan-guage and diagram my sentences as sets of possibilities. The ele-ments of each sentence can be shuffled within this hierarchy, to create a new order.

> *Young pines grow in advantageous exposures,*
> *where tall straight forests flourish,*
> *their trunks covered with bark all around;*
> *their shaggy sprays of foliage bow and bend,*
> *cluster dense and lawless on lee sides,*
> *diverge like hair charged by static electricity,*
> *in all directions,*
> *regarding gravity but not submitting,*
> *the needles themselves uneven,*
> *dense, and compact, fat and thin,*
> *like some digression or conflict*
> *blooming as if by inner compulsion,*
> *leaping out of symmetry or order, in endless iteration,*
> *tentative yet insistent, dark yet careless.*

> *Old trees,*
> *thick and contorted,*
> *knotted and twisted,*
> *the limbs themselves convoluted near their base,*
> *one or many of their craggy spikes*
> *isolated or clustered,*
> *high above the foliage,*
> *sometimes called aeries, but dead ends,*
> *so the trees seem to grow and stop and grow again;*

their lives have been pruned by relentless wind and drought and ice
   but persist,
   in a spiral of live bark up a single limb,
   like a seal struck by lightning,
      as it exposes and scours a bright strip of heartwood
      down the bark of a straight and healthy tree;
this line we call strip growth
   is to the lightning scar a negative,
   it does not indent but projects,
   like a glove turned inside out.

Mostly, heartwood meets the eye;
   naked, skeletal, gray, and split, caked with lime,
   or bright, sharp, and polished at the upper treeline;
      as if vision came from the direction of the wind;
   in many recognizable forms,
      some stark and striking,
      some that seem to multiply,
   almost always irregular;
past middle age, when anomalies become substance,
   diverging forms keep their distance on steep hillsides,
   ring by ring their differences multiply,
      by accretion, proliferation,
      the increments of their changes
      not quite coherent,
         like loose sentences,
            of the kind we are told to avoid,
               in series.

In the White Mountains

There is no sign for the Methuselah Tree, and the Forest Service
interpreter to whom visitors listen at the Schulman Grove before
taking a walk claims even the new district ranger doesn't know
which one it is.

All the old trees have little numbered aluminum tags nailed to
them. Near the likely region of the oldest one, even the scraps of
wood are tagged. TMC 281, TMC 290. There is no point in asking
about these tags. They are referenced to collections in Tucson, and
we are not supposed to see them. Searching is illegal. We are in-

structed to stay on the trail, because it is feared that we ourselves, as agents of erosion, will damage and undermine the remaining old trees. This is a reasonable fear. I have been told that sixty thousand people a year now visit the Schulman Grove, all during a very short summer season. Yet, knowing only a little about the nature of these trees and of the methods used by the early researchers, one knows, without doubt, where the Methuselah Tree ought to be.

People come here even though the tree is neither monumental nor labeled. They come here via a long and arduous drive. They batter their autos on the steep gravel track between the Schulman and the Patriarch Groves. They come even though there is only one camping spot in the region, down in the band of piñon and juniper, dusty and with no water. They come to see the oldest thing, and then they don't see it, or if they see it, they don't know it is THE ONE, and yet they seem mostly pleased.

These places, we are told, are not really for us but for scientific study. Thus continues the institutional idea that the trees and these mountains are primarily a scientific resource. That, we are told, is their value, or more precisely our value. Don't touch, don't leave the trail, we are told. Don't pick up anything.

I am a walker; I feel that now as I walk. I must saunter among the trees, even if on the trail. Indeed, I find myself often retracing my steps along the trail to make sure I have not missed anything or misunderstood. Yet everything seems quite simple around here. There are the trees and the rocky slope, the sun and the wind, life and death. The trail is like my mind, taking me to the place in a certain way and not in others, denying me certain things it would not have me know. I am told, for instance, that it used to pass close to the Methuselah Tree but was reconstructed to avoid this relic. I will not say whether I am ever tempted to leave the trail; I will not incriminate myself.

At one point, I see the oldest mountain mahogany I have ever seen, much older than the one outside my kitchen window; this one has been dated at more than 280 years, or so I am told. There is no sign. There is a bigger mahogany somewhere on Wheeler Peak, perhaps the biggest one in the world. It has a sign. Everything has been measured and has a date here, but no date is distinct. I see many old trees, am among so many old trees, that finally which is the oldest among them seems inconsequential.

Walking among these bristlecone pines is a great relief, for it has helped me to see myself more clearly, and what I see is that I am a fifty-year-old man who would walk for a long time among these trees whose lives are of a different order than himself, just for the pleasure in it. Surely there is something large and monumental as well as small and tortured in this realization.

But we want to interact with the trees, and consequently we break the rules. My teenage son climbs high up into the forked golden boughs of a dead and polished snag in the Patriarch Grove. I had forgotten to tell him not to do so. I walk by, oblivious; he speaks to me, but I cannot locate his voice. I do not expect to find my son twenty feet above the ground. And when I see him, I know he shouldn't be in a bristlecone, but it is too late. He knows too, and yet they are so beautiful together, I am silent. Because I do not know what it might mean to him to be within that tree, I respect his way of being in these woods.

My wife steals off the path too, as she has been doing for years, to find places where she can sketch. She has produced many paintings of these trees, and sold some. There will be more. As you can guess from my family's behavior, these groves are insufficiently policed.

Our walks, of course, are fanciful. When one writes it is of memories. So are my wife's drawings and paintings: she will draw every one of these trees, if only she lives long enough. At the university where I teach, its insignia an image of the bristlecone underscored by the motto "Learning Lives Forever," in the middle of our campus, at the base of a grassy knoll, there are some supine limbs of dead bristlecone, brought from the mountains, the wood gray and rotting. Some of my cynical colleagues have been heard to mutter, "Learning *takes* forever, you mean." That may be true, but it is a more universal dictum than they suppose. What has the bristlecone learned, absorbed, or recorded in its long life—ignoring for the moment whether it is conscious or not—that we may learn from it, now that we are ready? Or, more darkly put, what have we not learned from this bristlecone, we who will someday die, from these trees who seem to take forever dying?

The bristlecones seem to be at the source of so many kinds of knowledge that we acquire by looking at the inner and outer forms of the tree, at its surroundings, conversing, reading, drawing, painting, studying photographs, and writing. And yet here on this mountain, in the sky, there are still the trees themselves, inexhaustible, old and young, monumental and insignificant, living and dying, big and small, of the past and of the future. What little we know of them seems to have demolished so many singular or linear theories of ourselves, of the single source of civilization, of a single line of history, of simple cycles of weather. Look off to the northeast and see them trail across the mountainsides until they fade in the distance, with no end in sight, perhaps some of them older and more mysterious than any we have yet discovered.

Still, I wonder. People have only recently been ready to learn anything from the bristlecone; our relations to this tree until the mid-twentieth century have been very casual. Now, when things seem to have gotten serious, we have to ask another question. What are we trying to know?

We cannot escape the present. We do not have the luxury to evade history, except through deliberate ignorance, a path I cannot take. Consequently, when I go to the bristlecone forests, I carry with me all the language and all the perceptions I have read about the tree. Perhaps because I am conscious of the sources of these words and perspectives, I am less constrained by them than I would be if I went in ignorance. Perhaps I should pretend to see as a child. (As if I could enter the photos printed by the Nevada Commission on Tourism.) In fact, I know that knowledge limits, constricts, restrains, but also liberates by opening and widening my perspectives. All of my time in these woods is in some sense stolen time. I take my walks among these trees and choose.

Ron and Charlie

On September 11, 1995, I spoke on the telephone with Ranger Jay Pence in the office of the Humboldt National Forest in Ely, Nevada. I wanted to know about the bristlecone pines on Troy Peak in the Grant Range, through which John Muir had walked in the fall of 1878. The Grant Range is fifty miles from nothing, a hundred miles or so southwest of Ely. Muir claimed that the trees grew thick and healthy there, young and upright, foresting the ridges in shady profusion.

Ranger Pence told me that a couple of volunteers stayed out there from spring until the water froze: Ron and Charlie, retired fellows, fifty-five or sixty, but good walkers, all legs and lungs. They had a small white trailer and an orange van up near the end of the road. They would take me anywhere I wanted to go.

As I drove up Scofield Canyon the next day, I began to see signs of Ron and Charlie. Water bars, little ridges of gravel and soil that cut at diagonals across the hot road like speed bumps, but meant to divert water off to the sides. As the road got steeper, their frequency increased until I had eased the car over more than twenty-five of them. They were dug by hand; every one was perfectly straight and smoothly rounded. The one-lane track, as a result, was flat and even between them.

I found not a single can, Kleenex, or piece of litter in the entire canyon. There is a pipe at a spring and some mess at an old sawmill's ruin. Ron said the Forest Service wouldn't let them clean it up because it was supposedly an archaeological site. They had cut grass at the roadhead around a neatly constructed fire ring. They had made another ring at a nearly monastic campsite in the trees, adding a low bench and a small stove platform. The fire pits contained no ashes, and in the warm weather, I did not use one.

Now I first met Charlie, explaining that I was not lost but indeed looking for him. He said Ron had the maps and was off in Rimrock Canyon walking around. Charlie was waiting for a biologist who said he'd be up sometime this week, probably. So he couldn't go with me, but he advised a walk up the south fork of the canyon, then ascending the ridge and following it to Peak 11,028.

I didn't think I would make it that day, the time being about 12:30 P.M. and the elevation at the roadhead about 7,300 feet. But Charlie seemed to think that ridge was the right place for an afternoon. I asked if there was a trail, but he said maybe two or three people had gone up this year and then of course, he and Ron. He looked like he was in pretty good shape, said he was sixty-one. We talked about shoes. He said he and Ron waited for sales at Big 5 and went out buying all the sale boots in their sizes at the various stores around Las Vegas, which was OK as long as the shoes fit. They wore out fast on the limestone. I asked how much water he carried, and he said half a gallon, which he usually tried to refill at a spring on the way down, since their camp was dry. We discussed the route and trees in general, and he said looking at bristlecones always made him joyful. There were a lot of flies around, which didn't seem to bother him much. He said there was some steep loose rock up there, but after that the walking got better.

Virtually no water flows in the Grant Range. Sidehill and Bear Trap Springs come out of the limestone about twelve hundred feet above the area where Ron and Charlie hang out at the end of the road, flow for a few feet and then disappear again, never to resurface. Ron and Charlie say they have never seen water flow in the streambed by their little camp, not even in the heaviest cloudbursts. They have spent every summer here since the Grant Range was declared wilderness in 1989. Snowmelt never makes it down to their camp in the piñon-juniper.

I spent the afternoon walking up the ridge between Scofield and

Rimrock Canyons, saw a few footprints, about as many as you can count on both hands. And I saw a bristlecone forest.

In Indian summer, when grasshoppers snap in the dry golden grass, walking up through the aspens, past the spruces, into the "tallest and most evenly planted" growth of bristlecone he had ever seen, Muir found a true forest advancing north and south for miles along a waving ridge. Straight in the bole, these trees produced a shady growth. He thought some were more than eighty feet tall. Unlikely. (Ron accused Muir of hyperbole.) But the limestone ridge on which I found myself supports a forest of young and vigorous trees, young but many of them large, being six feet in diameter, dense yet airy, typically six to eight feet apart, and many of them are doubles.

In the Grant Range, the Limber Pine–Bristlecone Pine Zone is typical and yet not what people have come to expect when they visit bristlecones. Where there is scarcely a spring, and no running creek for miles, the ridges seem perfectly suited to the bristlecone pine. The ground is rocky but more than usually covered with bristlecone and limber needles and cones; the two species one often finds standing in pairs, next to each other as if asking for comparison. Such a density of life is wonderful and dangerous. This is a forest which can burn and has, near Bordoli Peak, south along the ridge. As I climbed higher, I watched the bristlecones predominate, but not entirely, for it is not accurate to speak of relations in the Grant Range as a competition. The bristlecones, for that is what I sought, were everywhere, remarkable and unremarkable, more like each other than different. On isolated, particularly rocky outcrops there are craggy trees, the kind you see in picture books. Yet in the forest itself, not distracted by individuals, I was impressed, as one is not normally in the bristlecone forests, by the profusion and extravagance.

This is nothing like the more famous and more frequently visited forest on Wheeler Peak. (Interesting: Muir himself reports seeing no bristlecones on Wheeler Peak.) The forest on Wheeler is justly famous for its old and picturesque trees, and for an old stump. I visited the site a couple of days later, but that is another story. The trees on Wheeler Peak give no sense of what the trees will do when in an environment conducive to their nature.

Strangely, walking the ridges of Troy Peak, in an isolated range of the Great Basin visited by scarcely more than a score of hikers each season, one feels one is in a domestic environment, yet when visiting the grove of Great Basin National Park, where one is scarcely ever out of sound or sight of other hikers, one feels a sense of isolation. One is, of course, attending to the way the trees themselves seem to fit or adapt to their environment. On a warm, clear fall afternoon, a light breeze waving the heavy thick foliage of the trees, walking in the shade and carrying plenty of water, it is always comfortable at elevations above 10,000 feet in the mountains of the Great Basin. Such weather may tempt one to overly expressive language, to say that the bristlecone is fully at home on Troy Peak, or that it is barely surviving on the moraine east of the Wheeler Peak glacial cirque, but these expressions also approach accurate representation.

The whole experience was, as Hemingway might have written, very satisfactory. I was moved. The great flat expanses of Railroad Valley and Coal Valley and Garden Valley, the canyons, and the thick forest of bristlecones, so thick I could at times scarcely see out, even though I was on a sharp ridge.

Here in the forests of Troy Peak one has such a sharp sense of differences, between the world up high and the world below, between the tree as it makes a forest and as it makes a monument, between the bristlecone forest as it is and the bristlecone as an attraction, between bristlecone as an everyday matter of fact and the tree as a source of curiosity. Here there are so many trees—at the moderate age of maybe a thousand years—they seem almost unremarkable, and it is a relief to know that there is nothing special to draw anyone to this place for any reason except to walk among them.

When I got back to camp, Ron was cleaning up and trimming his beard in preparation for meeting me, apparently, though neither they nor I had any reason to believe I was an important visitor. Now Charlie and Ron are both of medium height and slim. Charlie clean-shaven with short brown hair and Ron evenly gray on the top of his head and in his beard. Charlie wears trifocals, but Ron doesn't wear glasses. They have that loose way of walking that people have who are comfortable with their bodies and comfortable with the place where they live. Ron stutters, which doesn't stop him from talking a lot, almost as much as I talk. He said he was nervous with me, and when that passed he wouldn't stutter much.

We looked at maps, and they invited me to go on a walk the next morning. I told them I didn't think I could climb another four thousand feet to Troy Peak the next day, but I would go for a way with them. Charlie kept saying they would love to take me, and Ron said they liked to keep busy. This would be a way for them to go walking while keeping busy. Anyway, walking didn't make you any more tired than you already were.

The next morning we started up the north fork of Scofield Canyon, heading for the massive limestone wall that hangs below the east face of Troy Peak. Ron picked up an old shovel blade at the sawmill ruins, to scoop up and bury a dog dropping which we ran across about a hundred yards later.

I told them how much I admired the grassy hills that came down below the cliffs, steep hills like the ones on the coast range of California. These hillsides hadn't been grazed by domestic livestock for some years, not since the Forest Service had brought in bighorn sheep. Ron and Charlie believe the deep grass on these slopes, in such a dry range, constitutes an object lesson for the management of Great Basin National Park, where grazing permits continue.

About the time we got up a thousand feet or so, at Sidehill Spring, I was having such a good time I knew I'd follow these guys anywhere. I told them I thought I could make Troy Peak, if they wanted to go, but Ron said, "You've got two choices. We can go to Troy Peak, which is where everyone goes, or we can take you up to the big bristlecones on the ridge and the limestone arch we found." I told him we should go to the trees and arch and he said, "Good choice. The trouble with those peak-baggers is they only want to do one thing."

Now Ron and Charlie climbed Troy Peak about thirteen times that summer, which is about twice a week, and on one trip they spent five days at the top. They were disassembling a radio repeater station which didn't belong there. Maybe the ranchers had put it up there, they thought, or else it was a military installation. Nobody would tell them for sure. It went up by helicopter, they assumed, but the Forest Service said it would have to go down by foot. They were supposed to get help from some Nevada wilderness groups, but only two people showed up, and they were pretty old, so mostly Ron and Charlie carried the whole thing down themselves, with some help from Forest Service people. They used Shoe-Goo to seal the big batteries. They hacksawed all the pipe up into manageable sizes and packed the whole mess down.

Turns out, they found something interesting a couple of years ago on the ridges below the limestone cliffs: a big tree, maybe the biggest bristlecone in Nevada, and a big arch, fifty feet across. They believe it is bigger than Lexington Arch in Great Basin National

Park. The Forest Service was interested in the tree, though no Forest Service people had been to see it, and Charlie had sent pictures of the arch to the office in Ely, but nobody had visited it. You couldn't see the arch from the canyon. Turns out they had taken three people to the tree and arch. I would be the fourth.

The trees were spectacular as big old bristlecones often are. They were big, old, excellent examples of the so-called strip growth of weathered bristlecones, and in a spectacular position at somewhere around 10,000 feet on a ridge which sits in the middle of the huge amphitheater below the south ridge of Troy Peak. As Ron commented, climbing Troy Peak was fine, but on this walk you felt like you were *in* the mountains.

The ridge we ascended was steep rough country, and they followed a few small cairns they had put in the year before to remind themselves of the right route. Then there was a long traverse under overhanging limestone cliffs, with a lot of blind alleys and steep limestone ridges you had to pass to get to the arch. At one point Ron went ahead to check a gully. I asked Charlie how old Ron was. Charlie said Ron was his age, even though his hair was grayer. They had been high school hiking companions. Ron was surer on his feet, but I noticed he had to breathe a little harder than Charlie. They took care of each other.

When we got up to the base of the wall where Ron waited, we were standing at a tall, straight, symmetrical bristlecone, bark all around, that was nearly seven feet in diameter. They had measured it, of course. It was a short traverse to the arch, which stood out in a flying buttress, thick and massive yet graceful, like and unlike some of the sandstone arches in Canyonlands, but with that rough pocketed texture of limestone. Two straight bristlecones grew under the arch, and on its walls several bristlecone seedlings made a start in pockets. Walking through the arch, we followed a ledge into the center of an alcove whose overhanging wall provided shade. There were bedding sites where the mountain sheep rested, on a magical shelf where they could see everything below. Ron thought this might be a perfect office or study where I could write. He thought he could spend a lot of days here.

And then we started down the hill, into "slaughter canyon," as they called it, where one after another deer carcass marked a mountain lion's kills. Charlie said the deer had been killed last summer and watching the fresh kills, they could tell how carefully the lion consumed the flesh, the innards first, then the muscles, and last of all the fat, which it cleanly separated from the rest. The lion would follow you at night sometimes, Ron said, because it was curious at night, and you could hear it breathing behind you. They had brought some Sierra Club people through this canyon once, and the people had been appalled at the carnage. They didn't seem to understand that cats live by killing.

Which led to talking about places and being comfortable in places. People weren't very comfortable in Scofield Canyon, Charlie said, because there was no water. And one guy thought it was an outrage that there were no outhouses. Charlie said he and Ron used to go camping where there was water, but they discovered that everyone else was going to places like that. Most people who came to the range went down south to Cherry Creek, where there were a few campsites and a creek. Some of them would drive up this canyon on Labor Day, and it was amazing what a mess some of them could leave when they were only there for half an hour.

Well, we talked about a lot of other things, of the strategies of Earth First! and of the plan to make a Research Natural Area at Troy Peak, and about Glen Canyon—Ron said he would never forgive Brower for betraying it—and their climbs all over the Great Basin. I have the feeling they have been in places here I will never even imagine. By the end of the day Ron wasn't stuttering much at all. When I left, I told them I was going to have to get to work, teaching; Charlie was surprised. He said they kind of lost track of time up there, didn't realize it was time for that. But they'd probably be there for a couple more months this year, if I wanted to come back. For another lesson, I thought.

It just seems there is always somebody who surprises you, who knows more than you do, who knows more than you will ever know about a place, knows how to be there, and why to choose it. And is so completely open and generous with his time and knowledge. The Forest Service doesn't pay these guys a dime, even for expenses, but they are happy to be allowed the privilege of stewardship in a place most people don't think worthy of a visit.

The references below document the sources for specific passages and discussion in the preceding text. They constitute a small portion of the literature pertaining to the Great Basin and a larger portion of the literature about the Great Basin bristlecone pine. Grayson's and Trimble's volumes include extensive bibliographies on the natural history of the Great Basin. Henri Grissino-Mayor of the Laboratory of Tree-Ring Research at the University of Arizona keeps a chronological list of publications by its members from 1950 to the present and updates a thorough database of literature on dendrochronology and the Great Basin bristlecone pine (http://www.ltrr.arizona.edu).

I have also used a number of unpublished materials in the preparation of this book. Fred Frampton and Jim Whelan allowed me to use and copy U.S. Forest Service reports, memoranda, and correspondence relating to the trees in northeastern Nevada. These materials are uncataloged in the files of the Forest Service in Elko and Ely, Nevada. Also, I have a personal collection of brochures and handouts distributed by the Forest Service and the U.S. National Park Service over the past three decades. I have used correspondence with Darwin Lambert, and he has kindly allowed me to use copies of his correspondence with Dana K. Bailey, Charles Wesley Ferguson, Valmore LaMarche Jr., and Frits Went. Lambert also generously provided copies of memoranda written by Keith Trexler in 1964 and 1965.

In addition to my correspondence with Lambert, this text makes explicit references to interviews with Don Wilcox of the U.S. Forest Service, Joanne Garrett of Baker, Nevada, Linda Dufurrena of Winnemucca, Nevada, and Bryant Bannister, Rex Adams, and Lisa Graumlich of the Laboratory of Tree-Ring Research. Thomas Alexander, William Cronon, Edwin C. Rockwell, Patricia Wells, John Louth, Fred Frampton, Nick Van Pelt, Claude Fiddler, Pat Maespes, Jan Nachlinger, David Robertson, Jim Whelan, Ron Kniveton, Charlie Griffith, Peter Wigand, and Donald Worster also provided valuable perspectives in conversation.

I received support from my colleagues at Southern Utah University. Loralyn Felix, interlibrary loan officer, has served this project with patience and thoroughness. Steven Heath shared generously his own research on bristlecone pines. Part of this work was supported by a grant for faculty development from the Dean of Arts, Letters, and Humanities.

At the University of Nevada Press, I was encouraged through the entire project by Trudy McMurrin. This manuscript received the kind of scrupulous treatment I have come to expect from Sam Allen, whose wide knowledge and precise skills went quite beyond what is required for an editor. This was Sam's last project.

The manuscript has received thorough and constructive critical readings by Richard White, David Robertson, SueEllen Campbell, Cheryll Glotfelty, Michael Branch, Bryant Bannister, Rex Adams, Trudy McMurrin, Mary Thompson, and Peter Wigand. Sometimes I have included their own pertinent comments on certain issues. I have been truly fortunate in the help I received from many good friends.

Bibliography

Alexander, Thomas G. *The Rise of Multiple-Use Management in the Intermountain West: A History of Region 4 of the Forest Service.* F-399. U.S.D.A. Forest Service, 1987.

——. "Timber Management, Traditional Forestry, and Multiple-Use Stewardship: The Case of the Intermountain Region, 1950–85." *Journal of Forest History* 33 (1989): 21–34.

Anderson, Sherwood. *Winesburg, Ohio.* 1919. Reprint, New York: Viking Press, 1960.

"Andrew Ellicott Douglass, 1867–1992." *Tree-Ring Bulletin* 24 (1962): 2–10.

Arno, Stephen F., and Ramona P. Hammerly. *Timberline: Mountain and Arctic Forest Frontiers.* Seattle: The Mountaineers, 1984.

Axelrod, Daniel I., and Peter H. Raven. "Origins of the Cordilleran Flora." *Journal of Biogeography* 12 (1985): 21–47.

Bailey, D. K. "Phytogeography and Taxonomy of Pinus Subsection *Balfourianae.*" *Annals of the Missouri Botanical Garden* 57 (1970): 210–49.

Baillie, M. G. L. *A Slice Through Time: Dendrochronology and Precision Dating.* London: B. T. Batsford, 1995.

Bakker, Elna. *An Island Called California: An Ecological Introduction to Its Natural Communities.* Berkeley: University of California Press, 1971.

Barbour, Michael G. "Ecological Fragmentation in the Fifties." In *Uncommon Ground: Toward Reinventing Nature,* edited by William Cronon, 233–55. New York: W. W. Norton, 1995.

Barthes, Roland. *A Lover's Discourse. Fragments.* Translated by Richard Howard. New York: Hill and Wang, 1978.

Beasley, R. S., and J. O. Klemmedson. "Recognizing Site Adversity and Drought-Sensitive Trees in Stands of Bristlecone Pine (*Pinus longaeva*)." *Economic Botany* 27 (1973): 141–46.

——. "Ecological Relationships of Bristlecone Pine." *American Midland Naturalist* 104 (1980): 242–52.

Benjamin, Walter. *Illuminations.* Edited by Hannah Arendt and translated by Harry Zohn. New York: Schocken Books, 1969.

Betancourt, Julio L., Thomas R. Van Devender, and Paul S. Martin, eds. *Packrat Middens: The Last 40,000 Years of Biotic Change.* Tucson: University of Arizona Press, 1990.

Botkin, Daniel. *Discordant Harmonies: A New Ecology for the Twenty-first Century.* New York: Oxford University Press, 1990.

Bradley, R. S. *Quaternary Paleoclimatology: Methods of Paleoclimatic Reconstruction.* Boston: Unwin Hyman, 1985.

Brubaker, Linda B. "Forest Disturbance and Tree-Ring Analysis." In *International Symposium on Ecological Aspects of Tree-Ring Analysis in Marymount College, Tarrytown, New York,* edited by Gordon B. Jacoby and James W. Hornbeck, 101–18. U.S. Department of Energy, Conf-8608144, 1986.

Camus, Albert. *The Myth of Sisyphus and Other Essays.* Translated by Justin O'Brien. New York: Vintage Books, 1955.

Carlson, Helen S. *Nevada Place Names: A Geographical Dictionary.* Reno: University of Nevada Press, 1974.

Charlet, David Alan. *Atlas of Nevada Conifers: A Phytogeographic Reference.* Reno: University of Nevada Press, 1996.

Connor, Kristina F., and Ronald M. Lanner. "The Architectural Significance of Interfoliar Branches in *Pinus* Subsection *Balfourianae.*" *Canadian Journal of Forest Research* 17 (1987): 269–72.

——. "Effects of Tree Age on Secondary Xylem and Phloem Anatomy in Stems of Great Basin Bristlecone Pine (*Pinus longaeva*)." *American Journal of Botany* 77 (1990): 1070–77.

——. "Effects of Tree Age on Pollen, Seed, and Seedling Characteristics in Great Basin Bristlecone Pine." *Botanical Gazette* 152 (1991): 107–13.

Cook, E. R., L. J. Graumlich, P. Martin, J. Pastor, I. C. Prentice, T. W. Swetnam, K. Valenin, M. Verstraete, T. Webb III, J. White, and I. Woodward. "Biosphere-Climate Interactions During the Past 18,000 Years: Towards a Global Model of the Terrestrial Biosphere." In *Global Changes of the Past. Papers Arising from the 1989 OIES Global Change Institute in Snowmass, Colorado,* edited by R. S. Bradley. University of Colorado Atmospheric Research/Office for Interdisciplinary Earth Studies, 1991.

Critchfield, William B. "Hybridization of Foxtail and Bristlecone Pines." *Madroño* 24 (1977): 193–212.

Cronon, William, George Miles, and Jay Gitlin. "Becoming West: Toward a New Meaning for Western History." In *Under an Open Sky: Rethinking America's Western Past,* edited by William Cronon, George Miles, and Jay Gitlin, 3–27. New York: W. W. Norton, 1992.

Currey, Donald R. "An Ancient Bristlecone Pine Stand in Eastern Nevada." *Ecology* 46 (1965): 564–66.

Davis, Robert Con, and Ronald Schliefer. *Criticism and Culture: The Role of Critique in Modern Literary Theory.* London: Longman Group, 1991.

Douglass, Andrew Ellicott. *Climatic Cycles and Tree Growth.* Publication 289. Washington D. C.: Carnegie Institution, 1928.

——. "Secrets of the Southwest Solved by Talkative Tree Rings." *National Geographic* (December 1929): 736–70.

Eagleton, Terry. *The Ideology of the Aesthetic.* Oxford: Basil Blackwell, 1990.

Eardley, A. J., and William Viavant. *Rates of Denudation as Measured by Bristlecone Pines, Cedar Breaks, Utah.* Special Studies 21. Utah Geological and Mineralogical Survey, 1967.

Eco, Umberto. *Six Walks in the Fictional Woods. Charles Eliot Norton Lectures, 1993.* Cambridge, Mass: Harvard University Press, 1994.

"Edmund Schulman, 1908–1958." *Tree-Ring Bulletin* 22 (1958): 2–6.

Eliott, Russell R. *Nevada's Twentieth Century Mining Boom: Tonopah, Goldfield, Ely.* Reno: University of Nevada Press, 1966.

——. *Growing Up in a Company Town: A Family in the Copper Camp of McGill, Nevada.* Reno: Nevada Historical Society, 1990.

Emerson, Ralph Waldo. "Nature." In *Steven T. Whicher, ed. Selections from Ralph Waldo Emerson: An Organic Anthology,* 21–56. Boston: Houghton Mifflin. Riverside Editions, 1957.

Englemann, George. "Revision of the genus *Pinus,* and a description of *Pinus elliottie.*" *Trans. Acd. Sci. St. Louis.* 4: 161–90 (1880).

Feng, Xiahong, and Samuel Epstein. "Climatic Implications of an 8000-Year Hydrogen Isotope Time Series from Bristlecone Pine Trees." *Science* 265 (1994): 1079–81.

Ferguson, Charles W. "Bristlecone Pine: Science and Aesthetics." *Science* 159 (1968): 839–46.

——. "A 7104-year Annual Tree-ring Chronology for Bristlecone Pine, *Pinus Aristata,* from the White Mountains, California." *Tree-Ring Bulletin* 29 (1969): 3–39.

——. "Aspects of Research on Bristlecone Pine." In *The Ancient Bristlecone Pine Forest,* edited by Russ Johnson and Anne Johnson. 47–51. Bishop, Calif.: Chalfant Press, 1970.

——. "Dendrochronology of Bristlecone Pine, pinus aristata: Establishment of a 7484-Year Chronology in the White Mountains of Eastern Central California, U.S.A." In *Radiocarbon Variations and Absolute Chronology,* edited by Ingrid U. Olssun, 237–59. Stockholm Nobel Symposium 12, 1970.

——. *Terminal Report, Dendrochronology of Bristlecone Pine in East-Central Nevada.* Laboratory of Tree-Ring Research, University of Arizona, 1970.

Ferguson, Charles W., and D. A. Graybill. *Dendrochronology of Bristlecone Pine. A Terminal Report.* Laboratory of Tree-Ring Research, University of Arizona, 1981.

——. "Dendrochronology of Bristlecone Pine. A Progress Report." *Radiocarbon* 25 (1983): 287–88.

Fiero, Bill. *Geology of the Great Basin.* Max C. Fleishmann Series in Great Basin Natural History. Reno: University of Nevada Press, 1986.

Foucault, Michel. *Discipline and Punish: The Birth of the Prison.* Translated by Alan Sheridan. New York: Pantheon Books, 1978.

Fradkin, Philip L. *Fallout: An American Nuclear Tragedy.* Tucson: University of Arizona Press, 1989.

Fritts, Harold C. *Bristlecone Pine in the White Mountains of California: Growth and Ring-Width Characteristics.* Vol. 4. Papers of the Laboratory of Tree-Ring Research, Tucson: University of Arizona Press, 1969.

——. "Tree Rings and Climate." *Scientific American* 226 (1972): 92–100.

——. *Tree Rings and Climate.* London: Academic Press, 1976.

——. "Historical Changes in Forest Response to Climatic Variations and Other Factors Deduced from Tree Rings." In *Effects of Changes in Stratospheric Ozone and Global Climate,* edited by J. G. Titus, 3. Washington D.C.: U.S. Environmental Protection Agency, 1986.

——. *Reconstructing Large-Scale Climatic Patterns from Tree-Ring Data–-A Diagnostic Analysis.* Tucson: University of Arizona Press, 1991.

Fritts, Harold C., and T. W. Swetnam. "Dendroecology: A Tool for Evaluating Variations in Past and Present Forest Environments." In *Advances in Ecological Research,* edited by M. Bergon, A. H. Fitter, E. D. Ford, and A. Macfadyen. 111–88. 19. London: Academic Press, 1989.

Garb, Yaakov Jerome. "Perspective or Escape? Ecofeminist Musings on Contemporary Earth Imagery." In *Reweaving the World: The Emergence of Ecofeminism,* edited by Irene Diamond and Gloria Feman Orenstein, 264–78. San Francisco: Sierra Club Books, 1990.

Gates, David M. "An Amateur Botanist's Great Discovery: Dana K. Bailey and *Pinus longaeva.*" *Missouri Botanical Garden Bulletin* May, (1971): 39–48.

Gleick, James. *Chaos: Making a New Science.* New York: Viking Penguin, 1988.

Goetzmann, William H. *Exploration and Empire: The Explorer and the Scientist in the Winning of the American West.* New York: Alfred A. Knopf, 1966.

Gould, Stephen Jay. *Time's Arrow, Time's Cycle: Myth and Metaphor in the Discovery of Geological Time.* Cambridge, Mass.: Harvard University Press, 1987.

Graumlich, Lisa J. "Subalpine Tree Growth, Climate and Increasing CO_2; An Assessment of Recent Growth Trends." *Ecology* 72 (1991): 1–11.

—— ——. "A 1000-year Record of Temperature and Precipitation in the Sierra Nevada." *Quaternary Research* 39 (1993): 249–55.

——. "Long-term Vegetation Change in Mountain Environments. Palaeoecological Insights into Modern Vegetation Dynamics." In *Mountain Environments in Changing Climates,* edited by Martin Beniston, 167–79. London: Routledge, 1994.

Graumlich, Lisa J., and Linda B. Brubaker. "Long-Term Records of Growth and Distribution of Conifers: Integration of Paleoecology and

Physiology Ecology." In *Ecophysiology of Coniferous Forests,* edited by William K. Smith and Thomas M. Hinckley, 37–62. San Diego: Academic Press, 1995.

Grayson, Donald K. *The Desert's Past: A Natural Prehistory of the Great Basin.* Washington, D.C.: Smithsonian Institution Press, 1993.

Great Basin Planning Team. *Final General Management Plan/Development Concept Plans/Environmental Impact Statement, Great Basin National Park, White Pine County, Nevada.* Denver: National Park Service, Denver Service Center, U.S. Department of the Interior, 1992.

Hall, Clarence A., Jr., ed. *Natural History of the White-Inyo Range, Eastern California.* Vol. 55. California Natural History Guides. Berkeley: University of California Press, 1991.

Hall, Shawn R. *Romancing Nevada's Past: Ghost Towns and Historic Sites of Eureka, Lander, and White Pine Counties.* Reno: University of Nevada Press, 1994.

Harding, Walter. *The Days of Henry Thoreau: A Biography.* New York: Dover Publications, 1982.

Harmon, William, and C. Hugh Holman. *A Handbook to Literature.* 7th ed. Upper Saddle River, N.J.: Prentice Hall, 1996.

Harris, P. S., C. Lowry, and A. Nelson. *Plumbbob Series, 1957.* Technical Report DNA 001–78-C-0311. Defense Nuclear Agency, 1981.

Hart, John. *Hiking the Great Basin: The High Desert Country of California, Nevada, Oregon, and Utah.* Rev. ed., Sierra Club Totebook. San Francisco: Sierra Club Books, 1991.

Hendee, John C., George H. Stankey, and Robert C. Lucas. *Wilderness Management.* Miscelleaneous Publication no. 1365. Forest Service, U.S. Department of Agriculture, 1978.

Hiebert, Ronald D., and J. L. Hamrick. "Patterns and Levels of Genetic Variation in Great Basin Bristlecone Pine, *Pinus Longaeva.*" *Evolution* 37 (1983): 302–10.

Hirschboeck, K. K. "A New Worldwide Chronology of Volcanic Eruptions (with a Summary of Historical Ash-producing Activity and Some Implications for Climatic Trends of the Last One Hundred Years)." *Palaeogeography, Palaeoclimatology, Palaeoecology* 29 (1980): 223–41.

Hitch, Charles. "Dendrochronology and Serendipity." *American Scientist,* May–June 1982, 300–5.

Høeg, Peter. *Borderliners.* Translated by Barbara Haveland. New York: Dell Publishing, 1995.

Houghton, Samuel G. *A Trace of Desert Waters: The Great Basin Story.* 1976. Reprint, Reno: University of Nevada Press, 1994.

Hughes, M. K., P. M. Kelly, J. R. Pilcher, and V. C. LaMarche Jr., eds. *Climate from Tree Rings.* Cambridge: Cambridge University Press, 1982.

Hyde, Philip, and François Leydet. *The Last Redwoods.* San Francisco: Sierra Club, 1963.

Jackson, W. Turrentine. *Treasure Hill: Portrait of a Silver Mining Camp.* Tucson: University of Arizona Press, 1963.

Johnson, Russ, and Anne Johnson. *The Ancient Bristlecone Pine Forest.* Bishop, California: Chalfant Press, 1978.

Kelsey, Michael R. *Hiking and Climbing in the Great Basin National Park.* Provo, Utah: Kelsey Publishing, 1988.

King, R. T. *The Free Life of a Ranger: Archie Murchie in the U.S. Forest Service, 1929–1965.* Reno: University of Nevada Oral History Program, 1991.

Kundera, Milan. *Testaments Betrayed: An Essay in Nine Parts.* Translated by Linda Asher, 254–55. New York: Harper Collins, 1995.

LaMarche, Valmore C., Jr. *Origin and Geological Significance of Buttress Roots of Bristlecone Pines, White Mountains, California.* U.S. Geological Survey Professional Paper no. 475-c, 1963.

——. *Rates of Slope Degradation as Determined from Botanical Evidence, White Mountains California.* Geological Society Professional Paper no. 352-I. Washington D.C.: Government Printing Office, 1968.

——. "Environment in Relation to Age of Bristlecone Pines." *Ecology* 50 (1969): 53–59.

——. "Frost-Damage Rings in Subalpine Conifers and Their Applications to Tree-Ring Analysis with Special Reference to Northwest America." In *Tree-Ring Analysis with Special Reference to Northwest America,* edited by J. G. Harry and John Worrall Smith, 99–100. University of British Columbia, 1970.

——. "Holocene Climatic Variations Inferred from Treeline Fluctuations in the White Mountains, California." *Quaternary Research* Vol. 3, 4 (1973): 632–60.

——. "Paleoclimatic Inferences from Long Tree-Ring Records." *Science* 183 (1974): 1043–48.

——. "Tree-Ring Evidence of Past Climate Variability." *Nature* 276 (1978): 334–38.

LaMarche, Valmore C., Jr., and Harold C. Fritts. "Tree-Rings and Sunspot Numbers." *Tree-Ring Bulletin* 32 (1972): 21–35.

LaMarche, Valmore C., Jr., D. A. Graybill, H. C. Fritts, and M. R. Rose. "Increasing Atmospheric Carbon Dioxide: Tree Ring Evidence for Growth Enhancement in Natural Vegetation." *Science* 225 (1984): 1019–21.

LaMarche, Valmore C., Jr., and Thomas P. Harlan. "Accuracy of Tree Ring Dating of Bristlecone Pine for Calibration of the Radiocarbon Time Scale." *Journal of Geophysical Research* 78 (1973): 8849–58.

LaMarche, Valmore C., Jr., and Katherine K. Hirschboeck. "Frost Rings in Trees as Records of Major Volcanic Eruptions." *Nature* 307 (1984): 121–26.

LaMarche, Valmore C., Jr., and Harold A. Mooney. "Altithermal Timberline Advance in Western United States." *Nature* 213 (1967): 980–82.

———. "Recent Climatic Change and Development of the Bristlecone Pine (*P. longaeva* Bailey) Krummholz Zone, Mt. Washington, Nevada." *Arctic and Alpine Research* 4 (1972): 61–72.

LaMarche, Valmore C., Jr., and C. W. Stockton. "Chronologies from Temperature-Sensitive Bristlecone Pines at Upper Treeline in Western United States." *Tree-Ring Bulletin* 34 (1974): 21–45.

Lambert, Darwin. "Martyr for a Species." *Audubon* 70 (1968): 50–55.

———. *Great Basin Drama.* Niwot, Colo.: Roberts Rinehart, 1991.

Lambert, Darwin, and David Muench. *Timberline Ancients.* Portland, Ore.: Charles H. Belding, 1972.

Lanner, Ronald M. *The Piñon Pine: A Natural and Cultural History.* Reno: University of Nevada Press, 1981.

———. *Trees of the Great Basin: A Natural History.* Max C. Fleishmann Series in Great Basin Natural History. Reno: University of Nevada Press, 1983.

———. "Dependence of Great Basin Bristlecone Pine on Clark's Nutcracker for Regeneration at High Elevations." *Arctic and Alpine Research* 20 (1988): 358–62.

———. "Whatever Became of the World's Oldest Tree." *Wildflower* (winter 1996): 26–27.

Leavitt, Steven W. "Major Wet Interval in White Mountains Medieval Warm Period Evidenced δ13c of Bristlecone Pine Tree Rings." *Climatic Change* 26 (1994): 299–304.

Leigh, Rufus Wood. *Nevada Place Names: Their Origin and Significance.* Salt Lake City: Deseret News Press, 1964.

Libby, Willard F. *Radiocarbon Dating.* Chicago: University of Chicago Press, 1955.

———. "Accuracy of Radiocarbon Dates." *Science* 140 (1963): 278–80.

Limerick, Patricia Nelson, and Mark Klett. "Haunted by Rhyolite: Learning from the Landscape of Failure." *American Art* 6 (fall 1992): 18–39.

Lloyd, Robert M., and Richard S. Mitchell, eds. *A Flora of the White Mountains, California and Nevada.* Berkeley: University of California Press, 1973.

MacArthur, Robert H., and Edward O. Wilson. *The Theory of Island Biogeography.* Princeton: Princeton University Press, 1967.

Malusa, James. "Phylogeny and Biogeography of Pinyon Pines (*Pinus* subsect. *Cembroides*)." *Systematic Botany* 17 (1992): 42–66.

Maser, Chris. *The Redesigned Forest.* San Pedro, California: R & E Miles, 1988.

Mastrogiuseppe, R. J., and J. D. Mastrogiuseppe. "A Study of *Pinus Balfouriana* Grev. and Balf." *Systematic Botany* 5 (1980): 86–101.

McCarthy, Cormac. *The Crossing.* New York: Alfred A. Knopf, 1994.

McClelland, Gordon T., and Milford Zornes. *Milford Zornes.* Beverly Hills, California: Hillcrest Press, 1991.

McPhee, John. *Basin and Range.* New York: Farrar, Straus and Giroux, 1981.

Mehringer, P. J., Jr., and C. W. Ferguson. "Pluvial Occurrence of Bristle-cone Pine (*Pinus Aristata*) in a Mojave Desert Mountain Range." *Journal of the Arizona Academy of Science* 5 (1969): 284–91.

Melville, Herman. *Moby-Dick or, The Whale*. 1851. Reprint, edited by Charles Feidelson Jr. Indianapolis: Bobbs-Merrill, 1964.

Merchant, Carolyn. "Reinventing Eden: Western Culture as a Recovery Narrative." In *Uncommon Ground: Toward Reinventing Nature,* edited by William Cronon, 132–59. New York: W. W. Norton, 1995.

Mirov, Nicholas T. *The Genus Pinus*. New York: Ronald Press, 1967.

Mirov, Nicholas T., and Jean Hasbrouk. *The Story of Pines*. Bloomington: Indiana University Press, 1976.

Misrach, Richard, and Merrian Weisang Misrach. *Bravo 20: The Bombing of the American West*. Creating the North American Landscape, edited by George F. Thompson. Baltimore: Johns Hopkins University Press, 1990.

Misrach, Richard, and Susan Sontag. *Violent Legacies: Three Cantos*. New York: Aperture, 1992.

Mitchell, W. J. T. "Representation." In *Critical Terms for Literary Study,* edited by Frank Lentricchia and Frank McLaughlin, 11–22. Chicago: University of Chicago Press, 1990.

Mooney, Harold A. "Plant Communities and Vegetation." In *A Flora of the White Mountains, California and Nevada*. Berkeley: University of California Press, 1973.

Mooney, H. A., G. St. Andre, and R. D. Wright. "Alpine and Subalpine Vegetation Patterns in the White Mountains of California." *American Midland Naturalist* 68 (1962): 257–73.

Mozingo, Hugh N. *Shrubs of the Great Basin: A Natural History*. Max C. Fleishmann Series in Great Basin Natural History. Reno: University of Nevada Press, 1987.

Muir, John. *The Mountains of California*. 1894. Reprint, Berkeley: Ten Speed Press, 1977.

——. *Our National Parks*. Boston: Houghton Mifflin, 1901.

——. "Nevada Forests." In *Steep Trails,* 164–73. Boston: Houghton Mifflin, 1918.

——. "Nevada's Timber Belt." In *Steep Trails,* 174–83. Boston: Houghton Mifflin, 1918.

Murie, Adolph. "Ecological and Other Evaluations of the Wheeler Peak Area." In *Results of Field Investigations for Proposed National Park in the Snake Range of Eastern Nevada,* 19–40. San Francisco: National Park Service, Region Four Office, 1959.

Myers, Alan Arthur, and Paul Stanley Giller, eds. *Analytical Biogeography: An Integrated Approach to the Study of Animal and Plant Distributions*. London: Chapman and Hall, 1988.

Nash, Roderick. "The Value of Wilderness." *Environmental Review* 3 (1977): 14–25.

Nevada Commission on Tourism. *Nevada Visitor's Guide.* 1995

Noren, Ashee. *Ranger Al Noren.* Visalia, California: Jostens Printing, 1986.

Nowak, Cheryl L., Robert S. Nowak, Robin J. Tausch, and Peter E. Wigand. "Tree and Shrub Dynamics in Northeastern Great Basin Woodland and Shrub Steppe During the Late-Pleistocene and Holocene." *American Journal of Botany* 81 (1994): 265–77.

Nydal, Reidar. "Variations in C14 Concentration in the Atmosphere During the Last Several Years." *Tellus* 18 (1966): 271–79.

Overstreet, D. "The Man Who Told Time by the Trees: Dr. Andrew Ellicott Douglass, Father of the Science of Dendrochronology." *American West* 11 (1974): 26–29, 60–61.

Paul, Sherman. *Emerson's Angle of Vision: Man and Nature in American Experience.* Cambridge Mass.: Harvard University Press, 1952.

——. *For Love of the World: Essays on Nature Writers.* Iowa City: University of Iowa Press, 1992.

Peattie, Donald Culross. *A Natural History of Western Trees.* 1953. Reprint, Boston: Houghton Mifflin, 1991.

Peterson, Levi S. "Road to Damascus." In *The Canyons of Grace,* 35–56. Urbana: University of Illinois Press, 1982.

Pickett, S. T. A., and P. S. White, eds. *The Ecology of Natural Disturbance and Patch Dynamics.* New York: Academic Press, Inc., 1985.

Quintilian. Quoted in Edward P. S. Corbett, *Classical Rhetoric for the Modern Student,* third edition. New York: Oxford University Press, 1990.

Renfrew, Colin. *Before Civilization: The Radiocarbon Revolution and Prehistoric Europe.* New York: Alfred A. Knopf, 1973.

Robertson, David. "The Loneliest Road in America." *Terra Nova* 1 (1996): 41–51.

Ronald, Ann, and Stephen Trimble. *Earthtones: A Nevada Album.* Reno: University of Nevada Press, 1995.

Rowell, Galen. "The Rings of Life." *Sierra Club Bulletin,* September 1974, 5–7, 36–37.

——. *High and Wild: A Mountaineer's World.* San Francisco: Sierra Club Books, 1979.

Ruelle, David. *Chance and Chaos.* Princeton: Princeton University Press, 1991.

Scarry, Elaine. *The Body in Pain: The Making and Unmaking of the World.* New York: Oxford University Press, 1985.

Schama, Simon. "The Verdant Cross." In *Landscape and Memory,* 214–26. New York: Alfred A. Knopf, 1995.

Schaya, Leo. *The Universal Meaning of the Kabbalah.* Translated by Nancy Pearson. Penguin Metaphysical Library, edited by Jacob Needleman. Baltimore: Penguin Books, 1973.

Schulman, Edmund. "Longevity Under Adversity in Conifers." *Science* 119 (1954): 396–99.

——. "Tree-Rings and History in the Western United States." *Economic Botany* 8 (1954): 234–50.

——. *Dendroclimatic Changes in Semiarid America.* Tucson: University of Arizona Press, 1956.

——. "Bristlecone Pine, Oldest Known Living Thing." *National Geographic* 113 (1958): 354–72.

Scuderi, Louis A. "A 2000-Year Tree-Ring Record of Annual Temperatures in the Sierra Nevada Mountains." *Science* 259 (1993): 1433–36.

Shattuck, Roger. "Brinksmanship." *New York Review of Books,* January 11, 1996, 4–8.

Sloan, Jim. "The Oldest Living Thing." In *Nevada: True Tales from the Neon Wilderness,* 189–98. Salt Lake City: University of Utah Press, 1993.

Smith, Genny Schumacher, ed. *Deepest Valley: A Guide to Owens Valley, Its Roadsides and Mountain Trails.* Rev. ed. Los Altos, Calif.: William Kaufmann, 1978.

Snyder, Gary. *The Back Country.* New York: New Directions, 1968.

Sontag, Susan. *On Photography.* New York: Farrar, Straus and Giroux, 1977.

Soulé, Michael E., ed. *Conservation Biology: The Science of Scarcity and Diversity.* Sunderland, Mass.: Sinauer Associates, 1986.

Spaulding, W. G., and L. J. Graumlich. "The Last Pluvial Climatic Episode in the Deserts of Southwestern North America." *Nature* 319 (1986): 441–44.

Stockton, C. W., and G. C. Jacoby Jr. *Long-Term Surface-Water Supply and Streamflow Trends in the Upper Colorado River Basin Based on Tree-Ring Analysis.* Lake Powell Research Project Bulletin no. 18, 1976.

Stokes, M. A., and T. L. Smiley. *An Introduction to Tree-Ring Dating.* Chicago: University of Chicago Press, 1968.

Strauss, Steven H., and Allan H. Doerksen. "Restriction Fragment Analysis of Pine Phylogeny." *Evolution* 44 (1989): 1081–96.

Suess, H. E. "Bristlecone Pine Calibration of the Radiocarbon Time Scale." In *Radiocarbon Variations and Absolute Chronology,* edited by I. U. Olsson, 303–11. New York: John Wiley and Sons, 1970.

Swetnam, Thomas W. "Fire History of the Gila Wilderness, New Mexico." University of Arizona, 1983. Manuscript.

——. "Fire History and Climate Change in Giant Sequoia Groves." *Science* 262 (1993): 885–89.

Swetnam, Thomas W., M. A. Thompson, and E. K. Sutherland. "Using Dendrochronology to Measure Radial Growth of Defoliated Trees." In *Spruce Budworms Handbook,* 5–39. U.S.D.A. Forest Service, Agriculture Handbook, 1985.

Thompson, Robert S. "Late Quaternary Vegetation and Climate in the Great Basin." In *Packrat Middens,* edited by Betancourt, Van Deventer, and Martin, 200–39. Tucson: University of Arizona Press, 1990.

Thoreau, Henry David. *The Journal of Henry David Thoreau.* Vol. 14. Edited by Bradford Torrey and Francis Allen. Salt Lake City: Gibbs M. Smith, 1984.

——. *Walden and Resistance to Civil Government.* 2d ed., Norton Critical Edition, edited by William Rossi and Owen Thomas. New York: W. W. Norton, 1992.

Titus, A. Costandina. *Bombs in the Backyard: Atomic Testing and American Politics.* Nevada Studies in History and Political Science. Reno: University of Nevada Press, 1986.

Toll, David W. *The Compleat Nevada Traveler.* 1976. Reprint. Virginia City, Nev.: Gold Hill Publishing, 1993.

Trimble, Stephen. *The Sagebrush Ocean: A Natural History of the Great Basin.* Max C. Fleishmann Series in Great Basin Natural History. Reno: University of Nevada Press, 1989.

Van Pelt, N. S., and T. W. Swetnam. "Conservation and Stewardship of Tree-Ring Study Resources: Subfossil Wood and Living Trees." *Natural Areas Journal* 10 (1990): 19–27.

Vasek, Frank C. "Creosote Bush: Long-lived Clones in the Mojave Desert." *American Journal of Botany* 67 (1980): 246–55.

Waite, Robert Starr. "The Proposed Great Basin National Park: A Geographical Interpretation of the Southern Snake Range, Nevada." Ph.D. diss., University of California, Los Angeles, 1974.

Webb, George Ernest. *Tree Rings and Telescopes: The Scientific Career of A. E. Douglass.* Tucson: University of Arizona Press, 1983.

Whicher, Stephen T., ed. *Selections from Ralph Waldo Emerson: An Organic Anthology.* Boston: Houghton Mifflin. Riverside Editions, 1957.

White, Richard. *"It's Your Misfortune and None of My Own" : A History of the American West.* Norman: University of Oklahoma Press, 1991.

Williams, Raymond. *Keywords: A Vocabulary of Culture and Society.* Rev. ed. New York: Oxford University Press, 1985.

Williams, Terry Tempest. "A Letter of Solidarity." *Southern Utah Wilderness Alliance* 12 (1995): 3.

Wolfe, Linnie Marsh. *Son of the Wilderness: The Life of John Muir.* New York: Alfred A. Knopf, 1945.

Worster, Donald. *Nature's Economy: The Roots of Ecology.* San Francisco: Sierra Club Books, 1977.

Wright, R. D., and Harold A. Mooney. "Substrate-oriented Distribution of Bristlecone Pine in the White Mountains of California." *American Midland Naturalist* 73 (1965): 257–84.

Young, James A., and B. Abbott Sparks. *Cattle in the Cold Desert.* Logan: Utah State University Press, 1985.

Zavarin, Eugene, Karel Snajberk, Dana K. Bailey, and Edwin C. Rockwell. "Variability in Essential Oils and Needle Resin Canals of *Pinus long-aeva* from Eastern California and Western Nevada in Relation to Other Members of Subsection *Balfourianae.*" *Biochemical Systematics and Ecology* 10 (1982): 11–22.